"To Be Learned Is Good If..."

"To Be Learned Is Good If..."

Edited by
Robert L. Millet

Bookcraft
Salt Lake City, Utah

Library of Congress Catalog Card Number: 87-72364
ISBN 0-88494-645-2

First Printing, 1987

Printed in the United States of America

O that cunning plan of the evil one! O the vainness, and the frailties, and the foolishness of men! When they are learned they think they are wise, and they hearken not unto the counsel of God, for they set it aside, supposing they know of themselves, wherefore, their wisdom is foolishness and it profiteth them not. And they shall perish.

But to be learned is good if they hearken unto the counsels of God.

—2 Nephi 9:28–29

Contents

Preface

The Psalmist described with prophetic precision the attacks upon the faithful in the latter days: "The wicked bend their bow; lo, they make ready their arrow upon the string, that they may privily shoot at the upright in heart, *to destroy their foundation*" (JST, Psalm 11:2; italics added). Indeed, events and movements of recent decades evidence the nature of opposition to The Church of Jesus Christ of Latter-day Saints: an attack upon its foundation—foundational events, foundational doctrines, and the founding fathers of the faith.

The Church has always had its critics, its hecklers. From the very first, Joseph Smith was the object of an unrelenting assault by those *outside* the faith; he knew only too well the bitter and biting winds of religious bigotry and prejudice. Beyond this, unfortunately, there have always been those persons *in* the Church who have chosen to plant seeds of discord and doubt, persons whose membership records were to be found in the vaults of Zion but whose hearts and desires were more in harmony with the world-view of Babylon. In our day, as well as in the meridian dispensation, wherever the sheepfold of Christ is to be found, there are grievous wolves among us (see Acts 20:29–30), members of the Church who feel some sense of mission to steady the ark; a compulsion to bring the Church up to date; a desire to supersede traditional values, to liberate the "naïve" believer; and an inordinate zeal to revise the message of the Restoration in a manner that would be more palatable and acceptable to a cynical secular world.

The lessons of the past demonstrate that an unfortunate tendency to mingle the philosophies of men with the revealed word helped bring about the downfall of the primitive Church. The Great Apostasy is perhaps best exemplified by the hybrid heresy concerning the nature of God that evolved out of the compromises and conciliations between Christianity and Greek philosophy. Too eager for the praises of the learned and the flattery of the prominent, the early Christians sold themselves for a reward that neither soothed nor satisfied the soul. They became as salt that had lost its savor. We have the divine assurance that there will never again be an apostasy *of* the Church. There has been, however, is now, and will yet be many apostasies *from* the Church; too many fail to root and ground themselves in the basic theological verities and the spiritual experiences that ensure safety and serenity during the storms of opposition and dissidence.

This book has been prepared to suggest that one need not surrender cherished values to live in a modern world; that one need not suspend his intellectual faculties to be a faithful Latter-day Saint; that a member of the Church need not fall prey to the increasingly vocal voices of those who choose to preach from the forums of dissent; that one can have implicit trust in the Church and its leaders without sacrificing or compromising anything. All of the contributors to this volume are Mormon educators, men who have received academic training in some of the finest institutions of higher learning in the United States. Most important, the writers are possessed of faith in the Lord Jesus Christ and a loyalty to his Restored Church and its constituted leaders. But their faith is not blind nor their loyalty naïve. They have gained, after many years of study and prayer, a reason for the hope that is in them (see 1 Peter 3:15).

The things of God are only to be understood by the Spirit of God (see 1 Corinthians 2:11–14). The Lord and his plan are to be known by revelation or they will be known not at all. Peace and contentment in a day of spiritual turmoil are to be had, not by reasoned study alone, but by and through the power of the Holy Ghost. Only the peaceable followers of Christ—those who have gained knowledge by study and also by faith—are equipped with a sufficient hope to know the quiet rest of the Spirit here, and hereafter to come to enjoy that rest that is the fulness of God's glory (see Moroni 7:3; D&C 84:24; 88:118).

Robert L. Millet

How Should Our Story Be Told?

1

Robert L. Millet

"This is My Beloved Son. Hear Him!" (Joseph Smith—History 1:17.) The words were simple enough. But the implications of the message were and are remarkably profound. God has spoken again. The heavens have been opened. Prophets and Apostles walk the earth. Priesthoods and keys and authorities have been bestowed, giving mortal man power to bind and seal for eternity. Why, it is almost beyond belief! In fact, the God and Father of us all has begun to work a work which "shall be a great and a marvelous work" among all men; such that there are those who "will not believe it," although legal administrators and chosen messengers of God have begun to declare it. (See 3 Nephi 21:9.)

The dispensation of the fulness of times, or the dispensation of the fulness of dispensations, is that era—our era—wherein God has chosen to "gather together in one all things in Christ, both which are in heaven, and which are on earth; even in him." (Ephesians 1:10.) In the words of Joseph Smith the modern Prophet and Seer:

> It is necessary in the ushering in of the dispensation of the fulness of times, which dispensation is now beginning to usher in, that a whole

Robert L. Millet is Associate Professor of Ancient Scripture at Brigham Young University.

> and complete and perfect union, and welding together of dispensations, and keys, and powers, and glories should take place, and be revealed from the days of Adam even to the present time. And not only this, but those things which never have been revealed from the foundation of the world, but have been kept hid from the wise and prudent, shall be revealed unto babes and sucklings in this, the dispensation of the fulness of times. (D&C 128:18.)

The time of unveiling has begun.

In the spring of 1820 a young man in upstate New York sought a remission of his sins and likewise sought to know which church was approved of God. In answer to those humble requests, the "two personages who constitute the great, matchless, governing, and supreme power over all things, by whom all things were created and made"[1]—God the Father and his Son, Jesus Christ—appeared in a grove made sacred by the occasion. To young Joseph Smith, Jr., nothing was quite the same after that theophany. How could it be? Certainly his view of life and his perspective on the Lord's divine purposes would never be the same. And so it is with all the world—nothing is or will be quite the same since the spring of 1820. The Restoration has eternal implications and will have an everlasting impact on the world. "For the time cometh, saith the Lamb of God, that I will work a great and a marvelous work among the children of men; a work which shall be everlasting, either on the one hand or on the other—either to the convincing of them unto peace and life eternal, or unto the deliverance of them to the hardness of their hearts and the blindness of their minds unto their being brought down into captivity" (1 Nephi 14:7). The long night of apostate darkness is being brought to a close as the gospel sun has begun to shine once again. The age of restoration, "the times of restitution," begun in 1820, will continue with an accelerated pace into and through the Millennium (see D&C 101:32–34).[2]

Writing Our Story

We have a story to tell. It is one which must be told, and one which has, does now, and will yet have impact upon the lives of millions of souls on this earth. The story of the Latter-day Saints—the call of Joseph Smith, the recitation of the foundational events of this dispensation, and an account of those things which have brought the Church to its present state of growth and development—is one that deserves to be told. But it is one that must be told in the Lord's own way if it is to accomplish what the Savior and his anointed servants have envisioned.

It may well be that the perfect pattern for the writing of our story—a sacred history—is contained in the Book of Mormon.

Early in the small plates, Nephi wrote: "And it mattereth not to me that I am particular to give a full account of all the things of my father, for they cannot be written upon these [small] plates, for I desire the room that I may write of the things of God. For *the fulness of mine intent is that I may persuade men to come unto the God of Abraham, and the God of Isaac, and the God of Jacob, and be saved.* Wherefore," Nephi concluded, "*the things which are pleasing unto the world I do not write, but the things which are pleasing unto God* and unto those who are not of the world." (1 Nephi 6:3–5; italics added.) Jacob, in speaking of Nephi's instructions regarding record-keeping, explained: "He gave me, Jacob, a commandment that I should write upon these plates a few of the *things which I considered to be most precious;* that *I should not touch, save it were lightly, concerning the history of this people which are called the people of Nephi*" (Jacob 1:2; italics added).

So it is with the story of the Latter-day Saints. Like the story of the Book of Mormon peoples, ours is not simply a narrative of a religious movement; it is the "saga of a message,"[3] a prophetic history which may only be written and understood properly by the spirit of prophecy and revelation. In teaching of our history, therefore, we do not simply detail occurrences. Rather, in the words of President Ezra Taft Benson, "facts should be taught not only as facts; they should be taught to increase one's faith in the gospel, to build testimony."[4]

In the writing of our story there seems to be a temptation to let others "determine our agenda," to allow persons outside the faith to dictate not only *how* but *what* we say about our past. This may come in the form of attempting to rush about, putting out historical "fires" that some historians or thinkers feel to be significant issues; in doing so, at least sometimes, we dissipate valuable energy which might be more appropriately channeled toward primary causes and vital matters. Some seek to suggest naturalistic explanations for what in reality came about through divine intervention. Some are enamored with the use of academic jargon or theoretical models from other disciplines to interpret that which is only to be fully understood with an eye of faith. We have seen the handiwork of such approaches in regard to the holy scriptures: the Bible has been stripped of its divinity and historicity by many who see only through the lens of secular scholarship.[5]

President Joseph F. Smith warned that one of the great dangers facing the Latter-day Saints would be the flattery of prominent men.[6] It is frequently the case that when we aspire to the honors of men—adapting our work to make it acceptable in the eyes of the prominent—we offend the Lord. "For ye see your calling, brethren," Paul wrote, "how that not many wise men after the flesh, not many mighty, not many noble, are called: but God hath chosen the foolish things of the world to confound the wise; and

God hath chosen the weak things of the world to confound the things which are mighty'' (1 Corinthians 1:26–27). Why has he done so? ''That man should not counsel his fellow man, neither trust in the arm of flesh'' (D&C 1:19).

Often we hear of the need for an integration of the philosophies of men with gospel principles or insights. I am not so certain that *integration* is what is needed, since far too often we are attempting to integrate disparate views that do not successfully mix. ''When a teacher [or writer] feels he must blend worldly sophistication and erudition to the simple principles of the gospel or to our Church history so that his message will have more appeal and respectability to the academically learned,'' President Ezra Taft Benson warned, ''he has compromised his message. We seldom impress people by this means and almost never convert them to the gospel.'' President Benson then observed that ''disaffection from the gospel and the Lord's church was brought about in the past by the attempts to reconcile the pure gospel with the secular philosophies of men. *Nominal Christianity outside the restored church stands as an evidence that the blend between worldly philosophy and revealed truth leads to impotence.*''[7]

The crying need in our day is for academically competent Latter-day Saint thinkers to make judgments by the proper standards—the Lord's standards. ''Behold, I, the Lord, have made my church in these last days like unto a judge sitting on a hill, or in a high place, to judge the nations. For it shall come to pass that the inhabitants of Zion shall judge all things pertaining to Zion.'' (D&C 64:37–38.) ''We cannot safely substitute anything for the Gospel,'' Elder Orson F. Whitney stated in 1915.

> We have no right to take the theories of men, however scholarly, however learned, and set them up as a standard, and try to make the Gospel bow down to them; making of them an iron bedstead upon which God's truth, if not long enough, must be stretched out, or if too long, must be chopped off—anything to make it fit into the system of men's thoughts and theories! On the contrary, we should hold up the Gospel as the standard of truth, and measure thereby the theories and opinions of men. What God has revealed, what the prophets have spoken, what the servants of the Lord proclaim when inspired by the Holy Ghost, can be depended upon, for these are the utterances of a spirit that cannot lie and that does not make mistakes; while the teachings of men are often based upon sophistry and founded upon false reasoning. Uninspired men are prone to judge by outward appearances, and to allow prejudice and plausibilities to usurp the place of divine truth as God has made it known.[8]

Prophets: Weak and Simple, Mighty and Strong

Jesus of Nazareth was rejected by some for eating and drinking with publicans and sinners; surely, many thought, no true Messiah would lower himself to affiliate with the scourges of society. Joseph Smith was condemned for wrestling and joking and playing ball; certainly, some insisted, prophets ought to be made of more austere stuff!

"I can fellowship the President of the Church," said Lorenzo Snow, "if he does not know everything I know. . . . I saw the . . . imperfections in [Joseph Smith]. . . . I thanked God that he would put upon a man who had those imperfections the power and authority he placed upon him . . . for I knew that I myself had weakness, and I thought there was a chance for me."[9] Unfortunately, not all Latter-day Saints have been as sensitive or considerate of Joseph Smith and his successors as Elder Snow. It has become somewhat fashionable, in fact, to stress the humanity and weaknesses of those called to lead the Church; to cast aspersions on their motives or character; and to reveal personal and intricate historical details, the context and true meanings of which are often lacking. In the words of Elder Russell M. Nelson, to tell the truth (at least as we see it) is not enough; we must tell the truth *and more.* "We now live in a season," he explained, "in which some self-serving historians grovel for 'truth' that would defame the dead and the defenseless. Some may be tempted to undermine what is sacred to others, or diminish the esteem of honored names, or demean the efforts of revered individuals." To do so, he suggests, is the height of ingratitude. "They seem to forget that the greatness of the very lives they examine has given the historian the pedestal from which such work may have any interest."[10]

One who seeks either to degrade or to disseminate doubt may weaken or destroy another's faith. Such a person, in the words of Elder Boyd K. Packer, "places himself in great spiritual jeopardy. He is serving the wrong master, and unless he repents, he will not be among the faithful in the eternities."[11] "For what is a man profited, if he shall gain the [acclaim of the] whole world, and lose his own soul? or what shall a man give in exchange for his soul?" (Matthew 16:26). President Gordon B. Hinckley noted:

> We have critics who appear to cull out of a vast panorama of information those items which demean and belittle some men and women of the past who worked so hard in laying the foundation of this great cause. They find readers of their works who seem to delight in picking up these tidbits, in chewing them over and relishing them. . . .
>
> My plea is that as we continue our search for truth . . . we look for strength and goodness rather than weakness and foibles in those who did so great a work in their time.
>
> We recognize that our forebears were human. They doubtless made mistakes. . . .
>
> There was only one perfect man who ever walked the earth. The Lord has used imperfect people in the process of building his perfect

> society. If some of them occasionally stumbled, or if their characters may have been slightly flawed in one way or another, the wonder is the greater that they accomplished so much.[12]

The fact is, prophets are called and approved of God—what further and greater recommendation do we need? We ought to be grateful that God can utilize imperfect beings and that these men—molded into vessels of holiness over time—can prove such a benefit to their fellow imperfect humans. Joseph Smith, Brigham Young, Lorenzo Snow, Joseph F. Smith, or others of our leaders cannot be with us now to answer all the charges against them. But be it remembered again that God called them and God has evidenced his approbation of their labors. Those who attempt to mar the name or works of the Lord's anointed are covenant-breakers and will eventually answer to God himself for their actions. It was President George Albert Smith who, in speaking specifically of a book on the life of Joseph Smith which sought to mar the image of the Prophet, said: "Many have belittled Joseph Smith, but those who have will be forgotten in the remains of mother earth, and the odor of their infamy will ever be with them, but honor, majesty, and fidelity to God, exemplified by Joseph Smith and attached to his name, will never die."[13]

Patience and Perspective

The Lord warned the Latter-day Saints in August of 1831: "And in nothing doth man offend God, or against none is his wrath kindled, save those who confess not his hand in all things, and obey not his commandments" (D&C 59:21). Part of confessing the Lord's hand in our lives as members of the Church surely consists in acknowledging his personal involvement in our past, as well as his direction and approval of the actions of those who have led us. "The hand of the Lord may not be visible to all," President Joseph F. Smith stated. "There may be many who can not discern the workings of God's will in the progress and development of this great latter-day work, but *there are those who see in every hour and in every moment of the existence of the Church, from its beginning until now, the overruling, almighty hand of Him who sent His Only Begotten Son to the world* to become a sacrifice for the sin of the world."[14] It is a matter of perspective, an issue of where one has chosen to look for answers and causes. Those who look to God will live (see Alma 37:47). Those who do otherwise will be ever learning but never able to come to the knowledge of the truth (see 2 Timothy 3:7). President Gordon B. Hinckley thus observed that "those who criticize us most have lost sight of the glory and wonder of this work."

> In their cultivated faultfinding, they see not the majesty of the great onrolling of this cause. They have lost sight of the spark that was kindled in Palmyra which is now lighting fires of faith across the earth in many lands and in many languages. Wearing the spectacles of humanism, they fail to realize that spiritual emotions, with recognition of the influence of the Holy Spirit, had as much to do with the actions of our forebears as did the processes of the mind. They have failed to realize that religion is as much concerned with the heart as it is with the intellect.[15]

We simply do not have the whole story yet. Joseph and Brigham and John and Wilford are not here to fill in the gaps in our knowledge, nor are the rank-and-file members of the Church from bygone days always available for oral interviews and clarifications. We must do all that we can in the present to reconstruct the past, to write the story of the Latter-day Saints and prepare that sacred history, that saga of a message, which will yet touch the hearts and build the faith of many. But we must be patient in writing it, avoiding the temptation to attribute improper motivation or to jump prematurely to confusions, and seeking earnestly to give the leaders of the Church the benefit of the doubt. The Lord will vindicate the words and works of his anointed servants in time; of this I have no doubt. In the meantime we must receive their words, as the revelation declares, *"in all patience and faith"* (D&C 21:5; italics added). "The finished mosaic of the history of the Restoration," said Elder Neal A. Maxwell, "will be larger and more varied as more pieces of tile emerge, adjusting a sequence here or enlarging there a sector of our understanding." "There may even be," he added, "a few pieces of the tile which, for the moment, do not seem to fit. We can wait, as we must." In summary, "the final mosaic of the Restoration will be resplendent, reflecting divine design. . . . At the perfect day, we will see that we have been a part of things too wonderful for us. Part of the marvel and the wonder of God's 'marvelous work and a wonder' will be how perfect Divinity mercifully used us—imperfect humanity. Meanwhile, amid the human dissonance, those with ears to hear will follow the beckoning sounds of a certain trumpet."[16]

To have "an eye single to the glory of God" is to seek to build up the kingdom and establish his righteousness through any worthy means (JST, Matthew 6:38). It is to labor in primary causes, to fight maturely and manfully for things that matter most. It is to cultivate one's little garden and magnify his specific callings, assuming all the while that the Lord will give instructions regarding the cultivation of plots beyond his own. It is to know that intelligent devotion and loyalty to the Lord, his Church, and his appointed leaders are more highly prized by the Almighty than sheer intellect or native abilities. To have an eye single to the glory of God is to "earnestly contend for the faith which was once delivered unto the saints" (Jude 1:3). It is, finally, to feel and sing with conviction and commitment: "Faith of our fathers, holy faith, we will be true to thee till death" (*Hymns*, 1985, no. 84).

NOTES

1. *Lectures on Faith* (Salt Lake City: Deseret Book Co., 1985), 5:2.
2. See Bruce R. McConkie, "The Doctrinal Restoration," in *The Joseph Smith Translation: The Restoration of Plain and Precious Things*, ed. Monte S. Nyman and Robert L. Millet (Provo, UT: Religious Studies Center, 1985), pp. 1–22.
3. These words were used by Elder Boyd K. Packer in Conference Report, April 1986, p. 74.
4. "The Gospel Teacher and His Message," Address to Religious Educators, 17 September 1976, in *Charge to Religious Educators* (Salt Lake City: The Church of Jesus Christ of Latter-day Saints, 1982), p. 51.
5. A fascinating study of the effect of the writing of secular history upon Jewish culture is Yosef Hayim Yerushalmi, *Zakhor: Jewish History and Jewish Memory* (Seattle: University of Washington Press, 1982).
6. *Gospel Doctrine* (Salt Lake City: Deseret Book Co., 1971), pp. 312–13.
7. "The Gospel Teacher and His Message," pp. 50–51; italics in original.
8. From Conference Report, April 1915.
9. Cited by Neal A. Maxwell in Conference Report, October 1984, p. 10.
10. From "Truth and More," Address given at the annual university conference, Brigham Young University, 27 August 1985.
11. "The Mantle is Far, Far Greater than the Intellect," Address delivered to Church Educators, August 1981, in *Charge to Religious Educators*, p. 35.
12. "The Continuous Pursuit of Truth," *Ensign*, April 1986, p. 5.
13. Cited by Harold B. Lee in Conference Report, October 1973, p. 166.
14. Conference Report, April 1904, p. 2; italics added.
15. "The Continuous Pursuit of Truth," p. 5.
16. Conference Report, October 1984, pp. 11–12.

Traditions of Honesty and Integrity in the Smith Family

2

LaMar E. Garrard

Although our character is not completely determined by family traditions and the environment in which we are placed, still, these are factors that often influence and help to shape us. It is not hard to find instances where the character of a parent or grandparent set a pattern or tradition that affected the lives of his or her descendants. For example, a young naval aviator by the name of O'Hare exhibited great bravery during World War II. After discovering the enemy fleet while on patrol, he stayed in the vicinity until he had directed other airplanes to the area in an attempt to destroy that fleet. Although he was running low on fuel, he refused to return to his own ship until the enemy had been engaged in battle. This act of bravery cost him his life. Where did he get such character? No doubt a great influence on his life was his own father, who through an act of bravery also lost his life. He was a lawyer who was called upon to testify against certain participants in organized crime who threatened to kill him if he testified against them. O'Hare's father proceeded to give the testimony in spite of the threats against him. He was later killed by the mob.

LaMar E. Garrard is Professor of Church History and Doctrine at Brigham Young University.

The Prophet Joseph Smith inherited a tradition of honesty and integrity from his own father and grandfather. Both of these men had occasion in their lives in which they exhibited unusual honesty and integrity under severe conditions that caused them and their families great physical stress and economic loss.

Asael Smith

The Prophet's grandfather, Asael Smith, was the youngest of five children and the second son in the family of Samuel Smith. He was born in Topsfield, Massachusetts, in 1744, and his mother died when he was not yet a year old. He was raised on the family farm, sharing the work with his father and other brother. He married Mary Duty when he was twenty-three years old; they also lived and shared the work on the family farm until they had three children. However, "Asael was only the second son, so economic custom dictated his learning a trade and leaving the family homestead, allowing his older brother, Samuel Smith, Jr., to farm on shares with his father."[1]

Asael moved his family to Windham, New Hampshire, in May of 1772. While living there, one more child, Asael, Jr., was born as the family attempted to get ahead on their own. They then moved to Dunbarton, New Hampshire, in April of 1774. Approximately four years later they moved again, this time to Derryfield (Manchester), New Hampshire. During this four-year period two more children, Mary and Samuel, were born. Also, Asael enlisted in the army during the Revolutionary War, "an act of obvious hardship for a family head with six dependents."[2] This time in the army may have contributed to the poor health he experienced later on. After moving to Derryfield, Asael purchased a 100-acre farm, which he and his sons farmed during the summer. During the winter he and his sons worked at the cooper trade, making full round barrels. Four more children were born during the seven years on this farm.

On 14 November 1785 Asael's father, Samuel, died in Topsfield, Massachusetts. At that time Samuel Jr. (Asael's brother) was still living on the family farm with the stepmother, Priscilla Smith. Prior to the father's death, Asael had made a trip to visit his ailing father. The circumstances surrounding this visit were as follows:

> In 1785 Asael visited his father, Samuel, in Topsfield in his last sickness, and saw the old man at seventy-two jump out of bed in a delirium and head for the door, saying he must go to the mill or his family would suffer. Asael assured Samuel the family would be watched after. After Samuel's death on November 14, 1785, care of his widow first fell to Samuel, Jr. He was executor of the estate and initially took over the family farm. His listing as gentleman in the land records

as compared to Asael's cooper may reflect an aspiration to follow Samuel, Sr., into the town aristocracy. Within a few months of Samuel, Sr.'s death, however, Samuel, Jr., was ready to rid himself of the farm and settle for less. With the farm, he had inherited the responsibility for seeing that Priscilla Smith received one-third of its income, her widow's portion. In addition, he soon discovered that the estate was actually insolvent. The two burdens were greater than he chose to carry.[3]

What type of man was Samuel Smith? He had been a prominent member of the community of Topsfield, serving responsibly a half-dozen terms in the state legislature, many terms as governing selectman of Topsfield, and sometimes as town clerk. He was a captain in the militia and was active in the Congregational Church. His obituary described him as a man of integrity and uprightness. His involvement in civic affairs and lack of awareness concerning the condition of his personal finances no doubt accounted for his insolvency at death. Being insolvent at death often occurred among New Englanders.

> The insolvency of Samuel's estate is not surprising. In the absence of currency, New Englanders conducted their exchanges through debts and credits with neighbors, storekeepers, tradesmen, and city merchants. An active man could easily owe money to fifty or a hundred individuals and be owed by as many in turn. Debts were paid with services, commodities, and occasionally with small sums of money if any happened to come along. At a given moment it was difficult to know where one stood, because it was never certain which debtors would make good or when creditors would demand payment. Creditors were lenient while a man had earning power and closed in when he was in trouble. A person could be prospering while alive and working, and suddenly be insolvent at death.[4]

During the winter following the death of his father, Samuel Jr. made a trip to Derryfield to visit his brother Asael. He explained that his father's debts exceeded what others owed him, plus the real estate and personal property. He had come to Asael for help. However, at the time of his father's death Asael himself was "recovering from economic setbacks, and poor health,"[5] and at the time was father of eleven children. The conditions existing at this time were recalled and described by Asael's son John as follows:

> My uncle Samuel, who lived with my grandfather at the time of his death, after finding the condition his estate was in, came to New Hampshire to counsel with my father on the subject. He said it was not possible to pay the debts with the property that was left under the then existing circumstances. My father not being so well acquainted with the state of affairs as his elder brother Samuel, thought that it might be done. "For," said he, "I am not willing that my father, who has done so much business, should have it said of him that he died insolvent."

And [he] urged hard to have my uncle go on and settle the business, and he felt that the Lord would prosper him in the undertaking. But my uncle said that he had a large family and but very little property, and he could not undertake such a work without the means to do with.

My father was then in low circumstances, had been in a low state of health, entirely unable to labor for three years, during which time he was only able to keep the town record, as he had held the office of town clerk for many years. He owned a small farm in Derryfield, on Merrimack River, a large and growing family, and in consequence of his late sickness [they were] in very destitute condition. "Notwithstanding all my embarrassments," said my father, "I will undertake to settle my father's estate and save his name from going down to posterity as an insolvent debtor. . . ." After considerable conversation with my uncle, [they] agreed to change places. Accordingly, my father moved his family to Topsfield, Massachusetts and attend[ed] to the business above mentioned.[6]

Under these trying circumstances, Asael made good his promise to his dying father that he would take care of his family. But this "promise was kept by mental and physical blisters."[7] Asael and his family managed the farm in Topsfield in an attempt to take care of his stepmother and pay off his father's debts. Asael's attempts to pay off these debts were described by his son John as follows:

Here my father struggled hard for about five years and made out to support his family comfortably. His stepmother was on his hands during this time, who was sometimes rather childish. However, by prudence and industry he had paid some part of his father's debts. . . . [H]is old mother received her third, [and] after supporting a large family with the scanty means which was at his command, he could not pay the old debts which were crowding upon him. People showed no lenity, notwithstanding they knew that if he had not have come forward to pay them, they never could have got one-eighth part of what they [were] now determined to have.[8]

It was almost impossible to pay off the father's debts. Asael was industrious and a good manager, but sickness and poor economic times took away any profits. The economic conditions under which Asael labored to pay off his father's debts were described as follows:

Describing coming to Massachusetts in 1786, his son says that Asael "had lost considerable in the downfall of Continental paper," a grim condition that had also affected Samuel's estate. This paper dollar lost value during the Revolution, only to reach its low worth below a cent prior to Samuel's death. The decade after the Revolution saw much else that was "not worth a Continental." Debts incurred by the father during heavy inflation had to be repaid by the son during depression, when falling farm prices decreased the cash value of Asael's labors. At the time he sought to pay off his father's obligations, thou-

> sands of debtors in rural Massachusetts supported armed revolution (materializing in Shays's Rebellion) rather than face compulsory collection and foreclosure proceedings.[9]

During the five years of working the farm, Asael saw that the widow received her one-third, the children were fed, and an attempt was made to pay off the creditors. Asael finally realized, however, that he could not pay off all the creditors and still keep the farm, so in 1791 the farm was sold to pay off the creditors. This left Asael and his family practically destitute.

> But if a failing economy bequeathed impossibility, Asael was generous with his resources. The widow's right was met (perhaps on her demand) by renting a third of the land for her support, but the stepson voluntarily promised to pay necessities that she lacked. By entering the picture, Asael shouldered the burden of paying the widow plus the creditors; the latter obligation came largely out of his pocket, so he correctly said that honoring his father "cost me much money and trouble." Overall, he traded his own land for Samuel's farm; while running it he devoted excess profits to Samuel's creditors; when sold, he distributed virtually the entire return to settle his father's affairs. He might have walked away and let the creditors divide up the estate, with the widow assured of her dower. Instead, with his own labor he paid off all debts in full, by family tradition a net cost of $700 to him. Asael sold the farm but did not keep the proceeds: "He then paid all the debts . . . against the estate and left himself almost destitute of means to support his family." Five years of labor added little to his pocketbook but much to his moral stature.[10]

Asael did not sneak out of Topsfield owing large amounts of money, but rather he left as a respected member of his community, one who was morally upright and willing to pay off his debts, obligations not incurred by himself. He communicated with several members of the community for years after leaving for Vermont and was highly respected. In fact, fifteen years after Asael had moved to Vermont, one local investor in Topsfield loaned Asael and his sons seven hundred dollars.[11]

It is under stressful and opposing conditions that one's true character comes to light. Considering the conditions under which Asael lived during his last five years in Massachusetts, he proved himself to be an upright and honest man and a good example to his sons and grandsons. This tradition of integrity and honesty was carried on to his son Joseph Smith, Sr., who was careful to pay all the debts he owed to others, even when others had cheated him or had not paid the debts they owed to him. The events that are evidence of Joseph Sr.'s integrity took place later in the state of Vermont.

After selling the Topsfield farm in March of 1791, Asael moved his family temporarily to a dairy farm in the nearby town of Ipswich, Massachusetts. After they were settled there, he and his eldest son Jesse journeyed to Vermont while the rest of the family was left behind to manage the farm. While in Vermont he purchased eighty-three acres of uncleared land in the Tunbridge Gore. He intended to have his sons Jesse and Joseph clear the land that summer and winter and then move the entire family there in the spring of 1792. However, it was finally decided not to split up the family; so the crops were sold while still in the ground at Ipswich, and the entire family moved to Tunbridge, Vermont, in October of 1791.

Joseph Smith, Sr.

Two of the great challenges facing parents in those days were helping the children get off to a good start when they reached the proper age and also making preparations to care for themselves in their old age. "Adult life was a race to accumulate sufficient goods to give the children a start, and still have enough to be independent and comfortable in old age."[12] When he moved to Tunbridge, Asael had seven sons who shared the work on the farms with him. In the next few years following, Asael was able to purchase additional farms of one hundred acres each until he eventually had over three hundred acres in farms adjoining each other. As each son married he was helped to get started on a farm of his own. Jesse married shortly after arriving in Vermont and Joseph in 1796. Joseph was given the original farm of eighty-three acres in a partnership with his father while the new land was being purchased and cleared.[13] Joseph married Lucy Mack, a sister to a prominent member of the community, Stephen Mack. Stephen was a very prosperous businessman, at one time owning a sawmill, gristmill, blacksmith shop, and other establishments in Tunbridge. When Lucy married, Stephen gave her $500 and his partner also gave her $500. Joseph and Lucy then started their married life with a farm, and $1000 which Lucy laid away for future use. They farmed for six years and then decided to try their luck in business, as Stephen had done. They rented their farm and moved to nearby Randolph, where they established a mercantile business. "Joseph Smith opened his Randolph store with a line of goods purchased on credit from Boston. His inventory sold quickly, not for cash but for promise of payment in commodities at harvest."[14] The debt he incurred by the purchase of these goods in Boston came to about $1800.

At about this time, Joseph decided to make some money selling ginseng root. It grew wild in Vermont and after being gathered and processed, could be sold for considerable profit in China—it being "used as a remedy for the plague which was then raging there."[15] Joseph used all his means to obtain a quantity of this root and then process it and get it ready for shipment. In fact, he processed a quantity of it so large that he was offered $3000 for it by a merchant in Royalton named Stevens. However, Joseph felt he could make more profit by shipping and selling it himself, so he took the crystallized root with him to New York where he contracted with a ship's captain to take it to China and sell it for him. Mr. Stevens became aware of all this and shipped some crystallized root himself on the same ship, but sent his own son on the ship to manage the sale.

When the ship returned, the younger Stevens told Joseph Smith the venture was a failure, and the only payment Joseph received for all his efforts was a chest of tea. However, Stephen Mack discovered that Mr. Stevens had actually sold all the processed ginseng root for quite a profit and had pocketed Joseph's share. In fact, Mr. Stevens was setting up a plant to process the root when he was found out by Stephen Mack. He fled to Canada to escape punishment. Joseph pursued him but was unable to catch him.

After being cheated by Mr. Stevens and being unable to collect the $2000 owed him from sold merchandise, Joseph had nothing to pay the $1800 he owed to creditors in Boston for the merchandise he obtained from them. Lucy explained the predicament as follows:

> My husband pursued him a while, but finding pursuit vain, returned home much dispirited at the state of his affairs. He then went to work to overhaul his accounts in order to see how he stood with the world, upon which he discovered that, in addition to the loss sustained by the China adventure, he had lost about two thousand dollars in bad debts. At the time he sent his venture to China he was owing eighteen hundred dollars in the city of Boston for store goods, and he expected to discharge the debt at the return of the China expedition; but, having invested almost all his means in ginseng, the loss which he suffered in this article rendered it impossible for him to pay his debt with the property which remained in his hands. The principal dependence left him, in the shape of property, was the farm at Tunbridge, upon which we were then living, having moved back to this place immediately after his venture was sent to China. This farm, which was worth about fifteen hundred dollars, my husband sold for eight hundred dollars in order to make a speedy payment on the Boston debt; and, as I had not used the check of one thousand dollars, which my brother and Mr. Mudget gave me, I added it to the eight hundred dollars obtained for the farm, and by this means the debt was liquidated.[16]

As a result of his honesty, Joseph Smith, Sr., now had no property of his own. This necessitated many moves in the next few years.

> One of the misfortunes of the propertyless was the necessity for frequent moves. Tenants ofttimes rented farms that were in process of being sold and available only for a few years. When the farm was not sold out from under them, a better opportunity elsewhere impelled a move. Over the next fourteen years the Smiths moved seven times. Between 1803 and 1811 all the moves were in a tiny circle around Tunbridge, Royalton, and Sharon, immediately adjoining towns, and probably never involved a distance of more than five or six miles.[17]

According to Lucy, after the farm in Tunbridge was sold in 1802, the family moved to Royalton for a few months and then moved to Sharon, Vermont, where they lived on a farm rented from Lucy's father, Solomon Mack.[18] In order to make ends meet, Joseph taught school in the winter in addition to running the farm. It was while the family was living on this farm that the future prophet, Joseph Smith, Jr., was born on 23 December 1805. The family moved again, this time back to Tunbridge, where Samuel Harrison was born 13 March 1808. Again, they lived there for only a short while, then they moved to Royalton, where Ephraim was born in March 1810. A year later William was born.[19] In 1811 the family left Royalton and moved about twenty miles east to West Lebanon, New Hampshire, a town just across the Connecticut River from Vermont. Here they struggled to get ahead and also to send their children to schools conveniently located nearby. However, they suffered a setback here when every member of the family, except the parents, was struck with typhus fever. Sophronia suffered greatly and Joseph Smith, Jr., had to eventually have his leg operated on as a result of complications from the disease. This period of stress and disease lasted about a year. When health returned to the family, Lucy explained, "It found us in quite low circumstances. We were compelled to strain every energy to provide for our present necessities, instead of making arrangements for the future, as we had previously contemplated."[20] It was in 1814 that they moved again, this time to Norwich, Vermont, just five miles north of West Lebanon and back across the Connecticut River. By necessity they were required to again rent a farm, and they had crop failures for three years in succession, up to the year 1816. Evidently the family was destitute at this time, for they were "warned out of town," a legal procedure used by the town selectmen to absolve themselves from responsibility to take care of the poor. The constable was "required to summon Joseph Smith and family now residing in Norwich to depart said town hereof fail not but of this precept and your doings herein due return make according to law."[21] It was signed by the selectmen of Norwich on 15 March 1816. On 27 March 1816 the constable signed the town record attesting to the fact that he had served the warning to Joseph Smith.[22]

The crop failures, the advertisement of good land in New York, and the "warning out of town" were no doubt the factors which resulted in Joseph Smith, Sr.'s decision to leave Vermont and move to New York. However, Lucy explains that her husband Joseph was careful to be honest and settle his debts before he left for New York:

> This was enough; my husband was now altogether decided upon going to New York. He came in, one day, in quite a thoughtful mood, and sat down; after meditating some time, he observed that, could he so arrange his affairs, he would be glad to start soon for New York with a Mr. Howard, who was going to Palmyra. He further remarked, that he could not leave consistently, as the situation of the family would not admit of his absence; besides, he was owing some money that must first be paid.
>
> I told him it was my opinion he might get both his creditors and debtors together, and arrange matters between them in such a way as to give satisfaction to all parties concerned; and, in relation to the family, I thought I could make every necessary preparation to follow as soon as he would be ready for us. He accordingly called upon all with whom he had any dealings, and settled up his accounts with them. There were, however, some who, in the time of settlement, neglected to bring forward their books, consequently they were not balanced, or there were no entries made in them to show the settlement; but in cases of this kind, he called witnesses, that there might be evidence of the fact.[23]

Joseph Smith, Sr., then set out for Palmyra, New York, with Mr. Howard. Meanwhile, Lucy and the rest of the family made preparations to leave. When word came to Lucy from her husband to leave, she was confronted by unjust claims of creditors against her husband. She explained the situation as follows:

> We shortly received a communication from Mr. Smith, requesting us to make ourselves ready to take up a journey for Palmyra. In a short time after this, a team came for us. As we were about starting on this journey, several of those gentlemen who had withheld their books, in the time of settlement, now brought them forth, and claimed the accounts which had been settled, and which they had, in the presence of witnesses, agreed to erase. We were all ready for the journey, and the teams were waiting on expense. Under these circumstances, I concluded it would be more to our advantage to pay their unjust claims than to hazard a lawsuit. Therefore, by making considerable exertion, I raised the required sum, which was one hundred and fifty dollars, and liquidated the demand.

> A gentleman by the name of Flagg, a wealthy settler, living in the town of Hanover, also a Mr. Howard, who resided in Norwich, were both acquainted with the circumstances mentioned above. They were very indignant at it, and requested me to give them a sufficient time to get the witnesses together, and they would endeavor to recover that which had been taken from me by fraud. I told them I could not do so, for my husband had sent teams for me, which were on expense; moreover, there was an uncertainty in getting the money back again, and in case of failure, I should not be able to raise the means necessary to take the family where we contemplated moving.[24]

The above-named gentlemen then proposed to subscribe some money from those friends who understood the situation and present it to Lucy to help them out. She refused their offer, explaining that "the idea of receiving assistance in such a way as this was indeed very repulsive to my feelings."[25]

So we see that Joseph Smith, Sr., left for a new state—as did his father Asael—only after he had honestly tried to settle all of his debts. Many enemies of the Church have accused Joseph Smith, Sr., of being dishonest in one way or another. Such accusations, however, cannot be substantiated. I have spent considerable time and effort going over the civil court records of Orange and Windsor counties in Vermont and Grafton County in New Hampshire. The records were located in the county seats: Chelsea and Woodstock in Vermont, and Woodville in New Hampshire. All the court records were examined covering those years in which Joseph Smith, Sr., was a resident of each county. If he ever defaulted on a note or loan and a lawsuit was filed, it would have appeared in the court records. No such lawsuits were ever found filed against Joseph Smith, Sr.[26] Evidently he was like his father Asael, an honest and upright man. The Prophet Joseph Smith did indeed inherit a tradition of honesty and integrity from his father and grandfather.

NOTES

1. Richard Lloyd Anderson, *Joseph Smith's New England Heritage: Influences of Grandfathers Solomon Mack and Asael Smith* (Salt Lake City, Utah: Deseret Book Co. 1971), p. 91; hereafter referred to as Anderson.
2. Anderson, p. 92.
3. Richard L. Bushman, *Joseph Smith and the Beginnings of Mormonism* (Urbana and Chicago, Illinois: University of Illinois Press, 1984), p. 21; hereafter referred to as Bushman.
4. Bushman, p. 21.
5. Anderson, p. 95.

6. Anderson, pp. 95–97. The quote is from John Smith, Journal, 20 July 1839.

7. Anderson, p. 97.

8. Anderson, p. 97. The quote is from John Smith, Journal, 20 July 1839. The bracketed *were* replaces the ms. *was.*

9. Anderson, pp. 97–98.

10. Anderson, p. 98.

11. Anderson, p. 100.

12. Bushman, p. 32.

13. Bushman, p. 23.

14. Bushman, pp. 29–30.

15. Lucy Mack Smith, *History of Joseph Smith* (Salt Lake City: Bookcraft, 1957), p. 37; hereinafter referred to as Smith.

16. Smith, pp. 39–40.

17. Bushman, pp. 30–31.

18. Smith, p. 46.

19. Smith, p. 46.

20. Smith, p. 59.

21. Norwich Town Record (1813–17), p. 53.

22. Norwich Town Record (1813–17), p. 53.

23. Smith, pp. 59–60.

24. Smith, pp. 60–61.

25. Smith, p. 61.

26. The name of Joseph Smith, Sr., appears in the Supreme Court records of Vermont in connection with counterfeiting cases, but only as a witness who had been victimized by fraudulent paper. Rumors changing his role to that of conspirator found their way into print, but Richard L. Anderson looked at the cases in question and verified his innocence.

Joseph Smith's First Vision: Cornerstone of a Latter-day Faith

3

Milton V. Backman, Jr.

One of the most significant events in the history of mankind occurred in the spring of 1820. In that year, a fourteen-year-old farm boy, Joseph Smith, was called by God to introduce "the long-promised dispensation of the fulness of times." This transcendent experience initiated the "marvelous work of restoration," thereby becoming a cornerstone of the faith of Latter-day Saints.[1] "Of all the great events of the century," President Spencer W. Kimball declared, "none compared with the first vision of Joseph Smith."[2] Commenting on this same vision, a modern Apostle, Elder James E. Faust, observed, "There has been no event more glorious, more controversial, nor more important in the story of Joseph Smith than this vision. It is possibly the most singular event to occur on the earth since the Resurrection."[3]

Four Major Accounts

On at least four different occasions, Joseph Smith wrote or dictated to scribes accounts of his marvelous experience of 1820. Included in these accounts are descriptions of the reasons he launched a quest for religious truth, the historical setting of this

---

Milton V. Backman, Jr., is Professor of Church History and Doctrine at Brigham Young University.

experience, his encounter with Satan prior to his vision, personages who appeared to him, truths unfolded during the vision, and reflections regarding the aftermath of the sacred event.[4]

Although every major history pertaining to the rise of Mormonism prepared by Joseph Smith included a description of the First Vision, at no time did he write an account of everything he learned during this theophany. In the most detailed and complete recital, for example, he concluded with a statement, "Many other things did he say unto me, which I cannot write at this time."[5]

Historical Setting of a Latter-day Vision

Even though Joseph Smith never revealed everything he learned during his initial encounter with God, one's understanding of this vision may be enhanced by examining all known records containing Joseph Smith's testimony regarding his First Vision. From the age of twelve to fifteen, he wrote, he was involved in a quest for religious truth. This quest was initiated by his growing awareness that he had sinned and by his resolute desire to secure a remission of sins. After asking others questions regarding the means of salvation, he became confused. "I found," he added, "that there was a great clash of religious sentiment concerning the plan of salvation. If I went to one society they referred me to one plan, and another to another, each one pointing to his own particular creed as the summum bonum of perfection. . . . I felt to mourn for my own sins and for the sins of the world."[6] Deciding that "God could not be the author of so much confusion," Joseph Smith "determined to investigate the subject more fully. . . . If God had a church," he reasoned, it would not be split up into factions, and "if he taught one society to worship one way, and administer in one set of ordinances, he would not teach another principles which were diametrically opposed."[7]

Joseph Smith's description of the background of his First Vision also included an account of the unusual excitement on the subject of religion which occurred in the place where his family lived. "It commenced with the Methodists," he observed, "but soon became general among all the sects in that region of country. Indeed, the *whole district of country* seemed affected by it, and *great multitudes* united themselves to the different religious parties," precipitating a scene of great confusion—priest contending against priest, and convert against convert, so that any good feelings which might have been evident were entirely lost in a strife of words.[8]

During this war of words and contest of opinions, Joseph read in the epistle of James, "If any of you lack wisdom, let him ask of God, that giveth to all men liberally, and upbraideth not; and it shall be given him" (1:5). This passage of scripture penetrated his heart. Believing that if he did not follow the admonition of James he would remain in darkness and confusion, he retired to a secret place in a grove and knelt in prayer.[9] As he prayed, his tongue seemed to be swollen in his mouth, so that he could not utter a word. He heard a noise behind him, like someone walking toward him. He sprang to his feet, and after looking around, saw nothing that could have produced such a noise.[10] After kneeling again in prayer, he was seized upon by some power which entirely overcame him. Thick darkness gathered around him and he felt as if he were doomed to sudden destruction. Exerting all power within him, he asked God to deliver him from the power of this enemy. At this moment of great alarm, he saw a brilliant light which rested upon him.[11] "I was filled with the spirit of God," he said.[12] After the light rested upon him, he also saw two Personages, who resembled each other in feature and likeness.[13] One of them spoke to him, calling him by name, and said, pointing to the other, "This is my Beloved Son, Hear Him."[14]

Truths Unfolded in 1820

After perceiving that the power of evil was real and strong, but that the power of God was stronger, the fourteen-year-old boy learned that God hears and answers prayers and intervenes in the affairs of men. He also learned that the Father and Son are two separate and distinct personages who physically resemble each other.

Many close associates of the Mormon Prophet who heard Joseph Smith bear witness of his sacred experience of 1820 testified that the personage who introduced Jesus Christ was God, the Eternal Father, and that Joseph learned on this occasion that the Father and Son were separate and distinct personages. They also believed that this vision was a visitation in which the two Personages appeared in a brilliant light that penetrated the sacred grove.[15] George Q. Cannon echoed a theme that was frequently declared by other friends of the Prophet when he said that ignorance regarding the true concept of God prevailed in the early nineteenth century. But this ignorance "was swept away in one moment by the appearance of the . . . Father, and His Son, Jesus Christ, to the boy Joseph." "It was meant," he added, "that this knowledge should be restored first of all. It seems so, at least, from the fact that God Himself came; it seems that this knowledge had to be restored as the basis for all true faith to be built upon."[16]

Orson Pratt added his testimony concerning the reality of this visitation by the Father and Son when he declared:

> Now here was a certainty; here was something that he saw and heard; here were personages capable of instructing him, and of telling him

> which was the true religion. How different this was from going to an uninspired man. . . . One minute's instruction from personages clothed with the glory of God coming down from the eternal worlds is worth more than all the volumes that ever were written by uninspired men.[17]

Twentieth-century leaders have continued to bear witness of Joseph Smith's visitation by the Father and Son. President Spencer W. Kimball declared:

> The God of all these worlds and the Son of God, the Redeemer, our Savior, in person attended this boy. He saw the living God. He saw the living Christ. . . . Nothing short of this total vision to Joseph could have served the purpose to clear away the mists of the centuries. Merely an impression, a hidden voice, a dream could [not] have dispelled the old vagaries and misconceptions.[18]

As the vision unfolded, Joseph Smith learned many other truths. According to an account written by Joseph in 1832, Jesus told the young man that his sins were forgiven and that the Lord had taken upon Himself the sins of mankind. After learning about the reality of the Atonement, Joseph was told that prophecies regarding the second coming of Christ would be fulfilled.[19]

In nearly all accounts of the First Vision, Joseph Smith emphasized that he learned in 1820 that the Church of Christ was not upon the earth. In his first known draft of the First Vision Joseph Smith wrote that the Lord told him:

> the world lieth in sin at this time and none doeth good no not one they have turned aside from the gospel and keep not my commandments they draw near to me with their lips while their hearts are far from me and mine anger is kindling against the inhabitants of the earth to visit them according to their ungodliness and to bring to pass that which hath been spoken by the mouth of the prophets and Ap[o]stles.[20]

Six years later Joseph summarized this concept by writing:

> I was answered that I must join none of them, for they were all wrong, and the Personage who addressed me said that all their Creeds were an abomination in his sight, that those professors were all corrupt, that "they draw near to me with their lips but their hearts are far from me. They teach for doctrines the commandments of men, having a form of Godliness but they deny the power thereof."[21]

In the last account of the First Vision, written during the early 1840s at the request of a non-Mormon named John Wentworth, Joseph Smith emphasized again the reality of the Apostasy and need for a restoration. Instead of stating, however, that the Lord said their creeds were an abomination, he declared that one of the Personages told him that "all religious denominations were believing in incorrect doctrines." Then Joseph added a theme not found in any other account of the First Vision which he prepared. He received a promise in 1820 "that the fulness of the gospel should at some future time be made known unto" him.[22]

In the unpublished writings of Joseph Smith there are two additional concepts regarding this vision that are not found in his published works. In a diary entry of November 9, 1835, Joseph noted that during this "first communication" he "saw many angels."[23] And in his 1832 history, Joseph wrote that during this vision his soul was filled with love, and for many days following this experience he rejoiced with great joy, for the Lord was with him.[24]

Confirming Witnesses

All major themes included in Joseph Smith's writings regarding his 1820 vision, from its setting to its aftermath, were confirmed by contemporaries who described in their sermons and publications that which they learned from the Prophet. The first Latter-day Saint to publish an account of the First Vision was Orson Pratt. Elder Pratt included a description of that event in a missionary pamphlet, *Remarkable Visions*, published in Scotland in 1840. A comparison of this history with Joseph Smith's writings reveals that most major themes included in the Prophet's histories (especially the 1838 account) were included in that work. Since there are no direct quotations in Pratt's tract from the Prophet's manuscript histories and since the literary style in that work is very different from Joseph's pre-1840 writings, Orson Pratt probably based his history on that which he learned from listening to the Prophet rather than from reading his manuscripts.[25]

Although written and verbal statements by Orson Pratt and other close associates of the Prophet reiterate all major themes included in Joseph's accounts of the 1820 vision, they do not contribute substantially to our understanding of "other truths" unfolded in the spring of 1820. One possible exception was an elaboration of Joseph's prophetic call. Based on that which he learned personally from Joseph Smith, Orson Pratt said that Joseph Smith was not only promised during his First Vision that "at some future time the fulness of the Gospel should be made manifest to him," but was also told that "he should be an instrument in the hands of God in laying the foundations of the kingdom of God."[26] Brigham Young added that Joseph was told that "he had a work to perform, inasmuch as he should prove faithful."[27]

While explaining this magnificent vision, contemporaries discussed the meaning of the phrase "[they] had a form of godliness but denied the power of God." Brigham Young said that the Lord told Joseph that the churches lacked the holy priesthood and had strayed from the holy commandments.[28] Orson Pratt was more specific. He suggested that the Lord told Joseph in 1820 that all churches not only lacked authority but had departed from the apostolic order by denying a power of the New Testament Church, the gift of the Holy Ghost. They denied, he added, communication and revelation from heaven, including administration of angels, visions, prophecy, and miracles (such as the power to heal the sick). And because of their unbelief, Orson Pratt concluded, Joseph learned that others had lost the "power of godliness."[29]

Although contemporaries of Joseph Smith identified the two Personages who appeared to him in 1820 as the Father and Son, sometimes these same individuals said that an *angel* told Joseph not to join any of the churches. While speaking on the subject of the First Vision, President John Taylor said in March 1879 that an *angel* told Joseph that none of the churches were right.[30] Referring to this same vision less than one year later, President Taylor said, "The *Lord* appeared unto Joseph Smith, both the Father and Son."[31] Meanwhile, in 1864 George A. Smith quoted Joseph Smith's 1838 history that identified the Father and Son and summarized the vision by saying that *God* revealed truth to his servant Joseph.[32] This same leader in the late 1860s reported that the "*Lord* answered his prayer and revealed to Joseph, by the ministration of *angels*, the true condition of the religious world." He added that an "*holy angel*" told Joseph Smith that all the churches had gone astray.[33] And President Brigham Young on one occasion said that the Lord sent his angel, a messenger, to Joseph in 1820 and a few years later said that the Lord called upon Joseph Smith when he was fourteen years of age.[34]

Joseph Smith and many other early leaders of the Church used the term *Lord* to identify the Father and Son and used the words *Lord, Christ, personage, messenger,* and *angel* interchangeably. The Prophet taught others that the resurrected Christ was an angel. One kind of being in heaven, he said, is an angel or personage who is resurrected with a body of flesh and bones. To support this concept, Joseph quoted the Savior when he said to his disciples, "Handle me and see, for a spirit hath not flesh and bones, as ye see me have." (See D&C 129:1–2.) A similar pattern of expression is found in the Old Testament where *God* and *angel* are used interchangeably (see Genesis 48:15–16).

While discussing the Restoration, nineteenth-century Latter-day Saints generally used the language of their age. *Angel* was defined in the 1828 and 1844 editions of the Webster's *Dictionary* as a "messenger; one employed to communicate news or information from one person to another." "Christ, the mediator and head of the church" and "*Lord*" were two other definitions of *angel*. In this same dictionary *Lord* was not only defined as "Supreme Being" but as "Christ," the latter definition being identified as a New Testament usage.

Persecution of a Young Prophet

Joseph Smith declared that after informing others of his sacred experience of 1820 he endured bitter persecution and that relating his story precipitated a great deal of prejudice against him. He said that he felt much like Paul, when he made his defense before King Agrippa. "Some said he was dishonest, others said he was mad; and he was ridiculed and reviled. But all this did not destroy the reality of his vision." "So it was with me," Joseph continued, "I had seen a vision; I knew it, and I knew that God knew it, and I could not deny it."[35]

Writings of Joseph Smith's mother, Lucy Mack Smith, support his assertion that persecution erupted in the decade of the twenties. When Joseph was fourteen, she recalled, he was returning home from an errand and while passing through the dooryard, a gun was fired. The bullet apparently crossed a pathway, "with the evident intention of shooting him." Joseph "sprang to the door much frightened." Immediately after hearing the shot, members of the family "went in search of the [alleged] assassin, but could find no trace of him."[36]

There is also circumstantial evidence supporting Joseph Smith's claim of verbal abuse following his First Vision. Since persecutors generally do not write or publish accounts of their intolerant acts, historians must search for other evidence of unusual harassment and oppressive treatment. Such evidence is sometimes limited to declarations of the oppressed; and others living in western New York about 1820 endured the anguish of intolerance. David Marks, for example, claimed that in 1821, he received an impulse from heaven, commanding him to go forth and preach the gospel. This sixteen-year-old farm boy, who was about the same age as the Mormon Prophet and lived in the western part of the Finger Lakes country not far from Joseph's farm, left home and commenced preaching in the early 1820s. Probably because he was not a trained minister and was so young, others ridiculed him. In his reminiscences, he described the cruel treatment he endured. At times he was mocked and greeted with "contempt." He was especially harassed in Junius, the community where he lived; and said that in 1821 "one man gave notice that he would provide a handful of whips at my next meeting, and would give a gallon of whisky to anyone that would wear them out on me." Because of the "scandalous reports" concerning his character and the religion which he advocated, Marks left Junius to preach in other sections of the young nation. The only known evidence of persecution of this Free-will Baptist minister is his recorded testimony.[37]

Since many could not accept or appreciate Joseph's sacred experience of 1820, the Prophet cautiously unfolded to others that which he learned during his theophany near Palmyra. Joseph Smith was especially hesitant to identify the personages who appeared to him in 1820. Accounts addressed to nonmembers before and after Joseph wrote his 1838 history do not identify the two Personages.

All known accounts written or dictated by Joseph Smith were prepared during a ten-year period, between 1832 and 1842. The latter two accounts (1838 and 1842 histories) were initially published in the *Times and Seasons* (Nauvoo) in 1842. The first two accounts (1832 and 1835 histories) were left in an unpolished condition and were never published. Possibly, if Joseph had published the initial recordings of his impressions, he would have revised them and corrected possible mistakes, such as the approximate date of his vision.

Unfolding a Sacred Experience

There are many explanations of the fact that four surviving recitals of this theophany are different. They were prepared or rendered through different scribes, at different times, from a different perspective, for different purposes, and to different audiences. It is not surprising that each of them emphasizes different aspects of his experience. When Latter-day Saints today explain this remarkable vision to others, their descriptions often vary according to the audience or circumstances that prompt such reports. If one were to relate the incident to a group of adult Latter-day Saints, for example, he or she would undoubtedly tell it somewhat differently than if describing the vision to individuals who had never heard of the restoration of the gospel or of Joseph Smith. While the accounts contain different emphases, there is a striking harmony in the recitals.

Appearance of Two Personages

One difference in the four accounts of the 1820 vision prepared by Joseph pertains to that which he beheld during the vision. The thrust of the 1832 history was not who appeared but the Lord's message to him. In the 1835 diary reference, Joseph recalled that one Personage appeared and then another followed. He added that during this vision he saw many angels. In 1838 he identified the two Personages with the statement, "This is my Beloved Son." In the last account that he prepared, the Wentworth letter, he specified that the two Personages (without identifying the heavenly beings) resembled each other.

Some critics have suggested that prior to the mid-1830s Joseph Smith believed that the Father, Son, and Holy Ghost were three persons of one essence. After changing his belief regarding the Godhead, they contend, Joseph Smith altered his story of the First Vision, saying that two Personages, the Father and Son appeared. Responses to this criticism may follow different avenues of explanation. No one, for example, has located a publication (such as an article appearing in a Church periodical or statement from a missionary pamphlet) written by an active Latter-day Saint prior to the martyrdom of the Prophet that defends the traditional or popular creedal concept of the Trinity. One phase of the war of words of the early nineteenth century was the contest of opinions regarding the Godhead. Members of many faiths (such as Unitarians, many Universalists, and groups who called themselves "Christians," (including disciples of James O'Kelly, Barton Stone, Elias Smith and David Millard) rejected the decision of Nicaea regarding oneness in substance or essence. Instead many Americans in these and other churches believed that the New Testament clearly taught that the Father and Son were two separate and distinct beings. Moreover, there are no references in critical writings of the 1830s (including statements by apostates) that Joseph Smith introduced in the mid-thirties the doctrine of separateness of the Father and Son. On the other hand, whenever early Latter-day Saints articulated their belief on that subject they asserted that the Father and Son are separate beings. In a sermon delivered on June 16, 1844, Joseph Smith said that whenever he preached on the subject of the Godhead he declared God to be a distinct personage and Jesus Christ a distinct personage separate from God the Father. This doctrine, he added, had been preached for fifteen years.[38] Although the emphasis in his 1832 account was on the Savior's message, Joseph Smith did not write in that account that only one Personage appeared. Instead, he wrote that he prayed to the Lord and the Lord opened the heavens. Then he discussed the message the Lord (this latter "Lord" being identified as Christ) delivered to him. Instead of writing that the one Personage introduced his Son, Joseph possibly identified the Father in that account with the statement, "The Lord opened the heavens upon me."

Before writing a brief history in the latter part of 1832, Joseph Smith understood that the Father and Son were separate beings. These two personages had not only visited him in 1820, but had appeared to him on other occasions prior to the fall of 1832. On

February 16, 1832, Joseph Smith and Sidney Rigdon testified that they beheld the Son, "even on the right hand of God" (D&C 76:23). When these men wrote an account of this vision, they used a phrase located in the New Testament. Shortly before his death, Stephen saw the "Son of man, standing on the right hand of God" (Acts 7:55–56). When Joseph discussed the subject of three separate personages in the Godhead on June 11, 1844, he used Stephen's vision as scriptural support for that doctrine. As recorded by Willard Richards, Joseph said in essence, "Stephen . . . saw the son of man standing on the right hand of God.—3 personages—in heaven who hold the keys.—one to preside over all."[39]

Another reference to a vision of the Father and Son was recorded in 1831 by John Whitmer who was serving as Church historian. "He [probably referring to Joseph Smith] saw the heavens opened, and the Son of man sitting on the right hand of the Father."[40]

Non-Mormons recognized that the belief of Latter-day Saints regarding the Godhead conflicted with the popular creedal definition of God. In one of the first references by a non-Mormon to the LDS concept of God, Rev. Truman Coe, a Presbyterian minister (who prior to 1836 had lived among the Mormons for about four years) published an article in *The Ohio Observer* (1836) that discussed the distinguishing beliefs of Latter-day Saints. "They [Latter-day Saints] believe," he recorded, "that the true God is a material being, composed of body and parts; and that when the Creator formed Adam in his own image, he made him about the size and shape of God himself."[41] Belief in a material God precludes an endorsement of the traditional view of the Trinity (being of one essence).

While there are no known LDS publications prior to the martyrdom of the Prophet which defended the popular trinitarian view, there are many additional statements by Joseph Smith and his close associates recorded after 1834 that harmonize with the tenet that the Father and Son are separate and distinct beings. In one of the first published summaries of fundamental doctrines of Latter-day Saints, called *Lectures on Faith* (1835), a distinction was made in Lecture Five regarding the natures of the bodies of the two personages in the Godhead, the Father and Son.[42] One year after these lectures (which were delivered to the school of the elders in Kirtland) appeared in the Doctrine and Covenants, Joseph Smith testified that during a gathering of the priesthood in the Kirtland Temple (on January 21, 1836), he beheld the Father and Son in the celestial kingdom (D&C 137:3). Moreover, in one of the first missionary pamphlets written by a Latter-day Saint and published in 1838, Parley P. Pratt vehemently rejected a belief enunciated in the Methodist articles of religion, namely that God was three persons of one substance and was without body and parts. "We worship a God," he retorted, "who has both body and parts."[43] In another missionary publication that appeared two years later, this same modern Apostle claimed that others accused Latter-day Saints of denying the oneness of the Father, Son, and Holy Ghost. Such attacks he said were misrepresentations. Parley explained, however, that this oneness did not include unity of substance. "Whoever reads our books, or hears us preach, knows that we believe in the Father, Son, and Holy Ghost, as one God," he declared. Then he added, "The Son has flesh and bones, and . . . the Father is a spirit." Although apparently at that time he did not fully understand the nature of the body of the Father, Parley P. Pratt said that the Father's spiritual body resembled (in appearance) a temporal body. This personage of spirit (God, the Eternal Father) therefore has an "organized formation." He is an "individual identity," with "eyes, mouth, ears, &c; . . . hence it is said that Jesus is 'the express image of his (the father's) person.' "[44]

In another pamphlet published in 1840, Elder John Taylor compared the Methodist belief regarding the Godhead with that of the Latter-day Saints. After citing the Methodist articles of religion that referred to the Godhead as three persons of one essence, without body, parts, or passions, Elder Taylor quoted Parley P. Pratt: "Here, then, is the Methodist God without either eyes, ears, or mouth!!! and yet man was created after the image of God; but this could not apply to the Methodists' God, for he has not image or likeness!"[45]

In 1845, less than one year after the death of Joseph Smith, Elder John Taylor published an article on "The Living God" in the *Times and Seasons*, the official organ of the Church. After criticizing the most popular belief of Christians regarding the Trinity, he discussed his belief in a Godhead consisting of three separate and distinct personages. Although the Father, Son, and Holy Ghost are "one in power, one in dominion, and one in glory, constituting the first presidency of this system," he wrote, "they are as much three distinct persons as the sun, moon, and earth are three different bodies." The Savior, he explained, "never once said that he begat himself, or came into the world of his own accord. . . . On the contrary, He came to do the will of his Father who sent him."[46]

While discussing the belief of Latter-day Saints regarding the Godhead, Orson Pratt employed events described in the Bible and Church history to defend his conviction about the separate physical characteristics of the Father and Son. In an article appearing in the *Millennial Star* in 1849, this Apostle declared that visions of "both ancient and modern prophets . . . clearly demonstrate the existence of two distinct persons—the Father and Son." Although

Orson Pratt stated that the ancient and modern scriptures referred to the oneness of the Godhead and that Christ was called the Father and Son, he reasoned that such a belief did not conflict with the reality that God the Eternal Father was a being separate from his beloved Son. To support this doctrine, Orson Pratt described the vision of Stephen when he "saw two persons," Joseph Smith's vision of 1820 in which he "beheld both the Father and Son," and Joseph Smith's and Sidney Rigdon's vision of 1832 when they also "beheld the Father and Son" (see D&C 76:23).[47]

Dating the Vision

In only one account of the First Vision is there a reference to the date of that event. The Prophet wrote in 1838 that the vision occurred early in the spring of 1820 when he was in his fifteenth year. The only reference to an approximate date in the Wentworth letter was that the event occurred after the family moved to Manchester. According to this account, prior to moving to that township, the family settled in Palmyra where they lived for about four years. Since this history specified that Joseph Smith was ten when the family settled in Palmyra, it implied that the First Vision occurred when Joseph was about fourteen.[48] The 1835 diary reference also specified that Joseph Smith was "about fourteen" when he received his first communication from heaven. The 1832 history contains an insertion that is difficult to read regarding Joseph Smith's age at the time of that vision. This insertion states that he was in his "16th" year. The "16th" might have been written "15th." If Joseph wrote "16th" rather than "15th" he erred. Since this account was not published nor prepared for publication, no attempt was made to correct a possible error.

Recording the Vision

After learning that the earliest known recording of the First Vision by Joseph Smith was in 1832, some ask, "Why didn't Joseph Smith write an account of this experience at an earlier date?" Possibly he did and the manuscript was lost. But it is not surprising, considering Joseph Smith's limited formal education and the social and literary climate of that generation that he might not have written a history of that event until 1832. In 1836 many Latter-day Saints beheld visions in the Kirtland Temple. Few members, however, were keeping diaries at that time and most who described this event included the account in later reminiscences. Some referred to Joseph Smith's *History* and said they knew his account was reliable, for they were in Kirtland during this pentecostal season. Others said that the experience was so overwhelming that they could not express in human language that which they experienced.[49] Oliver Cowdery recorded in his diary under the date January 21, 1836, that the visions were too glorious to be described. Nevertheless, he added, many saw angels.[50]

Many living in early nineteenth-century America did not publish autobiographies or histories until many years after the events that shaped their lives had transpired. The possibility that Joseph Smith kept a diary in 1820 seems remote. As explained by Dean C. Jessee:

> Considering the youth of the Prophet, the frontier conditions in which he lived, his lack of academic training, the absence of any formal directive to motivate him to write, and the antagonistic reception he received upon first relating the experience, it is not strange that he failed to preserve an account of his First Vision during the decade between 1820 and 1830. However, once directed by an 1830 revelation to keep a history, Joseph acted with all the dispatch that time-consuming responsibilities and frustrating difficulties would allow.[51]

The first known recording by the Apostle Paul of his experience on the road to Damascus was made about twenty-four years after his vision.[52] And critics do not accept Joseph Smith and Sidney Rigdon's testimony regarding the vision of the Father and Son in February 1832 (D&C 76) even though this account was recorded and published within five months after the event occurred.[53]

A Reliable History

Joseph Smith not only wrote an accurate account of the message unfolded during his theophany near Palmyra but also aptly described the historical setting of that vision. He wrote that some members of his family, namely Lucy, his mother, and two brothers, Hyrum and Samuel, and a sister, Sophronia, had joined the Presbyterian faith.[54] There was only one meetinghouse in Palmyra in the early twenties, that being the Western Presbyterian Church. Records of this church prior to 1828 have not survived. An entry dated March 1830, however, disclosed that a committee interviewed the Smiths because they had neglected to attend church for one-and-a-half years. Since the committee reported that Lucy, Hyrum, and Samuel no longer desired to retain their membership, their request was granted. There is no reference in these minutes to Sophronia. Possibly she withdrew her membership after her marriage in the mid-1820s.[55]

A Powerful Awakening

Joseph Smith also wrote a vivid description of the religious quickening that was occurring in the area where he lived at the time of the First Vision. In the early nineteenth century, one of the great revivals in the history of evangelical Christianity erupted. While America was a land of liberty and religious pluralism, it was also a country in which many were unchurched. As settlers pushed westward, many lost contact with organized religion. At the time of the First Vision only about 11 percent of the people in this nation and in the immediate vicinity where Joseph Smith lived were members of a Christian society. Revivalists, however, attempted to alter this situation. Itinerant preachers carried messages of salvation to all who would listen. For the first time, many asked the question, "Which church should I join?" In the early nineteenth century, in unprecedented numbers, people united with different religious parties.[56]

While describing this awakening, Joseph wrote that religious excitement occurred in the place where he lived and that it commenced with the Methodists. He also declared that great multitudes united themselves to the different religious parties in the whole region or district of country.[57] The Prophet did not write that great multitudes joined churches in Palmyra village. When Joseph Smith used the terms *region* and *district*, he was writing a reminiscence in western Missouri. Prior to that recording, he had traveled to the east coast twice and to the western frontier five times. He was, therefore, viewing a historical event from a substantial distance in time and place, which makes plausible the assumption that he was considering general conditions in a large geographical area. Joseph Smith however, did not describe what he meant by "great multitudes" nor did he define whole region or district of country. When Joseph Smith (or scribes working under his direction) employed the terms *district* or *region* on other occasions in his *History of the Church*, he referred to multiple townships in northeastern Ohio and northwestern Missouri.[58] Methodist ministers sometimes also used this term to describe the circuit to which they had been assigned, and early circuits extended across many townships.[59]

Various historical sources substantiate religious quickenings initiated by Methodists in the area where Joseph Smith lived in 1819 and 1820. Methodism was the fastest growing religion in America at that time. These Protestants held more camp meetings than any other group and conducted such meetings in the neighborhood where Joseph Smith resided at the time of the First Vision.[60] In the summer of 1819 about one hundred Methodist ministers attended a conference in Phelps, the township adjacent to Manchester. Accompanying such conferences were multiple meetings, and following this gathering "a flaming spiritual advance" occurred in that region.[61]

Two non-Mormon contemporaries of Joseph Smith who lived in Palmyra in 1820 verified Joseph Smith's recollection of religious excitement in that place about the time of the First Vision. Orsamus Turner, who resided in Palmyra for several years prior to 1822, wrote that "after catching a spark of Methodism in the camp meeting, away down in the woods on the Vienna road, he [Joseph Smith] was a passable exhorter in evening meetings."[62] And Pomeroy Tucker said that Joseph Smith attended "protracted revival meetings" that were "customary in some of the churches." However, he wrote that after joining a probationary class of the Methodist Church in Palmyra he withdrew, saying that "all sectarianism was fallacious."[63]

Some critics insist that the only proper interpretation of Joseph Smith's 1838 account of the background of the First Vision is that of a revival which led to a significant increase in church membership in Palmyra and vicinity. This limited view fails to consider that the Prophet might have associated great increases in membership with a larger geographical region, an area extending beyond Palmyra and nearby villages. At least one contemporary of Joseph Smith, David Marks, "ranged over a fair sized area in the process of participating in certain religious revivals" about 1820. In 1821, for example, Marks learned that a great revival was progressing in Brutus and Camillus, communities located from twenty to thirty miles from Marks's home. Anxious to witness it, the young farmer left home and walked fifteen miles to Brutus, where he tarried with strangers. For approximately one month, Marks remained in that area, attending some forty-four meetings. When Marks later summarized his travels during his early years he wrote that they were "confined to a few towns in the vicinity of Junius." Commenting on this narrative, one Mormon scholar, Peter Crawley, aptly wrote, "Marks's narrative demonstrates . . . the fallacy in dogmatically requiring Joseph Smith's 'the place where we lived' [or whole district of country] to lie within 10 or 15 miles of the Smith farm. Marks, at least, in 1821 could refer to an area including towns 30 miles to the east and to the west of his home as 'the vicinity of Junius.' "[64]

There is much historical evidence supporting Joseph Smith's claim that great multitudes joined churches in the whole region of country. There are more reports of revivals in upstate and western New York in 1819 and 1820 than in any other section of the early republic. Reports of these revivals were announced in periodicals and newspapers, including the Palmyra *Register*.[65] Church records, newspapers, and periodicals reported unusual religious excitement and/or increases in membership in 1819–1820 in Phelps, Oaks

Corners, Geneva, Lyons, Manchester, Canandaigua, Bloomfield and other communities near the Smith farm.[66] Multitudes also joined churches east of the Finger Lakes and in the area of Albany.[67]

Brigham Young, who was living in Mendon in 1820, not far from the Smith farm, later affirmed Joseph's account of the historical setting of the First Vision by stating, "I very well recollect the reformation which took place in the country among the various denominations of Christians, the Baptists, Methodists, Presbyterians, and others—when Joseph was a boy . . . of fourteen."[68] Another contemporary of Joseph Smith, Daniel Wells, explained that he was born two or three counties from where the latter-day work emerged. "The days of my youth," he explained, "were days of religious excitement—the days of revivals, which so pervaded that section of country at that time—and I can well apprehend the effect these things must have had on the mind of Joseph. . . . I know how those revivals affected young minds in the neighborhood in which I lived."[69]

Canonizing a History

One account of Joseph Smith's theophany near Palmyra has been accepted by the Church as reliable history. During the October 1880 semi-annual conference, members of the Church sustained President John Taylor as prophet, seer, and revelator. Following this sustaining, Elder George Q. Cannon, First Counselor in the First Presidency, acting under the direction of President Taylor, presented to the assembly a new edition of the Doctrine and Covenants and the Pearl of Great Price. This latter work included Joseph Smith's 1838 account of the First Vision. Elder Cannon proposed that those present accept the books and their contents "as from God, and binding upon us as a people and as a Church." Then President Joseph F. Smith, Second Counselor in the First Presidency, moved that the membership accept the books as containing "revelations from God to the Church." By unanimous vote, leaders and members agreed that the First Vision and other material in the Pearl of Great Price and the Doctrine and Covenants was inspired of God.[70]

The Gift of Faith

Latter-day Saints testify that faith is a gift of God. By using the tools of secular historians, one cannot prove or disprove a vision. There is no tangible evidence of Paul's vision on the road to Damascus, and belief in Joseph Smith's First Vision is enclosed in the discipline of faith.

The vision that inaugurated a new gospel dispensation is a fundamental cornerstone of the restored Church. Latter-day Saints testify that Joseph Smith's 1838 description of his sacred experience in a peaceful grove is an accurate account of an actual historical event. Brigham Young, who met Joseph in 1832, and Daniel Wells, who met the Prophet almost ten years later, both testified that before meeting the Prophet Joseph Smith they did not understand the true character of God and his Son, Jesus. After meeting Joseph, however, they agreed that this latter-day Prophet knew more about religion and the things of God and eternity than any other individual they had known. He was the first, they testified, to explain to them the true "character" and "personality" of God.[71] "Joseph continued to receive revelation upon revelation, ordinance upon ordinance, truth upon truth," President Young added, "until he obtained all that was necessary for the salvation of the human family. . . . I know that Joseph Smith was a Prophet of God. . . . I have had many revelations; I have seen and heard for myself, and know these things are true. . . . Any one may dispute it, but there is no one in the world who can disprove it."[72]

NOTES

1. Gordon B. Hinckley, "The Cornerstones of Our Faith," Conference Report, October 1984, p. 68.

2. Spencer W. Kimball, *The Teachings of Spencer W. Kimball*, ed. Edward L. Kimball (Salt Lake City: Bookcraft, 1982), p. 428.

3. James E. Faust, "The Magnificent Vision near Palmyra," Conference Report, April 1984, p. 91.

4. Accounts of Joseph's recitals of the First Vision have been published as appendixes to Milton V. Backman, *Joseph Smith's First Vision*, 2nd ed. (Salt Lake City: Bookcraft, 1980) and in Dean C. Jessee, *The Personal Writings of Joseph Smith* (Salt Lake City: Deseret Book Co., 1984), pp. 5–6, 75–76, 199–200, 213. A harmony of the writings of the Prophet on the First Vision appears in Milton V. Backman, *Eyewitness Accounts of the Restoration* (Salt Lake City: Deseret Book Co., 1986). Manuscripts of three accounts are located in the Church Historical Department and these three accounts are identified in this work by the year in which they were written or dictated, 1832, 1835, and 1838. The manuscript of the last account has not been located but it was written in 1841 or 1842 and was the first to be published, being printed in the *Times and Seasons* in March 1842. This account is identified with the reference, "1842 History." Only one account, the 1832 History, is in the actual handwriting of Joseph Smith but the other accounts were either dictated by the Prophet or written under his direction.

5. 1838 History.

6. 1832 History; 1842 History.

7. 1842 History.

8. 1838 History. Italics were not included in the original manuscript. Spelling and punctuation of this and other manuscripts cited in this chapter, however, have been preserved in the form in which the information was recorded in the earliest known manuscript.

9. 1838 History; 1842 History.

10. 1835 History. This is an entry in Joseph Smith's 1835 Diary under the date, November 9. Book A-1 and Book B-1, Church Historical Department.

11. 1838 History. Joseph Smith used the terms *light* and *fire* interchangeably. See also 1835 History.

12. 1832 History.

13. 1842 History.

14. 1838 History.

15. For additional information on contemporary descriptions of the First Vision see Milton V. Backman, "Confirming Witnesses of the First Vision," *Ensign*, January 1986, pp. 32–37. Many references to the Father and Son appearing to Joseph Smith are found in the writings and discourses of early Latter-day Saints, such as Orson Pratt, "Are the Father and Son Two Distinct Personages?" *Millennial Star* 11 (1849): 310–11; *Journal of Discourses*, 26 vols. (London: Latter-day Saints' Book Depot, 1855–86), 21:65, 161; 24:372; 25:157; 26:106.

16. *Journal of Discourses* 24:372.

17. Ibid. 12:354.

18. Kimball, *Teachings*, p. 430.

19. 1832 History.

20. 1832 History.

21. 1838 History.

22. 1842 History.

23. 1835 History.

24. 1832 History.

25. Milton V. Backman, "Confirming Witnesses of the First Vision," *Ensign*, January 1986, p. 34. The 1838 History is in the handwriting of James Mulholland, who died on November 3, 1839. Consequently, the manuscript emphasizing Joseph Smith's visions and activities during the 1820s was completed between the spring of 1838 and the winter of 1839. Prior to publishing his missionary pamphlet in Scotland, Orson Pratt's last contact with Joseph was in December 1839. The two met in Philadelphia. Joseph was in the East attempting to secure redress for crimes committed against the Saints in Missouri, and Orson Pratt was en route to England. Prior to that date, Orson Pratt had been a close associate of Joseph Smith for eight years. If Orson Pratt had secured a copy of Joseph's history, there would probably have been a similarity in the usage of words in that history and Pratt's *Remarkable Visions*. On the other hand, there are striking parallels (in phrases) in the Wentworth history and the Orson Pratt pamphlet, indicating that Joseph Smith (or scribes who assisted him in writing the 1842 History) possibly used Orson Pratt's missionary pamphlet as an aid in preparing a reply to the editor of the *Chicago Democrat. Times and Seasons* 1 (February 1840):61.

26. *Journal of Discourses* 7:220–21.

27. Ibid. 2:171. See also a similar statement by George A. Smith in Ibid. 13:78.

28. Ibid. 12:67.

29. Ibid. 12:354; 14:141; 15:181.

30. Ibid. 20:166.

31. Ibid. 21:65.

32. Ibid. 11:2.

33. Ibid. 12:333–34; 13:77.

34. Ibid. 2:171; 8:354.

35. 1838 History.

36. Lucy Mack Smith, *Biographical Sketches of Joseph Smith, the Prophet and his Progenitors for Many Generations* (Liverpool: published for Orson Pratt and S. W. Richards, 1853), p. 73.

37. David Marks, ed., *Memoirs of the Life of David Marks* (Dover, N. H., 1846), pp. 17, 25–29. For additional information on this theme see Backman, *First Vision*, pp. 107–9, 114–21.

38. Andrew F. Ehat and Lyndon W. Cook, comp., *The Words of Joseph Smith* (Provo: Religious Studies Center, Brigham Young University, 1980), p. 378. See also pp. 63–64.

39. Ehat and Cook, *Words of Joseph Smith*, p. 212.

40. John Whitmer, *An Early Latter Day Saint History: The Book of John Whitmer*, F. Mark McKiernan and Roger D. Launius, eds. (Independence: Herald Publishing, 1980), pp. 66–67. Levi Hancock described the vision of the Father and Son to Joseph Smith on June 4, 1831. Levi W. Hancock, Diary, typescript, pp. 47–48, Brigham Young University Library, Special Collections.

41. *The Ohio Observer* (Hudson), August 11, 1836, p. 1; Milton V. Backman, "Truman Coe's 1836 Description of Mormonism," *BYU Studies* 17 (Spring 1977):347–55.

42. These lectures were initially published in the 1835 or first edition of the Doctrine and Covenants.

43. Parley P. Pratt, *Mormonism Unveiled: Zion's Watchman Unmasked, and its editor, Mr. L. R. Sunderland, Exposed: Truth Vindicated: the Devil Mad, and Priestcraft in Danger!* (New York: O. Pratt and E. Fordham, 1838), pp. 31, 43.

44. Parley P. Pratt, *An Answer to Mr. William Hewitt's Tract Against the Latter-day Saints* (Manchester: W. R. Thomas, 1840), pp. 8–9.

45. John Taylor, *Truth Defended and Methodism Weighed in the Balance and Found Wanting* (Liverpool: J. Tompkins, 1840), pp. 6–7.

46. John Taylor, "The Living God," *Times and Seasons* (February 15, 1845):808–9.

47. Orson Pratt, "Are the Father and Son Two Distinct Personages?" *Millennial Star* 11 (1849):310–11.

48. The Smiths probably moved to Manchester in 1818, two (rather than four) years prior to the First Vision.

49. For a description of the visions and witnesses of the visions of 1836 see Milton V. Backman, *The Heavens Resound: A History of the Latter-day Saints in Ohio, 1830–1838* (Salt Lake City: Deseret Book Co., 1983), pp. 287–308.

50. Oliver Cowdery, Sketch Book, January 21, 1836, Church Archives, reproduced in Leonard J. Arrington, "Oliver Cowdery's Kirtland, Ohio 'Sketch Book,' " *BYU Studies* 12 (Summer 1972):410–26.

51. Dean C. Jessee, "The Early Accounts of Joseph Smith's First Vision," *BYU Studies* 9 (Spring 1969):294.

52. Richard L. Anderson, "Parallel Prophets: Paul and Joseph Smith," *Brigham Young University Fireside and Devotional Speeches* (Provo, Utah: Brigham Young University Publications, 1983), pp. 178–79.

53. "A Vision," *The Evening and The Morning Star* 1 (July 1832).

54. 1838 History.

55. Backman, *Joseph Smith's First Vision*, pp. 67–69. See also Appendix K.

56. Milton V. Backman, *American Religions and the Rise of Mormonism* (Salt Lake City: Deseret Book Co., 1970), pp. 283–92, 308.

57. 1838 History.

58. Joseph Smith, *History of the Church of Jesus Christ of Latter-day Saints*, ed. B. H. Roberts, 7 vols. (Salt Lake City: The Church of Jesus Christ of Latter-day Saints, 1932–51), 2:323, 400; 3:97, 125.

59. Wade C. Barclay, *Early American Methodism, 1769–1844*, 2 vols. (New York: Board of Missions and Church Extension of the Methodist Church, 1949), 1:299–300.

60. *Palmyra Register*, June 28, 1820; July 5, 1820.

61. Backman, *Joseph Smith's First Vision*, pp. 81–82.

62. O. Turner, *History of the Pioneer Settlement of Phelps and Gorham's Purchase, and Morris' Reserve* (Rochester, 1852), p. 214.

63. Pomeroy Tucker, *Origin, Rise, and Progress of Mormonism* (New York, 1867), pp. 17–18.

64. Peter Crawley, "A Comment on Joseph Smith's Account of His First Vision and the 1820 Revival," *Dialogue* 4 (Spring 1971):106–7; Marilla Marks, ed., *Memoirs of the Life of David Marks* (Dover, N.H., 1846), pp. 17, 32; David Marks, *Life of David Marks*, p. 39.

65. Backman, *Joseph Smith's First Vision*, pp. 192–93.

66. Church records located at Cornell University, Ithaca, New York, gathered from the Finger Lakes region provide evidence of increases in church membership in Presbyterian churches located in Geneva, Junius, Seneca Falls, Truxton, Lyons, and Aurora; in Baptist churches of Solon, Marion, and Cortland; and in Congregational churches in Canandaigua, Williamson, and East Bloomfield. Moreover, Quaker records show an increase in 1819–1820 in Farmington (a part of which later became Manchester), the township where the Smith farm was located at that time. It is difficult to determine Methodist growth in the immediate area where Joseph Smith lived in 1820 because the Genesee District (an ecclesiastical unit containing circuits located in western New York between Lake Cayuga and Buffalo) was divided into two districts. The eastern part was called Ontario, and the western section (west of Rochester) retained the name Genesee. The membership reported in 1820 in the combined districts was 5,683 and in 1821 it was 7,568, the latter figure representing an increase of 1,885 members between the summer of 1820 and the summer of 1821, with a 398 increase in the Ontario District and 1,487 in the Genesee District, *Methodist Minutes* (1820), p. 27.

67. For additional information on the great revival of 1819 and 1820 in upstate and western New York, see Backman, *Joseph Smith's First Vision*, ch. 3.

68. *Journal of Discourses* 12:67.
69. Ibid. 12:71.
70. *The Latter-day Saints' Millennial Star,* November 15, 1880, pp. 723–24.
71. *Journal of Discourses* 12:71, 74; 16:46.
72. Ibid. 16:42, 46.

The Compassion of Joseph Smith

4

Bruce A. Van Orden

Joseph Smith remains an enigmatic person. The Angel Moroni prophesied to him on the night of 21 September 1823 that his name "should be had for good and evil among all nations, kindreds, and tongues, or that it should be both good and evil spoken of among all people" (Joseph Smith—History 1:33). On the one hand much has been said and written in recent years about his supposed weaknesses—that he was a libertine, that he was insensitive to his wife Emma, and that he had megalomaniacal fantasies, including paranoid delusions about his power and immortality. On the other side, Joseph Smith has been cast as a "choice seer," through whom God worked to bring forth His plan of salvation in these last days.[1]

While I sustain Joseph Smith as that "choice seer," the purpose of this essay is not to focus on his seership. Rather it is to demonstrate the qualities of friendship, kindness, charity, and compassion for which Joseph Smith was remembered by countless believing Latter-day Saints who knew him. Thus it will be demonstrated that his character was in harmony with his seership, that he was indeed the "good man . . . called by a perfect Lord, Jesus of Nazareth!"[2]

Bruce A. Van Orden is Assistant Professor of Church History and Doctrine at Brigham Young University.

Joseph Smith was not perfect; he didn't claim to be. "I never told you I was perfect," he told the Nauvoo Saints 12 May 1844 as he defended his prophetic calling.[3] Nevertheless he sought to keep the commandments and do God's will. One who knew Brother Joseph well, John Taylor, having been with the Prophet in private and in public and in councils of all kinds, declared, "I testify before God, angels, and men, that he was a good, honorable, virtuous man—that his doctrines were good, scriptural, and wholesome—that his precepts were such as became a man of God—that his private and public character was unimpeachable—and that he lived and died as a man of God and a gentleman."[4]

Joseph Smith was a man who made an impression on others, usually for good. For example, early in his ministry, even before the Church was established, Joseph became closely attached to the Joseph Knight family in Colesville, New York. "His noble deportment, his faithfulness and his kind address could not fail to win the esteem of those who had the pleasure of his acquaintance," reported Newel Knight.[5] And as Daryl Chase has observed, "The lives of scores of men and women were . . . changed from mediocrity or failure to lives of meaning and service" by Joseph Smith.[6]

A Life of Friendship and Compassion

By his own admission, Joseph Smith possessed "a native cheery temperament" (Joseph Smith—History 1:28). "I delight in the society of my friends," he confessed in his diary.[7] Everywhere he went he showed kindness and generosity, to friend and foe alike. One of his most dedicated disciples, Parley P. Pratt, observed, "His countenance was ever mild, affable, beaming with intelligence and benevolence; mingled with a look of interest and an unconscious smile, or cheerfulness, and entirely free from all restraint or affectation of gravity." Parley was convinced that Joseph's "benevolence [was] unbounded as the ocean." "Even his most bitter enemies were generally overcome, if he could once get their ears," Parley added.[8]

The discourses and letters of Joseph Smith are peppered with advice about love. "Love is one of the chief characteristics of Deity," Joseph wrote in 1840 to the Apostles on their mission in England, "and ought to be manifested by those who aspire to be the sons of God. A man filled with the love of God, is not content with blessing his family alone, but ranges through the whole world, anxious to bless the whole human race."[9] Speaking very personally to the infant Relief Society in 1842, Joseph confessed, "When persons manifest the least kindness and love to me, O what power it has over my mind, while the opposite course has a tendency to harrow up all the harsh feelings and depress the human mind."[10]

Showing love and kindness toward others seemed to come naturally to the Prophet. Whenever he saw someone in distress, his heart would melt with compassion and he would do what he could to help. This he did to all, without respect of persons, to members of his family, to little children, to the poor and the elderly, to his close friends, to enemies and former persecutors, to strangers, and to fellow Church leaders.

Family Members

Next to his love for Deity, Joseph Smith loved members of his family. One who knew him intimately, Benjamin F. Johnson, stated, "As a son, [Joseph] was nobility itself, in love and honor of his parents; as a brother he was loving and true, even unto death; as a husband and father, his devotion to wives and children stopped only at idolatry."[11]

Undoubtedly, much of Joseph Smith's kindly temperament came from his two loving parents. One of their descendants, Joseph F. Smith, wrote of Joseph Smith, Sr., and Lucy Mack Smith: "Love and good will to all found expression in their hearts and actions, and their children were imbued with like sentiments."[12] Joseph returned love to his parents, even though he was naturally busy with the affairs of the kingdom. In October 1835 in Kirtland, Joseph learned of his father's severe fever and dropped other duties to attend to him. After five days Joseph Sr. was failing fast and it appeared that he might die. But on the sixth day, a Sabbath, a miracle occurred:

> Waited on my father again, who was very sick. In secret prayer in the morning, the Lord said, "My servant, thy father shall live." I waited on him all this day with my heart raised to God in the name of Jesus Christ, that He would restore him to health, that I might be blessed with his company and advice, esteeming it one of the greatest earthly blessings to be blessed with the society of parents, whose mature years and experience render them capable of administering the most wholesome advice. At evening Brother David Whitmer came in. We called on the Lord in mighty prayer in the name of Jesus Christ, and laid our hands on him, and rebuked the disease. And God heard and answered our prayers—to the great satisfaction of our souls. Our aged father arose and dressed himself, shouted, and praised the Lord. Called Brother William Smith, who had retired to rest, that he might praise the Lord with us, by joining in songs of praise to the Most High.[13]

This type of compassion was also shown to members of Joseph's extended family. In October 1835 Joseph became aware of the failing health of Mary Bailey Smith, wife of his brother Samuel. Mary was nearly ready to deliver a baby. "I went out into the field and bowed before the Lord and called upon Him in mighty prayer in her behalf," recollected the Prophet. Joseph then received comfort that Dr. Frederick Williams would be given wisdom to deal prudently with Mary and that she would be spared and be delivered of a living child. "What God had manifested to me was fulfilled every whit," he recorded.[14]

While the Smith family usually exhibited much love toward each other, their internal relationships were not entirely without friction. This was especially true in the relationship of Joseph and his younger brother William, who had an excitable disposition. In late October 1835 Joseph and William disagreed on testimony that was presented before the high council on a case that was determining the fellowship of a family. Joseph and Hyrum Smith tried in the spirit of meekness to reason with their younger brother, but to no avail. William proceeded to prejudice the mind of their brother Samuel and to proclaim in the street his adverse feelings toward Joseph and Hyrum. "Where the matter will end I know not," fretted Joseph, "but I pray God to forgive him and them, and give them humility and repentance." Later in the day, Joseph recorded that, in answer to his prayer, "I obtained a testimony that my brother William would return to the Church, and repair the wrong he had done."[15]

Joseph maintained an especially close tie to his brother Hyrum, who was six years his senior. "Never in all my life have I seen anything more beautiful than the striking example of brotherly love and devotion felt for each other by Joseph and Hyrum," recalled a friend of the Smiths, William Taylor. "I witnessed this many, many times. No matter how often, or when or where they met, it was always with the same expression of supreme joy. It could not have been otherwise, when both were filled to overflowing with the gift and power of the Holy Ghost! It was kindred spirits meeting!"[16]

Joseph Smith's greatest filial affection was reserved for his wife and children. Next to "God and His Kingdom," Joseph Smith's greatest motto was "wives, children, and friends," recorded Benjamin F. Johnson.[17] In October 1832, Joseph went with several Church leaders to New York City to purchase goods for their mercantile business in Kirtland. Joseph was anxious for his wife Emma because she was pregnant with their fourth child (she had lost to death her previous three). "I feel as if I wanted to say something to you to comfort you in your peculiar trial and present affliction," wrote Joseph.

> I hope God will give you strength that you may not faint I pray God to soften the hearts of those arou[n]d you to be kind to you and take [the] burden of[f] your shoulders as much as possible and not afflict you I feel for you for I know you[r] state and that others do not but you must comfort yourself knowing that God is your friend in heaven and that you hav[e] one true and living friend on Earth your Husband.[18]

Dr. John M. Bernhisel, a close friend of the Prophet and a frequent guest in the Smith home in Nauvoo, indicated that Joseph was "kind and obliging, generous and benevolent, sociable and cheerful," but that it was "as the tender and affectionate husband and parent" that "the prominent traits of [Joseph Smith's] character are revealed."[19] Mercy Thompson, married to Robert Thompson, a scribe to the Prophet, remembered, "I saw him by the bedside of Emma, his wife, in sickness, exhibiting all the solicitude and sympathy possible for the tenderest of hearts and the most affectionate of natures to feel. And by the deathbed of my beloved companion, I saw him stand in sorrow, reluctantly submitting to the decree of Providence, while the tears of love and sympathy freely flowed."[20]

Children

Joseph Smith likewise dearly loved his children. Whenever he could, he would take time from his busy schedule and play and romp with his little ones. He took his turn with Emma in caring for them when they were sick. On one occasion, Benjamin F. Johnson, in visiting the Mansion House in Nauvoo, was introduced to two of Joseph's children, who had just come from their mother "all so nice, bright, and sweet." Joseph then exclaimed, "Benjamin, look at these children, how could I help loving their mother."[21]

The Prophet's tender feelings for children extended far beyond his own offspring. His nephew Joseph F. Smith claimed that "one marked illustration of his character was his love for children." Remembering that he as a youth sat upon his uncle's knee, Joseph F. Smith continued, "He never saw a child but he desired to take it up and bless it, and many he did so bless, taking them in his arms and upon his knee. . . . He was so fond of children that he would go far out of his way to speak to a little one, which is to me a striking characteristic of true manhood."[22]

Louisa Y. Littlefield, reminiscing in later years, remembered her first contact with the Prophet in 1834. "In Kirtland, when wagon loads of grown people and children came in from the country to meeting," she related, "Joseph would make his way to as many of the wagons as he well could and cordially shake the hand of each person. Every child and young babe in the company were especially noticed by him and tenderly taken by the hand, with his kind words and blessings. He loved innocence and purity, and he seemed to find it in the greatest perfection with the prattling child."[23]

Joseph Smith cared not only for the "prattling child," but also for emerging adolescents. Sister Littlefield's husband, Lyman, narrated an incident from the march of Zion's Camp when he was thirteen years old:

> The journey was extremely toilsome for all, and the physical suffering, coupled with the knowledge of the persecutions endured by our brethren whom we were traveling to succor, caused me to lapse one day into a state of melancholy. As the camp was making ready to depart I sat tired and brooding by the roadside. The Prophet was the busiest man of the camp; and yet when he saw me, he turned from the great press of other duties to say a word of comfort to a child. Placing his hand upon my head, he said, "Is there no place for you, my boy? If not, we must make one." This circumstance made an impression upon my mind which long lapse of time and cares of riper years have not effaced.[24]

In Nauvoo, two boys recently immigrated from England approached the Prophet as a last resort to find some kind of employment. Joseph asked them if they could dig a ditch. After they finished their job, Joseph looked at their work and said, "Boys, if I had done it myself, it could not have been done better. Now come with me." Joseph led them to the back of his store and told the boys to choose the best ham or piece of pork for themselves. They were too bashful, so he picked the two best pieces of meat and a sack of flour for each and asked them if that would do. "We thanked him kindly and went on our way home rejoicing in the kindheartedness of the Prophet of our God," related James Leech.[25]

Joseph Smith was particularly compassionate toward children in distress. "If he heard the cry of a child," recalled one of his plural wives, Helen Mar Kimball Whitney, "he would rush out of the house to see if it was harmed."[26] When Helen was a child, her father, Heber C. Kimball, related in a meeting an incident when Helen accidently broke several valuable dishes and then went outside under an apple tree and prayed that her mother's heart would be softened, that she might not whip her. Although Sister Kimball had warned Helen not to touch the dishes, she had no disposition to chastise the child when she returned home. "Joseph wept like a child on hearing this simple narrative and its application, and said it was well timed," remembered Heber C. Kimball.[27]

After Mercy Thompson had lost her husband to an untimely death, the Prophet displayed considerable interest in the widow and her daughter. "This indeed was a time of sorrow, but I can never forget the tender sympathy and brotherly kindness he ever showed toward me and my fatherless child," Mercy wrote, "When riding with him and his wife Emma in their carriage, I have known him to alight and gather prairie flowers for my little girl."[28]

While in Nauvoo, Joseph Smith took more than average interest in the twin daughters born to the Burgess family, since Emma had lost a child at birth at the same time. He loved to tend the little girls and comfort them whenever they fretted. Eventually little Mary Burgess died. Mary's older sister reminisced, "[Joseph] grieved as if he had lost one of his own. I remembered seeing him embrace the little cold form and say, 'Mary, oh my dear little Mary!' "[29]

Joseph was also wont to give blessings to little children. One notable example took place in Ramus (also known as Macedonia), Illinois, a Latter-day Saint settlement twenty miles from Nauvoo, in March 1843. In a gathering of the Ramus Saints, the Prophet conducted a blessing meeting where twenty-seven children were blessed, "nineteen of whom I blessed myself, with great fervency," noted Joseph. "Virtue went out of me, and my strength left me."[30] Benjamin F. Johnson recalled the same event in his memoirs:

> On one occasion, at Macedonia, after he had preached . . . and . . . blessed nineteen children, he said to me, "Let us go home." We went home, and I found my wife sitting with our first born still unblessed and said, "See now what we have lost by our babe not being at the meeting." Brother Joseph replied, "You shall lose nothing, for I will bless him too." Which he did, and then sitting back heavily in a big chair before the fire, and with a deep-drawn breath said, "Oh! I am so tired—so tired that I often feel to long for a day of rest."[31]

The Elderly and the Poor

Not only was Joseph Smith's heart moved when he saw little children, he felt compassion toward the elderly and the poor in their distress. "It was the disposition of the Prophet Joseph when he saw little children in the mud to take them up in his arms and wash the mud from their bare feet with his handkerchief," wrote Mosiah Hancock in his autobiography. "And oh how kind he was to the old folks, as well as to little children. He had a smile for his friends, and was always cheerful."[32] Orange L. Wight, son of Lyman Wight, observed this trait as well. "[Joseph] was very kind and sociable with both young and old."[33]

The Prophet was always ready to aid those who lacked funds to care for themselves. In the summer of 1838, when thousands of Saints were arriving in Missouri from Ohio, William Holden was engaged one day with many others in playing various outdoor games with Joseph Smith. After playing a while, Joseph urged the others to join him in building a log cabin for a widow. "Such was Joseph's way, always assisting in whatever he could."[34]

Elizabeth Ann Whitney, wife to Bishop Newel K. Whitney, related the story of a "Feast for the Poor" set up by her husband according to the desires of the Prophet. "The Feast lasted three days, during which time all in the vicinity of Kirtland who would come were invited, and entertained as courteously and generously as if they had been able to extend hospitality instead of receiving it. The Prophet Joseph and his two counselors were present each day, talking, blessing, and comforting the poor, by words of encouragement and their most welcome presence."[35]

Oliver B. Huntington remembered hearing Joseph Smith declare the following in a discourse: "Every man will fail sometime. Be charitable and liberal with your substance, for it is only a secondary consideration—the use you make of it is the primary consideration. You may do good to some one who is down today and who will rise and be on top of the wheel when you are down, for every man will fail sometime."[36]

Friends

Joseph Smith's favorite times seem to have been when he was in the presence of his friends. It was therapeutic for him to be jovial and at ease among people he trusted. And whenever any of his friends needed his help or sympathy, he was immediately ready to offer it. Lorenzo Snow came to Kirtland in 1836 and described the outgoing personality of Brother Joseph: "He was free and easy in his conversation with me, making me feel perfectly at home in his presence. In fact, I felt as free with him as if we had been special friends for years."[37]

Joseph was especially tenderhearted when he had seen his friends and Church members suffer. "Twelve days after the Prophet escaped from [Liberty Jail] Missouri, a General Conference of the Church was held at Quincy, Illinois," remembered Edward Stevenson. "His soul was filled with emotion, and it seemed as though he could not utter his feelings, only with a flood of tears. He looked calm, however, and a halo of brightness hovered about him. He was of a tender heart, as well as of a stern and firm disposition when occasion required it. I have known the Prophet to weep with tender affection."[38]

Some of Joseph Smith's greatest compassion was expressed during the malaria epidemic in Nauvoo in 1839 and 1840. Elizabeth Ann Whitney, who with her husband Newel K. Whitney, had hosted Joseph and Emma Smith in their distress in Kirtland in 1831, now had the favor returned to them. The entire Whitney family was sick with chills and fever and Sister Whitney was expecting her ninth child. "Joseph, upon visiting us and seeing our change of circumstances, urged us at once to come and share his accommodations. We went to live in the Prophet Joseph's yard in a small cottage," Elizabeth recorded. "We soon recruited in health, and the children became more like themselves."[39]

Elder Wilford Woodruff of the Twelve recorded the "day of God's power" when the Prophet on 22 July 1839 rose from his own bed of affliction and went about healing all about him on both sides of the Mississippi River. "The words of the Prophet were not like the words of man, but like the voice of God," remembered Wilford. On that day, Joseph received another request to heal two twins, five months old. Turning to Brother Woodruff, the Prophet said, "You go with the man and heal his children." "He took a red silk handkerchief out of his pocket and gave it to me, and told me to wipe their faces with the handkerchief when I administered to them and they should be healed," reported Elder Woodruff. "He also said unto me, 'As long as you will keep that handkerchief, it shall remain a league between you and me.' "[40]

During this same plague, Joseph was attended in the worst of his own sickness by his bosom friend and companion, Benjamin F. Johnson. As soon as the Prophet was recovered, Benjamin fell into a violent attack of the fever. Joseph then looked after his friend for the next two weeks until he recovered. A few months later, Benjamin needed to leave for the East to attend to his ailing parents, but was again sick himself. Joseph offered to bless his friend. "Placing his hands upon my head, he seemed to pour out his soul in blessing me," wrote Brother Johnson. "He told the Lord I had been faithful to care for others, but I was now worn and sick, and that on my journey I would need His care, and he asked that a guardian angel might go with me from that day and stay with me through all my life."[41]

Lucy Walker Kimball remembered how Joseph Smith invited her large family to stay with him and Emma while their mother lay dying with the chills and fever. After she died, the Prophet advised the father, Lorin, to find a new climate so that he himself would not die. "My house shall be their home. I will adopt them [the children] as my own," Joseph assured Brother Walker. Joseph and Emma then cared for the needs of the many children. "Our own father and mother could scarcely have done more or manifested greater solicitude for [our] recovery than did the Prophet and his wife Emma," reported Lucy. Joseph and Emma introduced the Walker children as their sons and daughters and every privilege was accorded them in the Mansion House. Young Lorin was referred to by Joseph as "his Edwin" and was his trusted friend—"arm in arm they walked and conversed freely on various subjects."[42]

Joseph Smith was always grateful for services rendered him by his friends. As an example, one day in Nauvoo Joseph poured out his soul in thanks to Dimick Huntington for all he had done for him. "Now, Dimick, in return for such acts, you may ask of me what you will and it shall be given you, even if it be to the half of my kingdom,'' exclaimed Joseph. Dimick replied that he had no interest in worldly honors or goods, but would be happy to be in the presence of Joseph Smith in the hereafter.[43]

Enemies and Former Persecutors

Like Jesus Christ, his Master, Joseph Smith throughout his life humbly held to the principle of showing mercy to his enemies. Joseph loved the ''parables of mercy'' and often preached about them to the Saints.[44] The Prophet recognized that the parables of the lost sheep, the lost coin, and the prodigal son condemned self-righteousness. In an 1842 discourse to the Relief Society sisters, he said, ''All the religious world is boasting of its righteousness—it is the doctrine of the devil to retard the human mind and retard our progress by filling us with self righteousness.'' Joseph then explained, ''The nearer we get to our heavenly Father the more are we disposed to look with compassion on perishing souls to take them upon our shoulders and cast their sins behind our back. . . . If you would have God have mercy on you, have mercy on one another.''[45]

Daniel Tyler wrote of two experiences where the Prophet forgave those who had trespassed against him. Once in Kirtland, when William Smith and many others had rebelled against him, Joseph Smith called a public meeting. ''Entering the school house a little before the meeting opened and gazing upon the man of God, I perceived sadness in his countenance and tears trickling down his cheeks,'' remembered Brother Tyler. In the meeting Joseph knelt in prayer and offered petitions that the Almighty would forgive those who had gone astray and open their eyes that they might see aright. ''That prayer, I say to the humble mind, partook of the learning and eloquence of heaven. . . . It was the crowning of all the prayers I ever heard.''[46]

On a later occasion early in the Nauvoo period, an unnamed man who had stood high in the Church in Far West, but who had apostatized, sought reinstatement in the Church. The man worked hard chopping cordwood to be able to earn money to take his family to Nauvoo. While he was traveling, the Lord revealed to Joseph Smith of his coming. ''The Prophet looked out of the window and saw him coming up the street. As soon as he turned to open the gate, the Prophet sprang up from his chair and ran and met him in the yard, exclaiming, 'O Brother, how glad I am to see you!' He caught him around the neck, and both wept like children.''[47]

Perhaps the most well-known example of Joseph Smith's forgiveness was his acceptance back into the fold of William W.

Phelps, who in Missouri had used Church money for his own purposes, was excommunicated, and then turned against Joseph and the members of the Church during the Battle of Far West. Phelps subsequently moved to Dayton, Ohio, where he was both poverty-stricken and penitent. Encouraged by Orson Hyde and John E. Page who discovered him in Dayton, Phelps decided to write to Joseph and ask forgiveness: "I am alive, and with the help of God I mean to live still. I am as the prodigal son . . . and I tremble at the gulf I have passed." The Prophet was moved to compassion and wrote back to his former friend:

> Inasmuch as long-suffering, patience, and mercy have ever characterized the dealings of our heavenly Father towards the humble and penitent, I feel disposed to copy the example, cherish the same principles, and by so doing be a savior of my fellow men.
>
> It is true, that we have suffered much in consequence of your behavior—*the cup of gall, already full enough* for mortals to drink, was indeed *filled* to *overflowing* when you turned against us. One with whom we had oft taken sweet counsel together, and enjoyed many refreshing seasons from the Lord. . . .
>
> However, the cup has been drunk, the will of our Father has been done, and we are yet alive, for which we thank the Lord. And having been delivered from the hands of wicked men by the mercy of our God, we say it is your privilege to be delivered from the powers of the adversary, be brought into the liberty of God's dear children. . . .
>
> Believing your confession to be real, and your repentance genuine, I shall be happy once again to give you the right hand of fellowship, and rejoice over the returning prodigal. . . .
>
> "Come on, dear brother, since the war is past,
> For friends at first, are friends again at last."[48]

Strangers

Joseph Smith was also kind and considerate toward strangers. He recognized that all individuals are children of God and he wanted to do his best by each one. He had this kindly trait when he was still a boy. A Mrs. Palmer, who at six years of age knew the teenaged Joseph as he worked at her father's farm, observed: "I remember going into the field on an afternoon to play in the corn rows while my brothers worked. When evening came, I was too tired to walk home and cried because my brothers refused to carry me. Joseph lifted me to his shoulder, and with his arm thrown across my feet to steady, and my arm about his neck, he carried me to our home."[49]

After the Prophet came out of prison in Missouri, a person approached him in Quincy, Illinois, and demanded any money he had, for Joseph had endorsed a loan of another man who owed the first man money. Joseph first pleaded that having come from prison, this was no time to ask him for money, but when the man was obstinate, Joseph cleared his pockets and gave the man four of his five silver dollars. Soon after that an ill sister came to Joseph asking him if he would recommend whether or not she should go to her friends in the East for care. When she said that she would rather stay with the Saints, Joseph replied, "Then stay, sister, and God bless you." He then put his hand in his pocket and gave her his last dollar. Christopher Merkley, who had witnessed both episodes, came to Joseph before he left for Commerce and gladly gave the Prophet a sovereign.[50]

One day in May 1842 while Joseph was talking to some townspeople in Nauvoo, a man approached and indicated that a poor brother some distance from town had had his house burn down the night before. Nearly all the men said they felt sorry for the man. Joseph put his hand in his pocket, took out five dollars and said, "I feel sorry for this brother to the amount of five dollars. How much do you all feel sorry?"[51]

On 17 May 1843, when Joseph Smith was giving instructions to the Saints in Ramus, Illinois, a Methodist minister by the name of Samuel Prior visited the meeting. Prior lived some sixty miles from Nauvoo and had heard sordid tales about the behavior of the Mormons. Deciding to see for himself what kind of people they were, he headed for Nauvoo. When he reached Carthage, a member of the Church offered to take him to meet the Mormon Prophet, who was then in Ramus. Prior was surprised: rather than seeing a wild-eyed fanatic, he saw in Joseph Smith a person who calmly and dispassionately delivered his discourse. In the evening, Reverend Prior was invited to speak to the congregation. "They paid the utmost attention," the minister related.

> This surprised me a little, as I did not expect to find any such thing as a religious toleration among them. After I had closed, Elder Smith, who had attended, arose and begged leave to differ from me in some few points of doctrine, and this he did mildly, politely, and affectingly; like one who was more desirous to disseminate truth and expose error, than to love the malicious triumph of debate over me. I was truly edified with his remarks, and felt less prejudiced against the Mormons than ever. He invited me to call upon him, and I promised to do so.[52]

Church Leaders

Finally, Joseph Smith was ever compassionate toward his fellow Church leaders. They could always count on him for a smile, a hearty handshake, and a listening ear. His patience with their weaknesses also seemed endless. For example, on the long and most difficult Zion's Camp trek from Ohio to Missouri, the Prophet was the epitome of self-restraint. According to George A. Smith,

"During the entire trip he never uttered a murmur or complained, while most of the men in the camp complained to him of sore toes, blistered feet, long drives, scanty supply of provisions, poor quality of bread, bad corn dodger, frowsy butter, strong honey, strong bacon and cheese." George A. added: "Joseph had to bear with us and tutor us like children."[53]

After he had become a loyal and devoted Apostle, Elder George A. Smith related that at the end of a conversation with the Prophet, Joseph wrapped his arms around his cousin and said, "George A., I love you, as I do my own life." Elder Smith then noted, "I felt so affected I could hardly speak, but replied, 'I hope, Brother Joseph, that my whole life and actions will ever prove my feelings and the depth of my affection towards you.' "[54]

Just days before his death, the Prophet paused on the outskirts of Nauvoo before heading for Carthage. In the presence of other Church leaders, he declared, "My friends, nay, dearer still my brethren, I love you. I love the city of Nauvoo too well to save my life at your expense. If I go not to them, they will come and act out the horrid Missouri scenes in Nauvoo. I may prevent it. I fear not death. My work is well nigh done. Keep the faith and I will die for Nauvoo."[55]

Thus we can see that Joseph Smith was no ordinary man. He rose above his fellows in his Christlike attributes. He reached out in the pure love of Christ to all he could. And thousands were the individuals he touched. Mary Alice Cannon expressed well that influence:

> The love the Saints had for him was inexpressible. They would willingly have laid down their lives for him. If he was to talk every task would be laid aside that they listen to his words.
>
> He was not an ordinary man. Saints and sinners alike felt and recognized a power and influence which he carried with him. It was impossible to meet him and not be impressed by the strength of his personality and influence.[56]

NOTES

1. Neal A. Maxwell, "A Choice Seer," *Ensign*, August 1986, pp. 6–15.

2. Neal A. Maxwell "A Choice Seer," p. 6.

3. *History of the Church* 6:366. Hereafter *HC*.

4. John Taylor, *The Gospel Kingdom*, ed. G. Homer Durham (Salt Lake City: Bookcraft, 1987), p. 355.

5. "Newel Knight's Journal," in *Scraps of Biography* (*Faith Promoting Series*, vol. 10) (Salt Lake City: Juvenile Instructor Office, 1883), p. 47.

6. Daryl Chase, *Joseph the Prophet* (Salt Lake City: Deseret Book Co., 1944), p. 41.

7. Diary of Joseph Smith, 11 January 1836, Joseph Smith Collection, LDS Historical Archives, as cited in Donald Q. Cannon, *The Wisdom of Joseph Smith* (Orem, Utah: Grandin Book Company, 1983), p. 10.

8. *Autobiography of Parley Parker Pratt* (Salt Lake City: Deseret Book Co., 1964), pp. 45–46.

9. *HC* 4:227.

10. *HC* 5:24.

11. "An Interesting Letter," Benjamin F. Johnson to George F. Gibbs, 1903, Benjamin F. Johnson file, LDS Church Historical Archives.

12. Joseph F. Smith, "Who Was Joseph Smith?" *Improvement Era*, December 1917, p. 168.

13. *HC* 2:288–89.

14. *HC* 2:292–93.

15. *HC* 2:297–98.

16. *Young Woman's Journal* 17 (December 1905):548.

17. Benjamin F. Johnson, "An Interesting Letter."

18. As cited in Dean C. Jessee, ed., *The Personal Writings of Joseph Smith* (Salt Lake City: Deseret Book, 1984), p. 253; spelling corrected.

19. Letter of John M. Bernhisel to Governor Thomas Ford, 14 June 1844, as cited in Hyrum L. Andrus and Helen Mae Andrus, *They Knew the Prophet* (Salt Lake City: Bookcraft, 1974), pp. 176–77.

20. *Juvenile Instructor*, 1 July 1892, p. 399.

21. Benjamin F. Johnson, "An Interesting Letter."

22. Joseph F. Smith, "Who Was Joseph Smith?" *Improvement Era*, December 1917, p. 168.

23. *Juvenile Instructor*, 1 January 1892, p. 24.

24. As cited in George Q. Cannon, *Life of Joseph Smith the Prophet* (Salt Lake City: Deseret Book Co., p. 344.

25. *Juvenile Instructor*, 1 March 1892, pp. 152–53.

26. Helen Mar Whitney, "Scenes and Incidents in Nauvoo," *Woman's Exponent* 10 (1 December 1881):97.

27. *Woman's Exponent* 9 (15 November 1880):90.

28. *Juvenile Instructor*, 1 July 1892, p. 399.

29. As cited in Andrus and Andrus, *They Knew the Prophet*, pp. 127–28.

30. *HC* 5:503.

31. Benjamin F. Johnson, *My Life's Review* (Independence, Missouri: Zion's Printing and Publishing, 1946), p. 97.

32. "Autobiography of Mosiah L. Hancock," typescript in Special Collections, Harold B. Lee Library, Brigham Young University, Provo, Utah.

33. As cited in Andrus and Andrus, *They Knew the Prophet*, p. 104.

34. *Juvenile Instructor*, 1 March 1892, p. 153.

35. As cited in Andrus and Andrus, *They Knew the Prophet*, p. 40.

36. As cited in Andrus and Andrus, *They Knew the Prophet*, p. 62.

37. *Improvement Era*, February 1937, p. 83.

38. "Autobiography of Edward Stevenson," Typescript, LDS Church Historical Archives.

39. As cited in Andrus and Andrus, *They Knew the Prophet*, p. 41.
40. As cited in Andrus and Andrus, *They Knew the Prophet*, pp. 82–84.
41. Benjamin F. Johnson, "An Interesting Letter."
42. *Woman's Exponent* 34 (November 1910):33–34.
43. As cited in Andrus and Andrus, *They Knew the Prophet*, p. 65.
44. See Richard Lloyd Anderson, "Parables of Mercy," *Ensign*, February 1987, pp. 20–25.
45. Andrew F. Ehat and Lyndon W. Cook, ed., *The Words of Joseph Smith* (Provo, UT: Religious Studies Center, Brigham Young University, 1980), p. 123.
46. As cited in Andrus and Andrus, *They Knew the Prophet*, pp. 51–52.
47. As cited in Andrus and Andrus, *They Knew the Prophet*, pp. 53–54.
48. *History of the Church* 4:163–64.
49. As cited in Andrus and Andrus, *They Knew the Prophet*, p. 1.
50. As told in Andrus and Andrus, *They Knew the Prophet*, pp. 121–22.
51. As told by Andrew Workman, *Juvenile Instructor*, 15 October 1892, p. 641.
52. *Times and Seasons* 4:197–98.
53. As cited in Andrus and Andrus, *They Knew the Prophet*, p. 48.
54. As cited in Andrus and Andrus, *They Knew the Prophet*, p. 49.
55. Dan Jones, "The Martyrdom of Joseph and Hyrum Smith," handwritten manuscript in LDS Church Historical Archives.
56. *Young Woman's Journal* 16 (December 1905):554.

Joseph Smith, the Book of Mormon, and the Nature of God

5

Robert L. Millet

Many Latter-day Saints have just begun to sense the power of the Book of Mormon. It is indeed a day of discovery. We have had a precious gift in our midst for over a century and a half and have just begun in a sense to remove the wrapping. But the excitement is mounting, and the thrill associated with intense spiritual encounter for an entire people is perhaps just around the corner.

Using the Book of Mormon

There has been some hesitation in the past to utilize the Book of Mormon as the supreme missionary tool it was intended to be. Some have worried that they would give offense to nonmembers of the Church by suggesting the need for another book of scripture. Some have sought to "prove" the Restoration from the Bible alone, trying to stay with what they perceive to be "common ground" between themselves and the rest of the Judaeo-Christian world. The Lord's plan for effective proselyting is set forth plainly in modern revelation. The following verses from the Doctrine and Covenants are but a few examples of that plan:

Robert L. Millet is Associate Professor of Ancient Scripture at Brigham Young University.

> . . . this generation shall have my word through you [Joseph Smith] (D&C 5:10).

> Lift up your heart and rejoice, for the hour of your mission [Thomas B. Marsh] is come; and your tongue shall be loosed, and you shall declare glad tidings of great joy unto this generation.
> *You shall declare the things which have been revealed to my servant, Joseph Smith, Jr.* (D&C 31:3–4; italics added.)

> Again I say, hearken ye elders of my church, whom I have appointed: Ye are not sent forth to be taught, but *to teach the children of men the things which I have put into your hands by the power of my Spirit* (D&C 43:15; italics added).

> Hearken unto my word, my servants Sidney [Rigdon], and Parley [P. Pratt], and Leman [Copley]; for behold, verily I say unto you, that I give unto you a commandment that you shall go and preach my gospel which ye have received, *even as ye have received it*, unto the Shakers.
> Behold, I say unto you, that they desire to know the truth in part, but not all, for they are not right before me and must needs repent.
> Wherefore, I send you, my servants Sidney and Parley, to preach the gospel unto them.
> And my servant Leman shall be ordained unto this work, *that he may reason with them* [the Shakers], *not according to that which he has received of them, but according to that which shall be taught him by you my servants; and by so doing I will bless him, otherwise he shall not prosper*. (D&C 49:1–4; italics added.)

Joseph Smith was a mature and independent witness of the truths of salvation. Parley P. Pratt related the following incident, which provides an important pattern for all those within the faith who desire to influence those outside the faith:

> While visiting with brother Joseph in Philadelphia, a very large church was opened for him to preach in, and about three thousand people assembled to hear him. Brother [Sidney] Rigdon spoke first, and dwelt on the Gospel, illustrating his doctrine by the Bible. When he was through, brother Joseph arose like a lion about to roar; and being full of the Holy Ghost, spoke in great power, *bearing testimony of the visions he had seen, the ministering of angels which he had enjoyed; and how he had found the plates of the Book of Mormon, and translated it by the gift and power of God.* He commenced by saying: "If nobody had the courage to testify of so glorious a message from Heaven, and of the finding of so glorious a record, he felt to do it in justice to the people, and leave the event with God."[1]

We will not accomplish the task of carrying the message of the Restoration to the ends of the earth through stressing the *similarities* between ourselves and other faiths. Only as we teach and proclaim those things which have been communicated specifically and by revelation to us (see D&C 84:61)—the *differences* between the Latter-day Saints and the rest of the world, the things which we have to offer to the world—will we make the difference we ought to make in the world. No one desires to be disliked or to be ridiculed for his peculiar beliefs. No one wants to be suspect or to be considered cultic or unchristian. At the same time, we have some truths to tell, truths not had as fully elsewhere. With the dawning of a brighter day, the knowledge of God and the authority to act in his behalf have been delivered to man again; a knowledge of Christ and the fulness of salvation available through him are to be had only by an acceptance of the doctrines and powers vested in The Church of Jesus Christ of Latter-day Saints.

The Book of Mormon is a guide to understanding persons and events in antiquity. The Nephite record provides, as it were, an interpretive lens through which we may view much in the Old Testament, for example, and supply missing or obscure parts to the story.[2] Much of what we understand about the Testaments is clear to us because of the Book of Mormon. There are those, however, who are hesitant to "read into" the biblical record what we know from modern revelation, those who feel that to do so is to compromise the "integrity" or unique contribution of the Bible itself. In response to this posture, let me suggest an analogy. If one were eager to locate a valuable site, should he utilize a map which is deficient in detail or inaccurate in layout, simply on the basis of the fact that the map had been in the family for generations and was highly prized? Should he choose to ignore the precious information to be had on a more reliable and complete map, if such were made available? Of course the whole matter is related to the question of whether the traveller is sincerely desirous of reaching his destination: maps have real value only to the degree that they guide us to a desired location. To change analogies, would a scholar in any discipline choose to maintain a position or defend a point of view when subsequent but available research had shed further (and perhaps clarifying) information on the subject? To do so would represent at best naïveté, and at worst shoddy and irresponsible scholarship. So it is with the Bible and the Book of Mormon: the latter is a supplementary doctrinal witness as well as a helpful historical guide. "Just as the New Testament clarified the long misunderstood message of the Old," Hugh Nibley observed, "so the Book of Mormon is held to reiterate the messages of both Testaments in a way that restores their full meaning."[3] Its strengths and supplementary contributions, however, will be fully appreciated only by those who are eager to be led to the fulness of truth, who seek the glory and approbation of God more than the praises of the secular synagogue.

"The Book of Mormon has not been, nor is it yet, the center of our personal study, family teaching, preaching, and missionary work. Of this we must repent," counseled President Ezra Taft Benson.[4] Our near neglect of the Book of Mormon has been a disturbance to the Lord for some time. "Your minds in times past," he warned the Saints in 1832, "have been darkened because of unbelief, and because you have treated lightly the things you have received—which vanity and unbelief have brought the whole church under condemnation." The condemnation, a "scourge and judgment" upon all the children of Zion, is to be lifted only as the members of the Church "remember the new covenant, even the Book of Mormon and the former commandments" which the Lord has delivered in this day of restoration (D&C 84:54–61). Our modern Church leaders have likewise warned us that the Church is still under condemnation, and have thus encouraged us to "daily sup from its pages and abide by its precepts." In so doing, President Benson has promised, "God will pour out upon each child of Zion and the Church a blessing hitherto unknown."[5]

The Doctrinal Superiority of the Book of Mormon

The Prophet Joseph Smith identified the Book of Mormon as the "most correct of any book on earth."[6] A modern Apostle has declared: "As far as learning the gospel and teaching the gospel are concerned, the Book of Mormon, by all odds, is the most important of the standard works, because in simplicity and in plainness it sets forth in a definitive manner the doctrines of the gospel."[7] Some things we simply understand better because of the Book of Mormon.

Some years ago at a university in the East I sat in a doctoral seminar on Paul. There were nine of us in the seminar: one Roman Catholic, three Southern Baptists, a Nazarene, a Jew, two Methodists, and a Latter-day Saint. The course was taught, interestingly enough, by a Jewish professor who obviously did not believe in the divinity of Jesus. In one particular session during the term, we centered our attention on 1 Corinthians 15. As the three-hour session rolled on, it became very clear to me that I was the only person in the group (including, of course, the instructor) who believed that the resurrection was a physical phenomenon, that the resurrected body is a tangible, corporeal entity. I wondered why such a plain and simple matter would have escaped their understandings. Then I read the chapter more carefully. Speaking of the resurrected body, Paul wrote: "It is sown a natural body; it is raised a *spiritual* body" (1 Corinthians 15:44). Suddenly it was clear why they misunderstood. But why did I understand that a "spiritual" body was a physical body, a glorified immortal body not subject to death? Only a moment's reflection was needed to remind me that I knew what I knew because of the Book of Mormon and modern revelation (see Alma 11:45; D&C 88:27; Moses 3:9). It was a sobering but soul-satisfying occasion.

Frequently the Bible will tell us *what* happened, while the Book of Mormon will tell us *why* it happened. We know from the Bible that there was a fall of Adam, but we learn from the Book of Mormon *why* there was a fall and thus why an atonement was necessary (see 2 Nephi 2). We learn early in the Old Testament that Jehovah gave a "law of carnal commandments" to rebellious Israel; we turn to the Book of Mormon to discover why he gave the Law of Moses and what the Law symbolized (see 2 Nephi 11:4; 25:24–27; Jacob 4:5; Mosiah 13:30; Alma 34:14). We know that Paul and the early Apostles preached the gospel, but we may come away from the New Testament lacking understanding on some essentials; the Book of Mormon leaves no doubt as to the meaning of the gospel and what its principles are. (See 2 Nephi 31–32; 3 Nephi 27). We are exposed to the doctrine of the election of Israel in the Old Testament and also read in Paul's writings about the status of the House of Israel (e.g., Romans 11), but we turn to the Book of Mormon for a more complete scriptural account concerning the destiny of the Lord's covenant people (see, for example, 1 Nephi 19–22; 2 Nephi 6:4–11; 10:3–8; Jacob 5–6; 3 Nephi 20–21).

And so it goes through most of the doctrines we might consider. In the words of Elder Bruce R. McConkie, in undertaking a serious doctrinal comparison between the stick of Judah and the stick of Joseph, "it will not be long before you know that Lehi and Jacob excel Paul in teaching the Atonement; that Alma's sermons on faith and on being born again surpass anything in the Bible; that Nephi makes a better exposition of the scattering and gathering of Israel than do Isaiah, Jeremiah, and Ezekiel combined; that Mormon's words about faith, hope, and charity have a clarity, a breadth, and a power of expression that even Paul did not attain; and so on and so on."[8] Elder McConkie's observation is in no way intended to denigrate the goodness and value of the Bible, but to point up the infinite worth of a supplementary scriptural source.

The Nature of God in the Book of Mormon

The Lord has chosen to bring about the restitution of all things in process of time; the truths of heaven, as well as the priesthoods and powers associated with establishing the kingdom of God, have been delivered to the Latter-day Saints "line upon line, precept upon precept," evidencing the Lord's sensitivity to our "bearing capacity," where the matters of salvation are concerned. What the Prophet understood as he left the Sacred Grove was no doubt a small amount when compared with what he had come to know by the time of his death in 1844. It is just so with the growth and development of the Latter-day Saints collectively: time and patience and maturity resulted in greater understanding. And yet the wisest among the Latter-day Saints—in Joseph Smith's day and certainly in our own—have come to recognize in the Book of Mormon not only a timely guide for living, but also a timeless sacred record and rich repository of doctrinal insights.

Some historians and writers have sought to contrast Joseph Smith's theology before 1835 with that which came to be taught in and after the Nauvoo experience. Of these treatments, there have been those who have included the Book of Mormon as a part of the doctrinal development, an integral aspect of the "early" thinking of the Mormon prophet. Some persons have gone so far as to suggest that the Book of Mormon represents a "trinitarian" concept of God, one beyond which Joseph Smith and the Church gradually evolved. What of such propositions?

1. *A Nineteenth-Century Product?* From the days of Alexander Campbell people have been eager to discount the divine story behind the Book of Mormon by suggesting alternative explanations for its origins. Campbell himself proposed that the Book of Mormon had been produced by Joseph Smith as a means of dealing with such commonplace issues in nineteenth-century America as "free masonry, republican government, and the rights of man."[9] Richard Bushman has successfully pointed up the fallacies of this approach to explaining the Book of Mormon, demonstrating convincingly that the socio-political setting of Nephite America is worlds apart from that of nineteenth-century America.[10] Others have suggested alternative authorship for the book, such as Sidney Rigdon[11] or Solomon Spaulding,[12] all of which are superficial but terribly resistant to extinction. In considering the whole question of alternative explanation—and here specifically the possibility of the Book of Mormon as a nineteenth-century book—Hugh Nibley has observed: "The idea that the Book of Mormon was simply a product of its time may be a necessary fiction to explain it but it is a fiction none the less. If they may be trusted in nothing else, the voluminous writings of the anti-Mormons [and of some misguided or myopic Mormons] stand as a monumental evidence for one fact: that Mormonism and the Book of Mormon were in no way a product of the society in which they arose."[13]

One of the things readily apparent to a careful reader of the Book of Mormon is what some would term "anachronistic" elements in the record. Matters such as faith and repentance and baptism, constant mention of Jesus Christ and his atonement, and repeated reference to the gift of the Holy Ghost are found throughout the Book of Mormon in the sermons of prophets who are supposed to have predated the Savior by many centuries. How do we explain such things? If he indeed wrote the Book of Mormon (as some contend), was Joseph Smith so careless or simple-minded as not to recognize that he was mixing time periods?

The answer to this query is quite simple to the person willing to fully accept Joseph Smith and his works and words: the Book of Mormon—with the Doctrine and Covenants, Pearl of Great Price, and Joseph Smith Translation of the Bible—restores many of the "plain and precious truths" lost before the Bible was compiled into its present form. One of the central verities of the Restoration—a matter totally hidden from the religious world until the "times of restitution" began—concerns "Christ's Eternal Gospel," the realization that Christian prophets have declared Christian doctrines and administered Christian ordinances since the days of Adam. In counseling with his errant son, Corianton, in approximately 73 B.C., Alma declared:

> And now, my son, I would say somewhat unto you concerning the coming of Christ. Behold, I say unto you, that it is he that surely shall come to take away the sins of the world; yea, he cometh to declare glad tidings of salvation unto his people.
>
> And now, my son, this was the ministry unto which ye were called, to declare these glad tidings unto this people, to prepare their minds; or rather that salvation might come unto them, that they may prepare the minds of their children to hear the word at the time of his coming.
>
> And now I will ease your mind somewhat on this subject. Behold, you marvel why these things should be known so long beforehand. Behold, I say unto you, is not a soul at this time as precious unto God as a soul will be at the time of his coming?
>
> Is it not as necessary that the plan of redemption should be made known unto this people as well as unto their children?
>
> Is it not as easy at this time for the Lord to send his angel to declare these glad tidings unto us as unto our children, or as after the time of his coming? (Alma 39:15–19; cf. Jacob 4:4.)

In the same vein, the Lord—after having spoken concerning the purposes for which the Book of Mormon was given to the world—explained in April of 1830 what doctrines and principles we now know as a result of the delivery of the Book of Mormon and modern revelation. Concerning the ministry of the Master, the Book of Mormon (with the Bible) testifies that "he was crucified, died, and rose again the third day; and ascended into heaven, to sit down on the right hand of the Father, to reign with almighty power according to the will of the Father; that as many as would believe," the account continues, "and be baptized in his holy name, and endure in faith to the end, should be saved." Now note the following, a recitation of truths which are made known primarily through the Book of Mormon and the revelations given to the Prophet Joseph Smith: "Not only those who believed after he came in the meridian of time, in the flesh, but *all those from the beginning, even as many as were before he came, who believed in the words of the holy prophets, who spake as they were inspired by the gift of the Holy Ghost, who truly testified of him in all things*, should have eternal life, as well as those who should come after, who should believe in the gifts and callings of God by the Holy Ghost, which beareth record of the Father and of the Son" (D&C 20:23–27; italics added). In short, the Book of Mormon is gospel centered and Christ centered and stands as a witness that all true believers and their scriptural records from the beginning have also been gospel centered and Christ centered.

Because some matters in the Book of Mormon (social, economic, political, religious, philosophical) seem so relevant to modern man—as those who have suggested alternative explanations have so adequately pointed out—must we therefore conclude that the book is a product of modern man? Could we not conclude just as easily—given a slight propensity to accept divine intervention, miracles, and angels—that the record was produced by ancient persons with prophetic insight to meet the needs and address issues of a modern time? Is that not what the Book of Mormon compilers/writers intended? In the words of President Ezra Taft Benson, "*The Book of Mormon was written for us today. God is the author of the book*. It is a record of a fallen people, compiled by inspired men for our blessing today. Those people never had the book—it was meant for us. Mormon, the ancient prophet after whom the book is named, abridged centuries of records. *God, who knows the end from the beginning, told him what to include in his abridgment that we would need for our day.*"[14] Moroni, the man who received the records from his father, finished the compilation and writing, and buried them in Cumorah, said: "Behold, I speak unto you as if ye were present, and yet ye are not. But behold, Jesus Christ hath shown you unto me, and I know your doing." (Mormon 8:35; cf. 9:30; 1 Nephi 19:21.)

2. *Joseph Smith's "Early" Theology*? To place the Book of Mormon within the developmental process is to accentuate the man (Joseph Smith) at the expense of the record (the Book of Mormon). Most believing Latter-day Saints accept without reservation that the process of translation involved a significant labor on the part of the Prophet and his scribes, and that mental exertion was frequently necessary to frame into words that which had been received by revelation. At the same time, to ascribe to Joseph Smith the *theology* of the Book of Mormon is to give him more credit than is due, and likewise to call into question the historicity of the record and its

ancient contents. For Joseph Smith to utilize the English language with which he was familiar in recording the translation is one thing; to create the theology (or to place the theology into the mouths of Benjamin or Alma or Moroni) is quite another. The latter situation would be tantamount to deceit and misrepresentation: it would be to claim that the doctrines and principles are of ancient date (which the record itself declares), when, in fact, they would be a fabrication of a nineteenth-century man.

In November of 1831 William E. McLellin, who later became one of the original twelve Apostles in this dispensation, criticized some of the revelations received by Joseph Smith. He was invited to write a revelation himself, one on a par with even the least of those recorded by the Prophet (see D&C 67:5–8). McLellin tried and failed miserably. In speaking of this episode, Joseph Smith said: "After the foregoing was received [D&C 67], William E. M'Lellin, as the wisest man, in his own estimation, having more learning than sense, endeavored to write a commandment like unto one of the least of the Lord's, but failed; *it was an awful responsibility to write in the name of the Lord.* The Elders and all present that witnessed *this vain attempt of a man to imitate the language of Jesus Christ*, renewed their faith in the fulness of the Gospel, and in the truth of the commandments and revelations which the Lord had given to the Church through my instrumentality."[15] It is difficult for me to imagine that a man who would make such a statement about the seriousness of imitating the language of Jesus Christ could be involved in the creation of a story about pre-Columbian Americans or insert Christian doctrine into their mouths. Why should we assume the theology of the Book of Mormon (and particularly, for our purposes here, the doctrines associated with the Godhead) to be a part of the doctrinal development of the modern seer and his followers? Because the Book of Mormon was published in 1830, must it be viewed as "early theology?" Is it not just as reasonable to suppose that the doctrines regarding the Godhead in the Book of Mormon reflect not the contemporary New England religious mind but rather the understanding had by the ancients?

My position is that the doctrine of the Godhead in the Book of Mormon is actually deeper and more penetrating than that found in any other book of scripture; that the Book of Mormon theology was not a part of a line-upon-line unfolding of doctrine in this dispensation; and that if Joseph Smith had been asked, prior to his death, to provide a reading list of recommended works detailing an in-depth look at God, Christ, and the Holy Ghost, the Book of Mormon would have been high on (if not at the top of) that list.

One of the perspectives a reader gains early in the Book of Mormon is the centrality of Jesus Christ, the majestic role he played as both premortal Jehovah and mortal Messiah. The Book of Mormon prophets declare with Christocentric consistency the fact that Jesus is not only the Christ but also the Eternal God (Title Page; 2 Nephi 26:12). In fact, the power and position of Christ is put forward with much more emphasis than in the Bible, the Doctrine and Covenants, and the Pearl of Great Price. Though, as we shall see shortly, God the Eternal Father (Elohim) is the ultimate object of worship in the Book of Mormon, Jesus Christ is the focus of the testimonies of all the prophets. Consistent with the teachings of latter-day prophets that all revelation since the fall of Adam has been by and through Jehovah-Christ,[16] the Nephites talk of Christ, rejoice in Christ, preach of Christ, and prophesy of Christ (see 2 Nephi 25:26). They stress that he is the God of Abraham, Isaac, and Jacob (1 Nephi 19:10); that he is the creator and upholder of all things and thus the very Eternal Father of heaven and of earth (Alma 11:39; 3 Nephi 9:15); and that he is the Holy One of Israel, the Eternal Judge of both quick and dead (1 Nephi 19:14–15; 2 Nephi 9:41; Moroni 10:34). The testimony of Elder Bruce R. McConkie echoes the testimonies of the Book of Mormon prophets:

> Christ-Messiah is God!
>
> Such is the plain and pure pronouncement of all the prophets of all the ages. In our desire to avoid the false and absurd conclusions contained in the creeds of Christendom, we are wont to shy away from this pure and unadorned verity; we go to great lengths to use language that shows there is both a Father and a Son, that they are separate Persons and are not somehow mystically intertwined as an essence or spirit that is everywhere present. Such an approach is perhaps essential in reasoning with the Gentiles of sectarianism; it helps to overthrow the fallacies formulated in their creeds.
>
> But having so done, if we are to envision our Lord's true status and glory, we must come back to the pronouncement of pronouncements, the doctrine of doctrines, the message of messages, which is that Christ is God. And if it were not so, he could not save us.[17]

Nephi wrote: "My soul delighteth in proving unto my people that save Christ should come all men must perish. For if there be no Christ there be no God; and if there be no God we are not, for there could have been no creation. But *there is a God, and he is Christ*, and he cometh in the fulness of his own time." (2 Nephi 11:6–7; italics added.)

The depth of the Book of Mormon doctrine of Christ is also to be seen in its treatment of the ministry of Jesus Christ as the Father and the Son.[18] Consistent with the other standard works, the Book of Mormon prophets revealed Christ as the Father by virtue of his role as *Creator* (Mosiah 3:8; D&C 14:9; Moses 1:33; 7:30), as well as through *spiritual rebirth* (Mosiah 5:5–7; D&C 25:1; Moses 6:58–60).

Christ is also called Father by *divine investiture of authority*. In the Doctrine and Covenants and the Pearl of Great Price we find numerous occasions wherein the Lord Jesus speaks in the name of his Father, on behalf of the Father, in the first person as though he were the Father (see D&C 29:1, 5; 49:5, 28; Moses 1:4, 6; 6:51–52).

One of the powerful witnesses of the Nephite-Jaredite record is that Jesus Christ is Father because Elohim has literally *invested* his Son with his own attributes and powers. Our Lord is Father "because he received power from his Father to do that which is infinite and eternal. This is a matter of his Eternal Parent investing him with power from on high so that he became the Father because he exercises the power of that Eternal Being."[19] Abinadi's penetrating testimony of Christ in Mosiah 15:1–5 might be paraphrased as follows:

a. God himself—Jehovah, the God of ancient Israel—will come to earth, take a body of flesh and bones, and accomplish the work of redemption for all mankind.

b. Because Jesus will have a physical body and dwell in the *flesh*—he will be known as the *Son* of God. His growth—like all men's—will be gradual, line upon line, precept upon precept.

c. The will of the Son is to be swallowed up in the will of the Father. That is, the *flesh* will be subject to the *spirit*, the mortal subject to the immortal. In short, Jesus will do what the Father would have him do.

d. Thus Christ will be known as both the Father and the Son. He will be called the Father because he was conceived by the power of God and inherited all of the divine endowments, particularly immortality, from his exalted Sire. He will be called the Son because of his flesh—his mortal inheritance from his mother, Mary. Therefore Christ will be both flesh (will have a physical body) and spirit (will possess the powers of the Spirit, the powers of his Father), both man and God, both Son and Father. "And they"—the Father and the Son, the spirit and the flesh, the God and the man—"are one God, yea, the very Eternal Father of heaven and of earth" (Mosiah 15:4). That is, the elements of mortality and immortality—flesh and spirit, Son and Father, man and God—are blended wondrously in one being, Jesus Christ.

Indeed, the Book of Mormon evidences a highly developed Christology, a doctrine of Christ as God which has no equal in the rest of our scriptural canon. Such views are neither primitive nor out of harmony with what Joseph Smith later taught the Saints, nor with what we teach today.

3. *A "Trinitarian" Concept of God?* Presumably persons who take this posture concerning the Book of Mormon assume that the book reflects the prevailing sentiments of the nineteenth century con-

cerning God. First of all, it is worth stating what is fairly obvious: trinitarian ideas concerning God—that the Father, Son, and Holy Ghost are simply three manifestations of one and the same being—are unscriptural, foreign to the spirit or content of the New Testament, and doctrinally untenable. Trinitarianism is a creation of man, a costly compromise between Greek philosophy and Christian doctrine, and a hybrid heresy which was perpetuated when the Christian Church had fallen into apostasy after A.D. 100. It certainly would have fallen into that category of creeds characterized by God in 1820 as abominable. (See Joseph Smith—History 1:19.)

Secondly, although the Book of Mormon prophets speak of the "oneness" of the members of the Godhead, this does not imply trinitarianism. There were, in fact, large groups of people in the nineteenth century who believed in the oneness of the Godhead but rejected the mysterious notions associated with trinitarianism. One religious leader, David Millard, a minister who organized an Eastern Christian church, published a pamphlet in 1818 in which he attacked the prevailing view of the Trinity. He undertook a scriptural analysis of the New Testament to prove his point. "The whole tenor of scripture," he asserted, "concurs in the testimony, that Christ is verily the Son of God, as really so as Isaac is the son of Abram." He further stressed the illogical nature of the Nicean concept: "Three Gods are not one God, any more than three times one are one or two and one are one: which not only destroys the rules of multiplication and addition, but is flat inconsistency."[20] Likewise, William Ellery Channing, the Father of Unitarianism, contended in a famous 1819 Baltimore sermon that God can no more be three persons than man can be.[21]

William W. Phelps wrote a letter dated 19 May 1835 concerning his beliefs before conversion. His perception might well reflect the views of other lay persons in nineteenth-century New England: "I was not a professor at the time, nor a believer in sectarian religion, but *a believer in God, and the Son of God, as two distinct characters*, and a believer in sacred scripture."[22] There is no reference in the *Messenger and Advocate* letter that such a belief was contrary in any way to the teachings of the restored Church; in fact, the statement implies that his preconversion beliefs were in harmony with the teachings of the Latter-day Saints.

The presentation of the Godhead in the Book of Mormon is remarkably similar to that in the New Testament concerning separateness yet oneness of the members of the Godhead. At the same time, and as we have observed already, the Book of Mormon is more complete in regard to establishing the centrality of Jesus Christ as God. The Book of Mormon is a mighty witness of the fact that although the Father, Son, and Holy Ghost are separate and distinct individuals, they are infinitely more one than they are separate. They are one God—one Godhead, united in purpose, power, and glory (see 2 Nephi 31:21; Alma 11:44; Moroni 7:7). And yet they are separate Persons. Consider the following areas in which the Book of Mormon establishes their individuality:

a. *We pray to the Father in the name of the Son.*

> But behold, I say unto you that ye must pray always, and not faint; that ye must not perform any thing unto the Lord save in the first place *ye shall pray unto the Father in the name of Christ,* that he will consecrate thy performance unto thee, that thy performance may be for the welfare of thy soul (2 Nephi 32:9; italics added).

> Therefore ye must always pray unto the Father in my name;
> And whatsoever ye shall ask the Father in my name, which is right, believing that ye shall receive, behold it shall be given unto you (3 Nephi 18:19–20).

> O then despise not, and wonder not, but hearken unto the words of the Lord, and *ask the Father in the name of Jesus for what things soever ye shall stand in need* (Mormon 9:27; italics added).

> Behold, when ye shall rend that veil of unbelief which doth cause you to remain in your awful state of wickedness, and hardness of heart, and blindness of mind, then shall the great and marvelous things which have been hid from the foundation of the world from you—yea, when *ye shall call upon the Father in my name,* with a broken heart and a contrite spirit, then shall ye know that the Father hath remembered the covenant which he made unto your fathers, O house of Israel (Ether 4:15; italics added).

> *O God, the Eternal Father, we ask thee in the name of thy Son, Jesus Christ,* to bless and sanctify this bread to the souls of all those who partake of it (Moroni 4:3; italics added; cf. 5:2; 10:4).

> I am mindful of you always in my prayers, *continually praying unto God the Father in the name of his Holy Child, Jesus,* that he, through his infinite goodness and grace, will keep you through the endurance of faith on his name to the end (Moroni 8:3; italics added).

b. *We worship the Father in the name of the Son.*

> And when that day shall come that they [the Jews] shall *believe in Christ, and worship the Father in his name,* with pure hearts and clean hands, and look not forward any more for another Messiah, then, at that time, the day will come that it must needs be expedient that they should believe these things (2 Nephi 25:16; italics added).

> For, for this intent have we written these things, that they may know that we knew of Christ, and we had a hope of his glory many

hundred years before his coming; and not only we ourselves had a hope of his glory, but also all the holy prophets which were before us.

Behold, *they believed in Christ and worshiped the Father in his name,* and also *we worship the Father in his name.* (Jacob 4:4–5; italics added.)

c. *Christ received powers from his Father.*

And because he [Christ] dwelleth in flesh he shall be called the Son of God, and having subjected the flesh to the will of the Father, being the Father and the Son—

The Father, because he was conceived by the power of God; and the Son, because of the flesh; thus becoming the Father and the Son (Mosiah 15:2–3; italics added).

And remember also the words which Amulek spake unto Zeezrom, in the city of Ammonihah; for he said unto him that the Lord surely should come to redeem his people, but that he should not come to redeem them in their sins, but to redeem them from their sins.

And he hath power given unto him from the Father to redeem them from their sins because of repentance. (Helaman 5:10–11; italics added.)

Know ye that ye must come to the knowledge of your fathers, and repent of all your sins and iniquities, and believe in Jesus Christ, that he is the Son of God, and that he was slain by the Jews, and *by the power of the Father he hath risen again,* whereby he hath gained the victory over the grave; and also in him is the sting of death swallowed up (Mormon 7:5; italics added).

d. *Christ's atonement reconciles us to God.*

For we labor diligently to write, to persuade our children, and also our brethren, *to believe in Christ, and to be reconciled to God;* for we know that it is by grace that we are saved, after all we can do (2 Nephi 25:23; italics added).

But God did call on men, in the name of his Son, (this being the plan of redemption which was laid) saying: If ye will repent, and harden not your hearts, *then will I have mercy upon you, through mine Only Begotten Son;*

Therefore, whosoever repenteth, and hardeneth not his heart, *he shall have claim on mercy through mine Only Begotten Son,* unto a remission of his sins; and these shall enter into my rest (Alma 12:33–34; italics added).

For behold, God knowing all things, being from everlasting to everlasting, behold, he sent angels to minister unto the children of men, to make manifest concerning the coming of Christ; and in Christ there should come every good thing. . . .

And after that he came men also were saved by faith in his name; and by faith, they become the sons of God. And as surely as Christ liveth he spake these words unto our fathers, saying: Whatsoever thing he shall ask the Father in my name, which is good, in faith believing that ye shall receive, behold, it shall be done unto you.

Wherefore, my beloved brethren, have miracles ceased because Christ hath ascended into heaven, and *hath sat down on the right hand of God, to claim of the Father his rights of mercy which he hath upon the children of men*? (Moroni 7:22, 26–27; italics added.)

e. *The voices of the Father and the Son are distinguished.*

And [Christ] said unto the children of men: Follow thou me. Wherefore, my beloved brethren, *can we follow Jesus save we shall be willing to keep the commandments of the Father*?

And *the Father said:* Repent ye, repent ye, and *be baptized in the name of my Beloved Son.*

And also, *the voice of the Son came unto me*, saying: *He that is baptized in my name, to him will the Father give the Holy Ghost*, like unto me; wherefore, follow me, and do the things which ye have seen me do.

Wherefore, my beloved brethren, I know that if ye shall follow the Son, with full purpose of heart, acting no hypocrisy and no deception before God, but with real intent, repenting of your sins, *witnessing unto the Father that ye are willing to take upon you the name of Christ*, by baptism—yea, by following your Lord and your Savior down into the water, according to his word, behold, then shall ye receive the Holy Ghost; . . . and then can ye speak with the tongue of angels, and shout praises unto the Holy One of Israel.

But, behold, my beloved brethren, *thus came the voice of the Son unto me*, saying: After ye have repented of your sins, and witnessed unto the Father that ye are willing to keep my commandments, by the baptism of water, and have received the baptism of fire and of the Holy Ghost, and can speak with a new tongue, yea, even with the tongue of angels, and after this should deny me, it would have been better for you that ye had not known me.

And *I heard a voice from the Father*, saying: Yea, *the words of my Beloved are true and faithful*. He that endureth to the end, the same shall be saved. (2 Nephi 31:10–15; italics added.)

The above passages are only a sample of a much larger group of scriptures that demonstrate that the Book of Mormon prophets understood very clearly the separate and distinct natures of the Father and the Son. Only eleven days before his death, Joseph Smith the Prophet said: "I have *always* declared God to be a distinct personage, Jesus Christ a separate and distinct personage from God the Father, and that the Holy Ghost was a distinct personage and a Spirit: and *these three constitute three distinct personages and three Gods.*"[23] Any thinking Latter-day Saint should ask the question: Would Joseph Smith expound doctrine—the distinctness of the Father and the Son—which was seemingly at variance with the teachings of a book he claimed to have received from God?[24] "Clearly," Elder

Neal A. Maxwell has written, "this book came *through* a 'choice seer'—Joseph Smith—but not *from* that seer."

> Some, desperate for an alternative explanation, almost seem to suppose Joseph was getting help from some theological mail-order supply house.
>
> To the human mind it is amazing that such rich revelations and translations should come through an untrained individual such as Joseph was. The reason, of course, is that, though Joseph did not spell perfectly, he came to know the grammar of the gospel, because he was God's apt pupil.[25]

In Perspective

It was in Nauvoo in 1841, during the zenith of his ministry, only three years before his death, that Joseph Smith made the statement that the Book of Mormon was "the most correct of any book on earth, and the keystone of our religion."[26] It would seem that by that time in his life and ministry he could speak not only with authority, but also with perspective. After having received literally hundreds of revelations from God, after having seen numerous visions and preached a myriad of doctrinal sermons, surely the modern Seer knew where truth and light were to be found. And those truly intent in this generation on growing in light and truth—those who literally seek for the glory of God (see D&C 93:36)—know where lasting inspiration is to be found. The Book of Mormon is indeed "the book that will save the world and prepare the sons of men for joy and peace here and now and everlasting life in eternity."[27]

NOTES

1. *Autobiography of Parley P. Pratt* (Salt Lake City: Deseret Book Co., 1972), p. 298; italics added.
2. See Joseph F. McConkie, "Modern Revelation: A Window to the Past," found in this volume.
3. From "The Book of Mormon: A Minimal Statement," in *Nibley on the Timely and the Timeless* (Provo, UT: Religious Studies Center, Brigham Young University, 1978), p. 150.
4. Conference Report, April 1986, p. 4.
5. Ibid., p. 100.
6. *Teachings of the Prophet Joseph Smith*, comp. Joseph Fielding Smith (Salt Lake City: Deseret Book Co., 1976), p. 194.
7. Bruce R. McConkie, "The Foolishness of Teaching," Address to LDS Church Educational System (Salt Lake City: The Church of Jesus Christ of Latter-day Saints, 1981), p. 6.

8. Conference Report, October 1983, p. 106.

9. Alexander Campbell, *Delusions: An Analysis of the Book of Mormon* (Boston: B. H. Green, 1832), p. 13.

10. Richard L. Bushman, "The Book of Mormon and the American Revolution," in *Book of Mormon Authorship*, ed. Noel B. Reynolds (Provo, UT: Religious Studies Center, Brigham Young University, 1982), pp. 189–211.

11. The ludicrous nature of this claim is to be seen in the fact that Sidney Rigdon was converted by the Book of Mormon.

12. See Rex C. Reeve, Jr., "Spaulding Theory and the Origin of the Book of Mormon," First Annual Symposium on the Book of Mormon, October 1985, for an excellent survey on the use and abuse of this theory.

13. Hugh Nibley, "Mixed Voices," *Improvement Era*, July 1959, p. 565.

14. Conference Report, April 1975, p. 94; italics added.

15. *History of the Church* 1:226.

16. See Joseph Fielding Smith, *Man: His Origin and Destiny* (Salt Lake City: Deseret Book Co., 1954), pp. 304, 312; *Doctrines of Salvation*, 3 vols., comp. Bruce R. McConkie (Salt Lake City: Bookcraft, 1954–56), 1:27; *Answers to Gospel Questions*, 5 vols. (Salt Lake City: Deseret Book Co., 1965–75), 3:58.

17. *The Promised Messiah: The First Coming of the Son of Man* (Salt Lake City: Deseret Book Co., 1978), p. 98.

18. For a detailed discussion of this subject, see my article entitled, "The Ministry of the Father and the Son," First Annual Symposium on the Book of Mormon, Religious Studies Center, Brigham Young University, October 1985. See also "The Father and the Son: A Doctrinal Exposition of the First Presidency and the Twelve," 30 June 1916, in James E. Talmage, *The Articles of Faith* (Salt Lake City: Deseret Book Co., 1975), pp. 465–73.

19. Bruce R. McConkie, *The Promised Messiah*, p. 371.

20. *The True Messiah Exalted, or Jesus Christ Really the Son of God, Vindicated; in Three Letters to a Presbyterian Minister* (Canandaigua, 1818), pp. 5–8.

21. William E. Channing, *The Works of William E. Channing* (Boston, 1886), p. 371; cited in Milton V. Backman, Jr., *American Religions and the Rise of Mormonism* (Salt Lake City: Deseret Book Co., 1970), p. 210.

22. *The Latter-day Saints' Messenger and Advocate*, vol. 1, no. 8 (May 1835), p. 115; italics added.

23. *Teachings of the Prophet Joseph Smith*, p. 370; italics added; cf. *The Words of Joseph Smith*, ed. Andrew F. Ehat and Lyndon W. Cook (Provo, UT: Brigham Young University, Religious Studies Center, 1980), pp. 63, 378.

24. I am aware of the fact that the early leaders of the Church in this dispensation did not always distinguish as clearly as we do today between the name-titles of Jehovah and Elohim. At the same time, there seems to have been no doubt in their minds as to the separateness of the Father and the Son. The issue is an issue of nomenclature, not theology. See my article, "The Ministry of the Father and the Son" for a more detailed treatment of this matter.

Some persons have even suggested that the Book of Mormon is "Calvinistic" in scope. Such an idea is even more radical than the proposition that the book is trinitarian. Do the Nephite prophets teach such doctrines as the total depravity of man (including man's inability to choose the right)? unconditional election of individuals to eternal life? a limited atonement (reserved only for the elect, those predestined to salvation)? irresistible grace? perseverance of the Saints (one's inability to fall from grace)? These ideas are as remote and foreign to the theology of the Book of Mormon as they could possibly be.

25. *"But for a Small Moment"* (Salt Lake City: Bookcraft, 1986), p. 44; italics in original.

26. *Teachings of the Prophet Joseph Smith*, p. 194.

27. Bruce R. McConkie, Conference Report, October 1983, p. 107.

Proving the Holy Scriptures Are True

6

Monte S. Nyman
Charles D. Tate, Jr.

The Lord revealed on April 6, 1830, that one of the purposes why he brought forth the Book of Mormon was to prove to the world that the holy scriptures are true (D&C 20:11). An examination of many of the teachings of the world and its so-called biblical scholarship through the last two centuries shows there is indeed a need for such verification. This need was recognized by President Brigham Young, the successor to Joseph Smith. "What do the infidel world say about the Bible? They say that the Bible is nothing better than last year's almanac; it is nothing but a fable of priestcraft, and it is good for nothing. The Book of Mormon, however, declares that the Bible is true, and it proves it; and the two prove each other true."[1] Although President Young's statement was made over a hundred years ago (May 1870), there is probably even a greater need for proving the scriptures today because of the sophistication of present-day scholarship.

Currently, scholars analyze the Bible from many different points of view: sociological, historical, linguistic, literary, and archaeological perspectives, to name a few. The basis of all these

Monte S. Nyman is Professor of Ancient Scripture at Brigham Young University.
Charles D. Tate is Professor of English at Brigham Young University.

analyses is to view the Bible as any other book rather than as scripture revealed from God.

The sociologists and the historians generally attempt to analyze the human element of the people who lived in the geographical area and explain the doctrine taught in the text as a product of that culture or civilization. The linguists look to the original meaning of the text, often refusing to acknowledge that we do not have any original texts but only copies that are hundreds of years old—and that the New Testament copies may not even be in their original language. From their conclusions, they attempt to correct supposed errors in translation or understanding. The literary critics compare the text to other literature not given by direct revelation, but whose authors may have been inspired. They draw their conclusions about the biblical text by using the same symbolic or figurative interpretation they have used with the other literature. Thus they often label the enlightenment of the divine revelations as myths and legends passed from one generation to another rather than as revelations from God. The archaeologists meticulously date their findings. And even though their dating processes are in constant revision, they tend to ignore the biblical dating in favor of their own theories and then base their interpretations of the biblical text on their understanding of the culture of those periods.

Thus the Bible is tossed to and fro with every wind of scholarly doctrine. While each of these fields of scholarship can help us gain a greater understanding of the biblical text, they cannot be considered the basis of interpretation for the revealed word of God.

Recognizing the great variance in beliefs about the Bible among scholars, denominations, peoples, and individuals, we will speak to the general trends of this scholarship rather than to specifics. We further recognize that in the changing world of scholarship what was believed a few years ago may no longer be believed today, and hardly ever have all the scholars agreed on any one point. Therefore, we will emphasize what the Book of Mormon and other modern scriptures teach rather than answer specific points of scholarship.

The Book of Mormon reveals that the Bible would be tampered with and that this tampering would cause the Gentiles in the latter days to stumble (1 Nephi 13:29; 2 Nephi 26:20). They stumble because they interpret the revealed word of God as a product of the human mind. The Prophet Joseph Smith stated: "I believe the Bible as it read when it came from the pen of the original writers. Ignorant translators, careless transcribers, or designing and corrupt priests have committed many errors."[2] To find the Bible as it came from the original writers, one must turn to the Book of Mormon.

Not only does the Book of Mormon prove that the Bible is true, but the Doctrine and Covenants and the Pearl of Great Price are also witnesses to its truth. Furthermore, the Prophet Joseph Smith was called by the Lord to translate the Bible and to restore the plain and precious truths that had been lost (D&C 35:20; 37:1). This work, now referred to as the Joseph Smith Translation (hereafter referred as JST), was never completed because he was martyred. Nonetheless, what he did complete makes a great contribution to our understanding of the Bible. Joseph was also commissioned to expound all scripture unto the Church (D&C 24:5, 9). An analysis of his teachings as recorded in the *History of the Church* reveals that Joseph commented on nearly every book of the Bible.[3] Because in our world the reasoning and intellect of man are often regarded as superior to revelation and scripture, it is expedient for us members of the Church to study what the Lord has confirmed about the truths contained in the Holy Bible. If we will ponder the revealed truths of the modern-day scriptures and the words of the Lord's mouthpieces—the Presidents of the Church (see D&C 107:91–92)—we will see that there is absolutely no reason not to believe in the truth of the Bible and its message; for the Lord has sustained it sufficiently to leave the world and the Church without excuse in accepting it as his word. We will all agree with another statement of Brigham Young: "We have a holy reverence for and a belief in the Bible."[4]

The Book of Mormon and other modern scriptures substantiate, verify, and prove the Bible is true by teaching the same doctrines it teaches, by quoting verses and chapters from it, and by referring to historical events and persons recorded in it. Often the modern reference is fuller and more complete than the biblical one, which testifies that plain and precious parts of the Bible have been lost; some of these have been returned to our knowledge by modern revelation.

An analysis of what modern revelation says about the Bible will follow. The plan is to treat a few examples with some detail and then to show in a chart the completeness of the coverage that the modern scriptures provide. A study of these sources will show how the Lord has restored such crucial doctrines as the nature of God; the relationship of the Father, the Son, and mankind; the purpose of mortality; the plan of salvation; and many other true teachings. These restored teachings form the basis for correctly interpreting the Bible.

The Old Testament

Although many scholars today question or reject the prophetic authorship of many of the Old Testament books, the Book of Mormon bears witness that the Old Testament is a record of the prophets (1 Nephi 13:39). The Doctrine and Covenants bears a similar testimony (D&C 52:9; 66:2). The traditional divisions of the Old Testament are the law, the prophets, the historical books, and the poetic books.

The Books of Moses

The first five books of the Bible are called the books of Moses, or the Law. The Book of Mormon says they were a part of the plates of brass, the accepted scriptures as early as 600 B.C., and contained then as the Bible does now, "an account of the creation of the world, and also of Adam and Eve, who were our first parents" (1 Nephi 5:11; see also 19:23). This Book of Mormon statement verifies the traditional authorship of those five books of the Bible and lays the foundation for other truths taught in the individual five books of the Law. Furthermore, the Pearl of Great Price gives the account of when these truths were revealed to Moses (see Moses 1). This latter account further substantiates the need for the latter-day restoration through Joseph Smith. "And in a day when the children of men shall esteem my words as naught and take many of them from the book which thou shalt write, behold, I will raise up another like unto thee; and they shall be had again among the children of men—among as many as shall believe" (Moses 1:41).

The book of Moses in the Pearl of Great Price is a restoration of the biblical text of Genesis 1:1–6:13 before the plain and precious parts were lost as referred to in 1 Nephi 13:24–29 and in *TPJS*, p. 327. The account of Satan's rebellion (Moses 4:1–4) and the prophecies of Enoch (Moses 6:26–7:69) are the major contributions of the book of Moses, although there are many other significant textual restorations for other chapters of Genesis. The Pearl of Great Price ends on the parallel account of Genesis 6:13 (Moses 8:30). Also the book of Abraham records some of the revelations given to him about the calling of noble and great leaders in the premortal life to be leaders upon the earth as mortals, an account of the Creation, and much information about Abraham's early life and God's covenant made to him.

In addition to the contributions of the books of Moses and Abraham, the Book of Mormon comments on twenty-three other areas of the book of Genesis. (See the chart at the end of this chapter for a list of these references.) The Doctrine and Covenants contains twenty-two references to Genesis. The JST makes additional changes in Genesis chapter six and also in thirty-four of the forty-four chapters that follow.[5] In addition to the teachings in the JST, the Prophet mentioned or expounded on the text of Genesis thirty-two different times in *TPJS*.

Even though modern revelation does not make specific comments about nine of the fifty chapters of Genesis, it verifies the reality of the main characters of these nine chapters. It is obvious that modern revelation testifies that the book of Genesis is basically a true account—especially as it is corrected through that modern-day revelation.

The other books of the Law are likewise supported by modern revelation, though not as thoroughly as is the book of Genesis. A study of the references in the accompanying chart will show that the major doctrines, messages, and history of each book are substantiated. For example, the exodus from Egypt and the miracles performed by Moses were emphasized by the Nephite prophets. The Doctrine and Covenants references to the Law deal primarily with the callings of Moses and of Aaron as his spokesman.

The books of Moses were the most highly esteemed among the ancient Israelites since they contained the law they were to live by. This law was a good one, but it was not the higher law; therefore, much of it does not relate to the latter days. Those parts that do relate, however, are definitely verified through modern-day revelation.

The Historical Books

The historical books include those from Joshua to Esther. Less is said in modern revelation about these historical books than is said about those in other divisions of the Bible, but there is enough said to sustain their validity.

The Book of Mormon says the plates of brass contained "a record of the Jews from the beginning, even down to the commencement of the reign of Zedekiah, king of Judah" (1 Nephi 5:12). In general it verifies Joshua's conquest of the land of Canaan (1 Nephi 17:32–33) and significant accounts in the books of Samuel and Kings, such as the marriages and downfall of David and Solomon. The Book of Mormon also confirms Solomon's building of a temple, the scattering of various tribes of Israel, and Elijah's historicity and translation into heaven.

The existence of the chief characters of the historical books of the Bible is affirmed by modern revelation.

The Poetic Books

The wisdom and devotional books of the Old Testament were not considered as authoritative as the Law or the Prophets. However, the poetic books do contain some great and eternal doctrinal concepts and principles of the gospel. Modern scriptures also verify much referred to in these books.

Book of Mormon references support the book of Job. Although some critics have accused Joseph Smith of copying from Shakespeare in referring to death as a place from which no traveler returns (*Hamlet* 3.1.78–9), the truth is that both Shakespeare and Lehi were paraphrasing Job (Job 10:21; 2 Nephi 1:14). This also has some bearing on the controversial dating of Job. If Lehi is quoting or paraphrasing Job from the plates of brass, the book of Job would have had to exist before 600 B.C.

Fifty-one of the one hundred fifty Psalms were changed in the JST. There are also fifteen comments on Psalms in the *TPJS*. Joseph Smith certainly recognized that there was value in the Psalms for our lives.

The poetic books of the Bible are given some credence in modern-day revelation. They should be read with the knowledge that comes from the contribution of latter-day revelation.

The Prophets

Much is said about the Prophets section of the Old Testament in the modern scriptures. The Book of Mormon states that the plates of brass contained "the prophecies of the holy prophets, from the beginning, even down to the commencement of the reign of Zedekiah; and also many prophecies which have been spoken by the mouth of Jeremiah" (1 Nephi 5:13). The Savior testified that "all the prophets from Samuel and those that follow after, as many as have spoken, have testified of me" (3 Nephi 20:24). His beginning with Samuel coincides with the Hebrew designation of Samuel as the first prophet following the reign of the Judges. Jesus further testified that he did "not destroy the prophets, for as many as have not been fulfilled in me, . . . shall all be fulfilled" (3 Nephi 15:6). This statement made in A.D. 34 indicates that the prophets also testified of the latter days, a concept sustained by several statements in the Doctrine and Covenants (1:18; 42:39; 52:9, 36; 59:22; 66:2; 84:2; 101:19).

There are more statements about Isaiah in modern revelation than about any other of the prophets. These references even include a commandment to search his writing (3 Nephi 20:11; 23:1; Mormon 8:23.)

There are extensive quotes from the book of Isaiah in the Book of Mormon, 425 of the KJV 1292 verses. Some 229 of the verses are quoted differently from those in the KJV, and 85 of those contain significant differences. Additionally, Isaiah passages are quoted or referred to 73 times in the Doctrine and Covenants, and *TPJS* features 35 statements about Isaiah.[6] The JST made extensive changes in the Isaiah text, showing corrections in 39 of the 66 chapters. All this evidence certainly labels Isaiah as one of the most important books of the Old Testament.

There are three references to Jeremiah in the Book of Mormon. Some of his prophecies were on the plates of brass (1 Nephi 5:13), and by beginning its narrative in the midst of Jeremiah's ministry, the Book of Mormon sustains the historical setting of the book of Jeremiah. It makes no reference to Ezekiel or Daniel. However, the famous two-stick prophecy of Ezekiel (Ezekiel 37:15–19) is sustained by a similar prophecy of Joseph of Egypt (2 Nephi 3:11–12), and the Doctrine and Covenants quotes Daniel regarding Adam and the latter days (D&C 65, 116). Joseph Smith made many comments about Daniel in *TPJS*.

The angel Moroni quoted Joel 2:28–32 to Joseph Smith on 22 September 1823, noting that that prophecy would soon be fulfilled (Joseph Smith—History 1:41). The JST made changes in five of the nine chapters of Amos. The *TPJS* refers to Obadiah's "saviors on Mount Zion" four different times.

When the resurrected Savior visited the Book of Mormon people, he quoted from Micah, although he implied he was referring to Isaiah. The Doctrine and Covenants quotes one of the same references concerning the Lord's threshing of the nations by the power of his spirit. The *TPJS* has one comment about the pure language spoken of in Zephaniah. The Doctrine and Covenants quotes three of his passages regarding Jesus' second coming to the Jews.

The angel Moroni quoted part of Malachi chapter three and all of chapter four to Joseph Smith on 22 September 1823 (Joseph Smith—History 1:36–37). He quoted 4:5–6 differently from the KJV as recorded in Doctrine and Covenants 2. The resurrected Savior also quoted chapters 3 and 4 to the Book of Mormon people. Earlier, Nephi quoted 4:1–2 showing that this part of the text was not unique to Malachi. The Doctrine and Covenants quotes extensively from Malachi, and *TPJS* comments freely on the book.

Much information about the prophets and their writings is revealed through latter-day scriptures. By searching the prophets as commanded (3 Nephi 23:5) and using this restored information, one can gain much knowledge of these writings.

Other Prophets

The Book of Mormon refers to several other prophets for whom we no longer have an Old Testament text, thus restoring at least some of the plain and precious parts lost from the Bible. These prophets are Zenos, Zenoch, Neum, Ezias, and others who were unidentified.

Apocrypha and Pseudepigrapha

There are two statements in the Doctrine and Covenants about books that were not canonized in the Bible—one refers to the book of Enoch (D&C 107:57) and the other notes that the Apocrypha contains both truth and human interpolation and is mostly translated correctly (D&C 91).

Conclusion

Of the thirty-nine Old Testament books, there are only four that have no helps for interpretation or sustaining quotations in the modern scriptures: Ruth, Esther, Lamentations, and Haggai. While other books have little said about them, many have enormous validation from modern scripture. Certainly the Lord has left us without reason not to accept the Old Testament in its traditional setting and message.

The New Testament

The restoration of truth through the Prophet Joseph Smith sustains the New Testament just as fully as it does the Old Testament. This is especially true for the Gospels and for the Revelation of John, but it also extends to almost all of the books in the New Testament canon.

The Book of Mormon bears witness that the Apostles and prophets were the authors of the New Testament books. This point is repeated four times in Nephi's account of his vision (1 Nephi 13:24–26, 39–41). The Doctrine and Covenants also confirms the apostolic authorship of the New Testament (D&C 52:9, 36; 66:2). These inspired revelatory statements give us an entirely different outlook on the formation of the New Testament from what we get from biblical scholars.

The Gospels

The books of Matthew, Mark, and Luke are called the synoptic Gospels because they are basically parallel accounts of the life of the Lord Jesus Christ. The references to Matthew are fully treated in the accompanying chart, but the parallel accounts are not, since to verify one account is to verify the parallel accounts. Also, the JST changes will be considered collectively with no attempt to designate which are parallel accounts.

The Book of Mormon records a sermon given to the Nephites that was nearly the same as the Sermon on the Mount recorded in Matthew 5–7 (3 Nephi 12–14). This allows us to make a comparison as well as to verify Jesus' declaration that what he was teaching the Nephites was what he had taught the Jews in his mortal ministry (3 Nephi 15:1). The presence of the complete sermon in the Book of Mormon restores some of the original teachings and refutes a current biblical criticism that the Sermon on the Mount is a compilation of an editor rather than an actual sermon. The Book of Mormon also confirms the mission of John the Baptist and the baptism of Jesus.

There are more quotations and commentary on the book of Matthew in the Doctrine and Covenants than on any other New Testament book (the synoptic parallels of Mark and Luke have not been counted here). The message of John the Baptist is also sustained. Jesus' reply to Satan's temptation and the instructions given to the Twelve when they were commissioned to preach the gospel are among many other events in Matthew verified by the Doctrine and Covenants.

Matthew chapter 24 was completely revised in the JST and is now included as Joseph Smith—Matthew in the Pearl of Great Price. The JST also made changes in every other chapter of Matthew. The total number of verses changed was 483. The title was also changed to "The Testimony of Matthew." The same was done to the titles of Mark, Luke, and John. There are ninety-eight Matthew references contained in the *TPJS*.

Every chapter in the book of Matthew has some verification in latter-day revelation, and many of the chapters have extensive help given for their interpretation.

Other New Testament books will not be analyzed here as thoroughly as the book of Matthew. A few selected examples supporting various books will be cited. Readers are encouraged to study the references in the accompanying chart.

The Book of Mormon confirms the last four verses of the Gospel of Mark as a valid teaching of the Savior, a concept questioned in the scholarly world. The Book of Mormon teachings on the spirit world (Alma 40:9–14) provide a second witness to Luke's parable of Lazarus (16:13–19).

The Gospel of John is unique as a more spiritual treatise of Jesus' work. There are in the Doctrine and Covenants thirty-three quotations or concepts from John's Gospel. These enlighten us on such controversial doctrines as whether man may see God and the ordinance of the washing of feet, and they confirm several other teachings. The ninety-third section is a firm endorsement of John's Gospel. As with the other Gospels, every chapter of John benefits from supporting and enlarging understanding from modern scriptural sources. Its importance should be recognized by Latter-day Saints.

The Acts of the Apostles

Four major teachings in the book of Acts are confirmed by the Book of Mormon: (1) the gospel taken to the Gentiles, which is the theme of the book of Acts; (2) the identification of Jesus Christ as the prophet spoken of in chapter three; (3) Jesus as the only name for salvation; and (4) the existence of the Church in the Old Testament times. That the Church functioned through the Apostles following Jesus' crucifixion and resurrection is clearly verified by modern revelation.

The Epistles of Paul

Fourteen epistles are traditionally attributed to the Apostle Paul. This study accepts this traditional number and shows modern-day confirmation of each book.

Romans is one of the more difficult books to understand in the New Testament, but by using all the helps shown in the accompanying chart, the student of modern scripture can understand it better.

Mormon gave a great sermon to the faithful members of the Church that teaches concepts very similar to those found in 1 Corinthians 13 (Moroni 7). Although critics have charged plagiarism, they have not carefully studied the text of Mormon's discourse, which adds much to our understanding of Paul's writings.

The Book of Mormon relates to the teachings of Galatians about the purpose of the law of Moses. It also makes a great statement that helps us understand what Paul meant when he wrote to the Ephesians about being saved by grace. The Doctrine and Covenants also testifies about putting on the armor of God. It speaks several times of being caught up in the cloud to be received by Christ, a teaching found in Paul's first epistle to the Thessalonians; and it quotes two phrases from 1 Timothy 4—about the danger of being seduced by evil spirits or doctrines of devils, and forbidding to marry and commanding to abstain from meats. The JST shows changes in all six chapters.

Modern revelation contributes much to understanding the book of Hebrews. The Book of Mormon sustains three concepts of Hebrews: God cannot lie; a definition of faith; and the sameness of Jesus Christ. The JST shows changes in all of its thirteen chapters. There are also thirty-five statements in the *TPJS* about the book of Hebrews.

There is help through modern revelation in understanding all of Paul's epistles, except the little epistle to Philemon. The difficult books of Romans and Hebrews have received much emphasis so that we can better understand Paul's writings, which Peter said were hard to understand (2 Peter 3:15–16).

The General Epistles

Modern revelation also gives insight into most of the seven other New Testament general epistles.

The little book of James is very important to this dispensation because it helped usher in the Restoration: Joseph Smith's reading of James 1:5–6 led him to the First Vision and subsequent events (see Joseph Smith—History 1:11–17).

The vision of President Joseph F. Smith, now Doctrine and Covenants 138, came as he pondered Peter's first epistle. The JST shows changes in all five chapters of 1 Peter, and the *TPJS* comments eight times on that book. There are changes in the JST in all three of the chapters in 2 Peter, and *TPJS* has seventeen references to it.

The JST also shows changes in five chapters of 1 John. The epistle 2 John is written to the elect lady, and Emma Smith is addressed similarly in Doctrine and Covenants 25:3. The Doctrine and Covenants also refers to the wicked being kept in chains of darkness and garments "spotted by the flesh" as taught in Jude 23.

All of the general epistles except 3 John are clarified by modern scripture. While some books receive limited attention, the longer books are made considerably clearer by modern revelation.

The Revelation of John

Many modern scripture references help us understand the apocalyptic text of Revelation. In fact, the book of Revelation is one of the most often commented-on books in the New Testament. This is understandable because it is difficult to understand.

The Book of Mormon verifies four of the teachings in Revelation: the fall of Satan; his church's being the whore of all the earth; Satan's being bound; and death and hell's delivering up their dead.

Doctrine and Covenants 77 gives the key to understanding Revelation. The rest of the Doctrine and Covenants also quotes many different passages from that book. All but five of its twenty-two chapters are altered in the JST, and the *TPJS* comments forty times on the text.

To most people the book of Revelation is a mystery. With all of the helps from modern revelation, the serious student of latter-day revelation can decipher it at least to some degree.

Conclusion

Of the twenty-seven New Testament books, only 3 John is unconfirmed by modern-day revelation. Second John and Philemon are referred to only once, but the major books are heavily supported. The Lord has left modern man without excuse in accepting the New Testament in its traditional setting and message.

This chapter is intended to be an overview, not a comprehensive study! Many other observations and conclusions may be drawn from studying the compilations on the following chart, but these will be left for a further study. We hope that our readers will gain a deeper appreciation for both the Bible and modern scriptures from reading this overview and studying the references in the accompanying chart.

Explanation of the Bible/Modern Scriptures Chart

The purpose of the following chart is to show how widely and at the same time how deeply modern revelation supports, verifies, and explains the events and teachings in the Bible. We built it after years of studying the Bible, the Book of Mormon, the Doctrine and Covenants, and the Pearl of Great Price—the standard works of The Church of Jesus Christ of Latter-day Saints. As we saw the same doctrines being taught both anciently and in this modern dispensation, we felt the need to show how widely modern scripture supports and substantiates the Bible, which has fallen on bad days at the hands of biblical criticism.

While we have made every effort to be as complete as possible, we know we must have missed some references. We offer what we have found to both scholar and lay reader alike to assist them in finding cross-references for biblical topics from all the modern scriptures now available. We have included references to the Joseph Smith Translation (JST) and the *Teachings of the Prophet Joseph Smith* (TPJS) since Joseph was specifically called to receive and expound the scriptures to this dispensation.

We are very heavily indebted to Dr. Robert J. Matthews, dean of religious education at Brigham Young University, for his masterful book, *"A Plainer Translation": Joseph Smith's Translation of the Bible, A History and Commentary* (Provo, Utah: Brigham Young University Press, 1975). We have used the listing in his Appendix B as the basis for our references to the JST. Where his listings are detailed verse by verse, limitations of space and purpose dictated our using inclusive numbers when there were a great many verses listed in his work for a given chapter in the Bible. We unreservedly recommend Dean Matthews's book as essential reading in any study of the JST.

For space reasons we have listed the Pearl of Great Price (PofGP) references in the same column with those from TPJS, since they can readily be identified by their scriptural form and the TPJS ones by their Arabic numeral page references.

BIBLE	BOOK OF MORMON	DOC. & COV.	JST	PofGP/TPJS
GENESIS-DEUT	1N 5:11; 19:23			
GENESIS 1-3	1N 5:11; 2N 2:15; Al 18:36; 22:13	29:34-42		
1-11	Ether 1:3	107:39-53		Moses 1-8; Abr 4-5
1			1:1-33	Moses 1; Abr 4
1:1			1:1-2	348, 371
1:2				181
1:3-5		95:7		
1:14				132
1:26-27	Mos 7:27; Al 22:12			157, 345, 372
1:28		132:63		
2			2:1-29	Moses 3; Abr 5
2:4				350
2:7				301, 352
2:15-17	2N 2:15; Al 12:21-23			345
3	2N 2:17		3:1-5:3	Moses 4
3: 1-5	2N 2:18; Mos 16:3; Al 22:12; 42:2-5			
3:9-10				168
3:24	2N 2:19-25; Al 12: 21-23			
4			5:4-6:8	Moses 5:1-6:4
4: 1-5		124:75		58, 169
4:8	Ether 8:15	84:16; 138:40		
5			6:9-8:1	Moses 6:5-8:13
5:3-8		107:43; 138:40		170
5:24		38:4; 45:11-14		
5:28-29				171
6			8:2-28	
6:1-13				171, 327; Moses 8:14-30
7			8:29-45	
8			8:47-9:7	
9			9:8-30	
9:5-6		49:21		
9:13				340
9:20-27				193, 269
10			10:3-20	
10:25		133:24		
11		138:41	11:1-18	
11:27-32				Abr 1:1-2:2
12:1-13	1N 13:23; 15:18; 17: 40; 22:9; 3N 20:25-27	27:10; 110:12; 124: 58; 132:21, 29-37	12:2-9,11,14	189; Abr 2:3-25
Abraham				Abr 3:1-28
13:10			13:1-14	249
14:18	Al 13:14-19	107:2-4	14:1-40	
15:5		132:30	15:1-21	
15:16		103:3		
16:2		132:34, 65	16:5-18	

BIBLE	BOOK OF MORMON	DOC. & COV.	JST	PofGP/TPJS
17:7		110:12		
17:11			17:1-32	264
18:18		124:58	18:1-42	
19:24-25			19:1-44	271
20-21			20:1-21:32	
22:1-14	Jacob 4:5	101:4; 132:36	22:1-21,26	
22:17-18	1N15:18; 22:9; 3N 20:25-27	110:12; 132:30		
23-24			23:3-24:68	
25:1-6		132:37	25:7,17,21,22,32	
25:12-34	1N 3:3			
26:2-5	1N 13:23; 17:40		26:7,9,35	
27			27:12,33	
28:12			28:12,22	12, 305
29-32			29:4,21-24,30	
			30:3-4,9,16	
			31:22	
			32:11	
35:10-12	1N 13:23; 17:40	124:58		
37:12-30	2N 3:4		37:2	
37:31-35	Al 46:23-26			
38-39			38:2,8,9,16,18	
			39:8,22	
42-49	1N 5:14; Ether 13:7		44:8-15	
			45:1	
47:1-12		105:27		
48			48:1-16	
49:22-26	2N 3:5; 9:53; 101; Jacob 2:25; Al 46: 23-26	10:60; 50:44	49:1,24	39
50:2,3,7,24-26	2N 3:4-22; 4:1-2		50:24,25-38	232, 295
EXODUS 1:1			1:1	
Moses		110:11; 132:1,38; 138:41		Moses 1:1-42
1:7-14	1N 17:25			
2:18-21		84:6		
3:2-3			3:2-3	
3:7-18	1N 17:24	38:18		
4:14-16	2N 3:17	28:3		252, 363
4:21,24-27			4:21,24-27	
5:1-9	1N 17:25		5:4	
6:3-4,8,12,14,26-29			6:3-4,8,12,14,26-29	
7:1				363, 375
7:1-4,9,13			7:1-4,9,13	
7:10-12				202
9:12-13,17			9:12-13,17	
9:16				189
10:1,20,27			10:1,20,27	
11:8-10			11:8-10	
12-17	1N 5:15; 19:10			
12:33,37			12:33,37	
12:21-36	1N 17:23			

BIBLE	BOOK OF MORMON	DOC. & COV.	JST	PofGP/TPJS
13:20-22	1N 17:30			
14:4,8,17,30			14:4,8,17,30	
14:13-31	1N 4:2; 17:26-27; Mos 7:19; Al 36:28; Hel 8:11	8:3		
16:14-21	1N 17:28; Mos 7:19			
17:6-7	1N 17:29; 2N 25:20			
18:1			18:1	
19:5-11ff		84:23-26		
19:13, 19		29:13		
20:1-17	1N 17:55; Mos 12: 33-36; 13:5-17			
20:5		98:46; 103:26; 124: 50		
20:7		63:6164		
20:13-17		42:18-20; 59:6		127, 256
20:18-21				247, 322
20:23			20:23	
21:6,8,20-21			21:6,8,20-21	
22:18,28			22:18, 28	
22:25				328
23:3			23:3	
27:8			27:8	
30:31-32			318	
32:1,12,14,23,35			32:1,12,14,23,35	
32:7				207
33:1,20-23			33:1,20-23	
33:14-15		103:19-20		254
34:1-2,4,7,14,35			34:1-2,4,7,14,35	
34:29	Mos 13:5			
40:15		68:15-20; 84:18,27, 30-32		319
LEVITICUS 2: 2-3				172
8:1-13		84:23		
12:3-5			12:3-5	
21:1,11			21:1,11	
22:9			22:9	
25:36				328
NUMBERS 2: 34		61:25		
9:15-21	1N 17:30			
14-16	1N 17:30-31,42	84:24		207
16:10			16:10	
21:5-9	1N 17:41; 2N 25:20; Al 33:19-20; Hel 8: 14-15			
22:20			22:20	
23:19				327
DEUTERONOMY 2:30			2:30	
5:9		98:46; 103:26; 124:50		

BIBLE	BOOK OF MORMON	DOC. & COV.	JST	PofGP/TPJS
6:5		59:5		
7:2				256
8:3		84:44; 98:11		306
10:1-2			10:1-2	
14:21,26			14:21, 26	
16:22			16:22	
18:15-19	1N 22:20-21; 3N 20: 23; 21:11	1:14; 133:63		
19:15	2N 11:3	6:28; 128:3		
30:1-4, 7	3N 5:23-26			85
33:17		58:45		
34:5-6	Al 45:19	84:25	34:6	
JOSHUA thru 2 KINGS 23	1N 5:12			
JOSUHA 1-11	1N 17:32-33			
5:2-6				264
7:10-21				207, 227
11:20			11:20	
JUDGES 2:18			2:18	
RUTH	no commentary			
1 SAMUEL 15: 11, 35			15:11, 35	
15:22				253
16:14-16, 23			16:14-16,23	
18:10			18:10	
19:9			19:9	
28:9, 11-15				289, 11-15
2 SAMUEL 11: 26-27	Jacob 1:15; 2:23-24	132:1, 38-39		
12:1-14	Jacob 1:15; 2:23-24	132:1, 38-39	12:13	
24:16-17			24:16-17	
1 KINGS 3:1-9,12,14			3:1-9,12,14	
3:5-14				256
5-7	2N 5:15-17			
11:1-6	Jacob 1:15; 2:23-24	132:138-39		
11:4-6,33-39			11:4-6,33-39	
13:18			13:18	
14:8			14:8	
15:3,5,11-12			15:3,5,11-12	
15:5	Jacob 1:15; 2:23-24	132:38-39		
17-2 KINGS 1: 11		110:13; 138:46-47		
2 KINGS 1:10-14				340
1:10,12,14			1:10,12,14	
8:10			8:10	
17:6	2N 10:22			
19:35			19:35	
1 CHRONICLES 10:13			10:13	
13:9-10		85:8		239
21:15, 20			21:15,20	

BIBLE	BOOK OF MORMON	DOC. & COV.	JST	PofGP/TPJS
2 CHRONICLES 2:3-5,7-8,18			2:3-5,7-8,18	
6:17			6:17	
7:22			7:22	
13:3			13:3	
18:12-27				207
18:20-22			18:20-22	
20:2,6-7,11,17			20:2,6-7,11,17	
22:2			22:2	
24:9,22			24:9,22	
25:18			25:18	
34:16			34:16	
36:15-16	1N 1:4			
EZRA 2:61-62		85:12		
NEHEMIAH 6: 11,13			6:11,13	
7:10-62			7:10-62	
10:29,30			10:29,30	
ESTHER	no commentary			
JOB		121:10		
1:6			1:6	
1:7				208
2:1			2:1	
7:9;10:21;14:12-13	1N 18:18; 2N 1:14			
19:25-27	2N 9:4			
38:4-7		128:23		167, 220
PSALMS 1:5				17
8:2				321
10-143			10-143	
19:1		104:14		56
34:18		59:8		
37:1				239
45:7				245
46:10		101:16		
47:7				252
50:1-5				183
67:6				248-49
68:18		88:6		
82:6		76:58; 121:28		374
85:10-11				13
93:3-4				185
102				17
110:4				265
118:22-23	Jacob 4:16			
144:15				252
PROVERBS 1-9	Mos 8:20			
16,18,22,30			16,18,22,30	
16:18				137
22:6	2N 4:5			
26:27		109:25		
29:2		98:9		

BIBLE	BOOK OF MORMON	DOC. & COV.	JST	PofGP/TPJS
ECCLESIASTES			3:1	
3:1				
7:20		82:6		
11:1				316
SONG OF		5:14; 105:31; 109:73		
SOLOMON 6:10				
SAMUEL to	1N 5:13; 3N 20:24			
JEREMIAH				
ISAIAH 1:9			189	
1:16			1:16	
1:18		50:10-12		
1:19-20		64:34		
1:26			93	
2	2N 12			
2:2		133:12-13		
2:2-3				252, 367
2:2-21			2:2-21	
2:3-4		115:4-5		
2:4			248, 251	
3	2N 13			
31-26			3:1-26	
4	2N 14			
4:1-5			3:27-4:4	
4:3		112:23-26		
4:5		45:63-75; 84:2-5		
4:6		115:4-6		
5	2N 15			
5:1-30			5:1-30	
5:1		101:43-62		
6	2N 16			
6:2		38:1; 77:2-4		
6:7,9-13			6:7,9-13	
7	2N 17			
7:1-23			7:1-23	
8	2N 18			
8:1-22			8:1-22	
8:16		88:84; 133:72		
8:20			373	
9	2N 19			
9:1-17			9:1-17	
10	2N 20			
10:2-21			10:2-21	
11	2N 21			
11:1		113:1-4		
11:4		19:15		
11:6-9				71, 93, 316
11:10		90:2-4;113:5-6		
11:11				14
11:16		133:26-32		
12	2N 22			
13	2N 23			
13:1		133:14		
13:2-22			13:2-22	

BIBLE	BOOK OF MORMON	DOC. & COV.	JST	PofGP/TPJS
13:2-6		86:1-7; 133:4-14		
13:10		29:14;34:9;45:42; 88:87;133:49		
13:10-13				29, 71
13:12-13		21:6;35:24		
14	2N 24			
14:2-32			14:2-32	
14:7		43:31;88:110;101:28		
14:12		76:25-27		
14:14		29:36; 76:28; 88:35		
14:21		88:21-35		
14:32		97:21		
16:6			16:6	
22:23-25		45:48-53		
23:10			23:10	
24:5		1:15		
24:16-20		49:23;88:87		
24:20-22				29, 71, 219
25:6		58:8-12		
25:7		121:26-33		
26:20-21		45:43-47		17
28:9		19:21-22		
28:10	2N 28:30			
28:15		5:19;45:31;97:23		
28:19				87
28:21		95:4;101:95		267
29:2-23			29:2-32	
29:3-5	2N 26:15-18			
29:6-24	2N 27:3-35			
29:14		4:1;6:1;11:1;12:1; 14:1;18:44		
32:1-12		58:17-22		
32:14			32:14	
33:2,18			33:2,18	
33:14				361
33:20				33
33:22				252
34:4				29
34:5-6		1:12-14, 36		
34:7,16-17			34:7,16-17	
35:1-2		49:24-25;117:7		
35:3-7		81:5		
35:8			35:8	
35:8-10		45:71;66:11;101:18; 133:26-34		
35:10				17, 34
36:5			36:5	
36:20-21				17
37:17,32,36			37:17,32, 36	
38:15-17			38:15-17	
39:2			39:2	
40:3	1N 10:8	33:10;65:1;88:66		319, 335

BIBLE	BOOK OF MORMON	DOC. & COV.	JST	PofGP/TPJS
40:4		133:22		
40:5		101:23		
40:6				274
40:28-31		89:20		
41:8-9		93:46;133:30-32		
41:28			41:28	
42:6-7		128:22		
42:7				219, 222
42:19-25			42:19-25	
43:5-6				183
43:8-10		76:1		
43:13			43:13	
44:21			44:21	
45:22-24				82
45:23		76:110;88:104		
46:7			46:7(1867)	
48	1N 20			
49	1N 21			
49:2		5:10;6:2;86:8-9; 103:7;133:30-34		
49:6		86:11		
49:22		45:9;115:3-5		
49:23,25			49:23,25	
50	2N 7			
50:1-11			50:1-8	
50:2-3		133:66-69		
50:11		133:70-74		
51-52:2	2N 8			
51:1-20			51:1-20	
51:3				249
51:11-12		45:71;66:11; 101:18-19		
52:1-3, 6-15	3N 20:32-45			
52:1		82:14;113:7-8		
52:2,6		113:9-10		
52:6-7,9			52:6-7,9	
52:7		19:29;31:3;79:1		
52:8		84:98-99		80
52:10		133:2-4		
52:11		38:42;133:5-6		
52:12		133:15		
52:15		101:94		
53	Mos 14			
53:9-10		34:3		
54	3N 22			
54:2		82:14;133:9		
54:10,15			54:10,15	
54:13		45:58		
55:1-2	2N 9:50-51			
55:6-7		88:62-63		
57:5			57:5	
59:17		27:15-18		
60:2		45:62-75;112:23		

BIBLE	BOOK OF MORMON	DOC. & COV.	JST	PofGP/TPJS
60:22		133:58	60:22	
61:1		128:22		
62:3		133:32		
62:4-5		133:23-24	62:4-5	
63:1-2		133:46-48		
63:3-4		76:107;88:106; 133:50-52		
63:7,9		133:52-53		
63:17			63:17	
64:1		133:40		
64:2		34:8;133:41-42		
64:3		133:43-44		
64:5-6			64:5-6	
65:1-2,4,20			65:1-2,4,20	
65:17		101:25		
65:18-19		101:27-29		
65:20		63:50-51;101:30-31, 101		
65:24		101:32-34		
65:25		101:26		
66:1-2		38:17		
66:22		29:23		
66:24		76:44		
JEREMIAH	1N 5:13;7:14; Hel 8:20			
1:13-16	Hel 8:20			
2:24			2:24	
3:2-3			3:2-3	
5:19			5:19	
8:20		45:2; 56:16		
12:5			12:5	
17:5			17:5(1867)	
18:8,10,14			18:8,10,14	
23:5-6	Hel 8:20			
25:31			25:31	
26:3-20			26:3-20	
27:7,11			27:7,11	
29:12,18-19			29:12,18-19	
30:11		87:6		
30:12-16			30:12-16	
31:21			31:21	
31:31-34		1:22;45:9;49:9; 84:98		
33:11			33:11	
34:15			34:15	
35:14-15			35:14-15	
36:30,32	1N 5:13		36:30	
37:15-20	1N 7:14		37:16	
42:10,14,21			42:10,14,21	
44:4			44:4	
50:6			50:6	
LAMENTATIONS	no commentary			

BIBLE	BOOK OF MORMON	DOC. & COV.	JST	PofGP/TPJS
EZEKIEL 1:26-28		110:2-3		
14				237-38
14:9			14:9	
18:32			18:32	
19:10			19:10	
20:30			20:30	
23:17,22,28,34			23:17,22,28,32	
34:3				315
34:11-13				17
35:6			35:6	
36:36			36:36	
37:1-14		138:43		
37:15-20	2N 3:11-12			
37:16-17		27:5		
38:2-3				280
38:14-23		29:21		
48:35			48:35	
DANIEL 2:21		121:12		
2:35				13
2:44-45		65:2,6; 109:73; 138:44		365
5:27				362
5:28			5:28	
6:5			6:5	
6:10				161
7				157, 161
7:3-7				289
7:9,13				167, 253
7:9-27		27:11;Section 116; 138:38		
7:16				289
7:21-22				159
9:27;11:31;12:11		88:85		
10:11			10:11	
HOSEA 6:2				286
11:8			11:8	
13:14	Mos 16:7-8			
JOEL 1:6			1:6	
2:2				141
2:10-11,31		29:14;34:9;43:18 84:118		
2:13-14			2:13-14	
2:28 (28-32)		95:4		JS-H 1:41
2:30-31				71
2:32				17
3:16		21:6;35:24		
AMOS 3:6-7			3:6-7	265, 280
4:3,5-6			4:3,5-6	
6:10			6:10	
7:3,6			7:3,6	
9:8			9:8	

BIBLE	BOOK OF MORMON	DOC. & COV.	JST	PofGP/TPJS
OBADIAH vs 21				189, 191, 223, 330
JONAH 3:9-10			3:9-10	
MICAH 4:11-13	3N 20:18-19	133:59		
5:8-9	3N 16:14-15;20:16-17			
5:8-15	3N 21:12-21	87:5		
NAHUM 1:8			1:8	
HABAKKUK 1:5	3N 21:5			
ZEPHANIAH 3:9				93
HAGGAI	no commentary			
ZECHARIAH 4:7				163
4:10,14			4:10,14	
6:5,7,13			6:5,7,13	
8:7,13			8:7,13	
12:10		45:51,53		
13:6		45:52		
14:4		133:20		
14:20				93
MALACHI 3-4	3N 24-25	138:46		JS-H 1:36-37
3:1		36:8;45:9;133:2		
3:2-3		13;128:24		172
3:17		101:3		
4:1		29:9;64:24;133:64		
4:2	1N 22:15,24; 3N 25:13;26:4,9	45:58		
4:4-6		2;27:9;35:4;98:16-17;110:14-15;128:17		160, 172, 321, 323, 330, 337, 356
OTHER PROPHETS				
Zenos	1N 19:10-17; Jacob 5;Al 33:15-16; Hel 8:20;15:11; 3N 10:16-17			
Zenoch	1N 19:10; Al 33:15-16; Hel 8:20; 3N 10: 15-16			
Neum	1N 19:10			
Ezias	Hel 8:20			
Unnamed	1N 15:11; Al 34:36			
Apocrypha and Pseudepigrapha		91:1-6; 107:57		

BIBLE	BOOK OF MORMON	DOC. & COV.	JST	PofGP/TPJS
NEW TESTAMENT	1N 13:24-26, 39-41	52:9, 36; 66:2		
MATTHEW 1: 6-25			1:3-2:8	
2:2-22			3:2-26	
3:1-3		33:10; 34:6; 35:4; 39:19-20; 42:7; 65:3		335
3:1-12	1N 10:7-10			
3:2-3				273, 341
3:3-17			3:29-46	
3:9				319
3:10		97:7		341
3:11				335, 360
3:13-17	1N 11:26-27; 2N 31: 4-9; Mor 7:10			266, 276, 319
4:1-23			4:1-22	
4:4		84:44; 98:11		306
4:21				349
5-7	3N 12-14			
5:1-48			5:1-50	
5:5		88:17		
5:11-12				124, 259
5:13	3N 16:15	101:37-40; 103:10		
5:17-18				318
5:26				359
5:28-29		63:16		127
5:29-30				35
5:32		42:74		
5:37		124:120		
5:45				218, 317
6:1-23			6:1-39	
6:12				313
6:15		132:56		
6:22		88:67		
6:23				124
6:25-34		84:81-85; 101:37		
6:27				199
6:31	Al 31:37			
6:33	Jacob 2:17-19			256
7:1-29			7:1-37	
7:1				163
7:2				129
7:6		41:6		77
7:7	2N 32:4	49:26; 66:9; 75:27; 88:63; 103:31, 35		13, 257
7:13-14	Jacob 6:11, 3N 27: 33	132:22, 25		67
7:20	Moro 7:5			
7:23	Mos 26:27	29:28		
7:24-27	Hel 5:12; 3N 11:39-40; 18:12-13	6:34; 90:5		376
8:1-29			8:1-30	

BIBLE	BOOK OF MORMON	DOC. & COV.	JST	PofGP/TPJS
8:12				288
8:29				208
9:1-30			9:1-36	
9:12-13	Moro 8:8			240
10:2-42			10:2(1867)-38	
10:9-10		24:18; 70:12; 84:77-79		
10:11-15		24:15; 60:15; 75:19-22; 84:92-95; 109:39		
10:16		111:11		
10:18-19		84:85; 100:6		
10:39		98:13; 103:27		
10:40-42		39:22; 84:36-38, 89-91; 99:2; 112:20-21		261
11:2-28			11:2(1867)-29	
11:5		35:15		
11:11				275-76
11:12-13				318
11:22		75:22		
11:28-30				82, 270
12:3-50			12:3-44	
12:20		52:11		
12:30	2N 10:16			
12:31-32		76:34; 132:27		219, 356, 361
12:34		121:23		358
12:39				157
12:49-50				121
13:5-54			13:5-55	
13:3-9				94
13:10-17				94-5
13:19-40				95-98, 100
13:20-22		40:2		
13:36-43		38:12; 86:1-7; 101:65-66		
13:41-52				101-02, 159
14:3-23			14:2(1867)-20	
14:11				261
15:4-33			15:4-31(1867)	
16:1-29			16:1-29	
16:4				157, 278
16:16-19		10:69; 21:6; 98:22; 124:93; 127:7; 128:8,10; 132:46		
16:18				274, 318
16:19	Hel 10:7			265
16:24		56:2; 112:14		
17				13
17:1-11		27:12-13; 63:21; 138:45		158
17:5-25			17:4-24	
17:5				312
18:4-5		99:3		

BIBLE	BOOK OF MORMON	DOC. & COV.	JST	PofGP/TPJS
18:6-7		54:5; 121:22		124, 261
18:8-27			18:7-27	
18:16	2N11:3	6:28; 128:3		
18:18	Hel 10:7			265
18:20		6:32; 61:36		
18:22		98:40		238
19:1-30			19:1-30	
19:28	1N 12:9; Mor 3:18	29:12		
19:30	Ether 13:12	29:30		
20:1-31			20:1-31	
20:16	Ether 13:12	95:5; 121:34-40		321
21:1-46			21:1-56	
21:16				321
21:22		29:6		
21:33-41		101:44ff		
22:3-35			22:3-34	
22:2-14		58:11		
22:14		95:5-6; 121:34-40		331
22:21		63:26		
22:23-32		132:15-17		
22:35				261
22:37		59:5		
23:3-39			23:2-41	
23:12		101:42; 112:3; 124:114		
23:23				332
23:35-36				222
23:37	3N 10:4-7	10:65; 29:2; 43:24		307, 310, 312
24:1-43	(complete rewrite)		24:1-56	JS-Matthew
24		45:16-75		
24:4-5,31		49:23		365
24:14-15				364
24:30		76:63; 88:93		
24:32-33		35:16		
24:35		56:11		274
24:36		39:21-24; 49:7; 133:11		
24:42-51		51:19-20; 61:38; 124:10		
25:1-45			25:1-46	
25:1-13		33:17; 45:56; 63:54; 133:19		36
25:14-30		52:13; 60:3; 70:17; 78:15,22; 82:18; 101:61; 117:10; 124:113; 132:53		68
25:18				257
25:29				257
25:33		29:27		
25:40-42		42:38		
26:2-73			26:2-73	
26:24		76:32		
26:26-29		27:2-4		

BIBLE	BOOK OF MORMON	DOC. & COV.	JST	PofGP/TPJS
26:29				65
26:39	3N 11:11	19:18		
26:41				363
27:4-65			27:5-66(1867)	
27:52-53		133:54-56		
27:59				232
28:19-20		105:41		262
MARK 1:1-11	1N 10:7-10; 11:26-27; 17:21			
1:5-45			1:4-40	
1:7				273
1:10				276
1:24				213
2:1-28			2:1-27	
2:22				192
3:2-31			3:2-26	
3:28				219
4:8-37			4:7-30	
5:3-42			5:2-34	
6:2-54			6:2-57	
6:7		42:6; 52:10		
7:4-36			7:4-35	
8:1-38			8:1-43	
8:35				129
9:1-50			8:44-9:50	
9:34		64:6-8		
9:48		76:44		
10:1-51			10:1-51	
10:13-15	3N 9:22; 11:37-38; 17:21			
10:16				314
11:2-32			11:2-34	
12:1-44			12:1-50	
13:1-37			13:1-51	
14:1-72			14:1-82	
14:38				315
15:1-46			15:2-50	
16:4-13			16:3-13	
16:15-18	2N 9:23-24; 3N 11:33-34; Mor 9:22-25; Ether 4:8	35:8-9; 58:64; 63:9; 68:8-10; 80:1; 84:62-74; 112:28-29		15, 71, 206, 224, 262, 265
LUKE 1:1-79			1:1-78	
1:5-17				272, 319
1:17-19		27:6-7; 110:12		
2:1-51			2:1-51	
3:2:38			3:2-45	
3:5		49:23		
3:16-22	1N 10:7-10; 11:26-27; 2N 31:4-9			
3:22				276
4:2-43			4:2-43	

BIBLE	BOOK OF MORMON	DOC. & COV.	JST	PofGP/TPJS
4:18				219
5:2-39			5:2-39	
6:1-48			6:1-48	
6:39				311
7:1-43			7:1-43	
8:1-50			8:1-51	
8:46				281
9:1-61			9:1-61	
10:1-39		(See Matt 10)	10:1-40	
11:1-53			11:1-54	
11:28				253
12:1-58			12:1(1867)-67	
12:32		82:24		
12:48		82:3		
13:1-35			13:1-36	
13:32				258
14:2-35			14:2-38	
15:1-32			15:1-32	
15:1-2				277
15:4-7				277
15:7				77
15:8-10				277
15:11-30				276
16:1-31			16:1-36	
16:9		82:22		
16:13-19	Al 40:9-14			
16:16				314
17:1-37			17:1-40	
18:1-43			18:1-43	
18:1-8		101:81-84		
19:2-40			19:2-39	
20:2-47			20:2-47	
21:1-38			21:1-38	
21:25				250, 252
21:26		88:91		
21:36				253
22				63
22:2-71			22:2-71(1867)	
22:31		52:12		
22:32				241
23:1-51			23:1-52	
23:43				309
23:56				232
24:1-53			24:1-52(1867)	
24:36-39				325
24:39-40		6:37; 129:2		
24:45-47				81
24:46-48				262
JOHN 1:1-51			1:1-51	

BIBLE	BOOK OF MORMON	DOC. & COV.	JST	PofGP/TPJS
1:1-14		6:21; 10:57-58; 11:28-30; 34:2; 35:2; 39:2-4; 45:7-8; 84:46; 88:49; 93:2,4,6-11		
1:7-9				335
1:10-11	3N 9:15-16			
1:16		93:16		
1:18		67:11-12; 84:22		
1:19-34	1N 10:7-10; 11:26-27; 2N 31:4			
1:28	1N 10:9			
1:32		93:15		276
1:47		41:11		
2:1-24			2:1-24	
2:15		117:16		
3:1-5	Mor 7:10			12, 162, 198, 264, 274, 314, 328
3:2-36			3:2-36	
3:16-17		34:3; 49:5		
4:1-54			4:1-56	
4:14		63:23		
4:35		4:4; 6:3; 11:3; 12:3; 14:3; 33:3,7		
5:3-45			5:3-46	
5:19				312, 347, 373
5:26				181
5:29		76:15,17,50		
5:36		93:5		
6:12-65			6:12-65	
7:3-39			7:3-39	
8:1-47			8:1-47	
8:11		82:7		
8:12	3N 9:18; 11:11; Ether 4:12			
8:56				60
8:58		39:1		
9:4-32			9:4-32	
9:5	3N 9:18; 11:11; Ether 4:12			
10:1				266
10:7-14			10:7-14	
10:11				300
10:14-16	1N 22:25; 3N 15:14-24; 16:1-4; 17:4	10:59; 50:44		
10:17-18				312, 346, 373
10:30	3N 11:27,36; 28:10	50:43; 93:3		
10:34-36		76:58		374
11:1-57			11:1-57	
12:7,14			12:7,14	
13:5-12		88:140-41		111
13:8,10,19			13:8,10,19	

BIBLE	BOOK OF MORMON	DOC. & COV.	JST	PofGP/TPJS
14:2-3	Enos 1:27; Ether 12: 34-37	59:2; 72:4; 76:111; 98:18		311, 331, 359, 366
14:3,30-31			14:3, 30-31	
14:6		132:12		
14:10		93:3		
14:16		88:3		
14:23		130:3		
14:26	2N 32:3,5			243
14:30		127:11		
15:1-6	1N 15:15-16			194
15:13				195
15:16	3N 27:28	42:3; 50:29; 88:64		
15:26				243
16:10,13			16:10,13	
16:13-14	2N 32:3,5			243
16:16		38:8		
16:33		64:2		
17:3		132:24		344, 346
17:9-11				311, 372
17:21		35:2		
18:38			18:38	
19:11,17,29			19:11,17,29	
19:39-40				232
20:1,10,17			20:1,10,17	
20:20		6:37		
20:23		132:46		
20:31	Mor 7:5			
21:15-17				241
21:20-23	3N 28:6-7	Section 7; 112:14		
ACTS 1:3-4			1:3-4	
1:4-8				263, 265, 274
1:9-11		34:7		
2:1-4		109:37		274, 310
2:3,27			2:3,27	
2:3-6				149, 195
2:13				246
2:27				339
2:29				188
2:37-38		33:11; 49:11-14		149, 199, 263
2:39-41		36:6		81, 190
3:1-21			3:1-21	
3:15				265
3:17-19				188, 190, 339
3:21				252
3:22-23	1N 22:20-21; 3N 20: 23	133:63		
4:10-12	2N 25:20; 31:21; Mos 3:17; 5:8	18:23		265
4:21			4:21	
5				62
5:13,39			5:13,39	
6:2				109

BIBLE	BOOK OF MORMON	DOC. & COV.	JST	PofGP/TPJS
6:9			6:9	
7:38	2N 9:2			
7:39-40,44,59			7:39-40,44,59	
7:55-56		49:6		312
8:5-17				336
8:14-19		35:6		
9:5-6				265
9:7-40			9:7-40	
9:18				265
10:1-42	1N 10:11			
10:2-6				265
10:45-48				199
12:7			12:7	
13:8-10				99
13:36,48			13:36,48	
13:46				15
14:14			14:14	
15:24			15:24	
16:13			16:13	
16:16-18				206
17:19,27,31			17:19,27,31	
17:28		45:1		
19:1-6				99, 246, 263, 336
19:15				99, 199, 208
20:21			20:21	
21:25			21:25	
22:10,29-30			22:10,29-30	
23:5,15,27			23:5,15,27	
25:16-17			25:16-17	
ROMANS 1:1-32			1:1-32	
1:16		68:4		263
2:1,16			2:1,16	
2:12		76:72		218
3:1-30			3:1-30	
4:2,4-7,16			4:2,4-7,16	
4:15	2N 9:25-26			
5:3,13-16			5:3,13-16	
5:13	2N 9:25-26			
6:3-6		128:12		265
6:7,14,17,19			7:7,14,17,19	
7:1-25			7:1-27	
8:6	2N 9:39			
8:8-31			8:8-31	
8:15				375
8:26				141, 278
8:28		100:15		
8:29		93:21		
9				189
9:3				189
9:3-32			9:3-32	
9:17				189

BIBLE	BOOK OF MORMON	DOC. & COV.	JST	PofGP/TPJS
9:22		76:33		
9:28		52:11		
9:29				189
10:14-15				100, 221
10:16-19			10:16-19	
10:17				148, 149
11:2-26			11:2-26	
11:13-24	1N 10:11-14; 15:12-18; Jacob 5-6			
11:25--27				14
12:2,9			12:2,9	
13:1-14			13:1-14	
14:11,15,23			14:11,15,23	
14:11	Mos 27:31			
15:5,24			15:5,24	
16:10-11,16,25			16:10-11,16,25	
1 CORINTHIANS 1:1-28			1:1-28	
1:12		76:99		
1:21				300
1:27		1:19; 35:13; 124:1		
2:9	3N 17:16-17	76:10		
2:11			2:11	202, 205, 247
3:2,15			3:2,15	
3:16-17		93:35		
4:2,4-5			2:2,4-5	
5:3-5,12			5:3-5,12	
5:5		78:12; 82:21; 132:26		338
6:12,18			6:12,18	
7:1-38			7:1-38	
7:14-19		74:1-7		
8:5-6		76:58		
8:4			8:4	
9:24			9:24	
9:22				306
10:1-2				264
10 : 11,23 24,27,33			10 : 11,23 24,27,33	
10:13	Al 13:28			
11:10,19-21,29			11:10,19-21,29	
11:27-29	3N 18:28-29; Mor 9:29			
12				15, 207, 223
12:1,31			12:1,31	
12:1				244
12:3				223, 243
12:4-13	Moro 10:8-19	46:8-33		243, 245, 270
12:12-27				231, 245, 328
12:14-23		84:109-10		
12:27-30				243, 244, 265
13				195
13:1-2				228
13:2-8	Moro 7:44-46			

BIBLE	BOOK OF MORMON	DOC. & COV.	JST	PofGP/TPJS
1:9-10		27:13		159, 168, 231, 252
1:13-14		76:53		149
2:2				208
2:8-9	2N 25:23		2:8,11	
3:1-3			3:1-3	
4:4-28			4:4-28	
4:5				266
4:8,11		88:6		244
4:10-11				206
4:11-12		124:143		
4:12				265
4:14		76:75		
5:7,17			5:7,17	
5:22-31				88
5:26		76:41		
6:13-18	2N 1:23	27:15-18; 35:14; 112:7		
PHILIPPIANS 1:4-30			1:4-30	
2:10	Mos 27:31	76:110; 88:104		
2:17			2:17	
3:1,11,18-19			3:1,11,18-19	
3:20-21				65
4:6			4:6	
COLOSSIANS 1:4,6			1:4,6	
1:16		121:29; 132:13		
2:2,7,20-23			2:2,7,20-22	
3:3		86:9		
3:18-22				89
4:11			4:11	
1 THESSALONIANS 1:1-2,8			1:1-2,8	
2:16			2:16	
4:16-17		76:102; 78:21; 88:96-97; 109:75	4:15,17	
5:4-5				286
5:26			5:26	
2 THESSALONIANS 1:1,9			1:1,9	
2:2-3,7-9			2:2-3,7-9	
1 TIMOTHY 1:1			1:1	
2:4-5,12,15			2:4-5,12,15	
3:8,15-16			3:8,15-16	
4:1		46:7		
4:2			4:2	
4:3-4		49:15-19		
5:1				212
5:10,23-25			5:10, 23-25	
6:15-16			6:15-16	
2 TIMOTHY 2:5,8,11			2:5,8,11	

BIBLE	BOOK OF MORMON	DOC. & COV.	JST	PofGP/TPJS
3:16			3:16	
4:1-2,15,22			4:1-2,15,22	
TITUS 1:15			1:15	
2:11			2:11	
PHILEMON 1:25			1:25	
HEBREWS 1:2-3		76:23-24		
1:6-7			1:6-7	
1:9				245
1:14				168
2:16			2:16	
3:3			3:3	
4:2				60
4:2-3,5,12			4:2-3,5,12	
5:4		132:59		264, 272
6:1-10			6:1-10	
6:1-3				99, 188, 328, 338, 360
6:5-6		76:35		83, 339
6:18	Enos 1:6; Ether 3:12			
7:1				321
7:3		84:17		323
7:3,19-20,26-27			7:3,19-20,25-26	
7:4				322
7:11-12				308
7:17				265
8:4			8:4	
9:8-28			9:8-28	
10:1,10,13,21			10:1,10,13,21	
11:1	Al 32:21; Ether 12:6			
11:1-40			11:1-40	
11:4				169
11:5				170
11:6		63:11		
11:10				159
11:35				170
11:40		128:15		159, 337, 356
12:6-8		95:1		194
12:22-24		76:66-69		12, 158, 320, 325, 366
12:29				361, 367
13:3,5			13:3,5	
13:8	Mor 9:9	35:1		264
JAMES 1:2,4,12,21,27			1:2,4,12,21,27	
1:5-6	2N 4:35	42:68; 46:7		
1:17	Omni 1:25, Moro 7:12			
2:1-26			2:1-25	
3:1			3:1	
3:8				239
4:3	2N 4:35	46:9		
5:14		42:43-44		198

BIBLE	BOOK OF MORMON	DOC. & COV.	JST	PofGP/TPJS
5:16				342
5:17-18				89
1 PETER 1:9-11			1:9-11	
1:13		73:6; 75:22; 112:14		
1:20				265
2:7,8,12			2:7,8,12	
2:9				202
3:1-20			3:1-20	
3:18-20		Section 138		219, 222, 309
4:1-11			4:1-11	
4:5-6		76:73; Section 138		223
4:8				193, 316
5:13			5:13	
2 PETER 1:5-8		88:40		16, 217, 297, 306, 368
1:10				305
1:16-19				297-98, 303, 306, 312
1:19-20		131:5-6	1:19-20	
1:21				243
2:1,3,19			2:1,3,19	
2:4		38:5		
3:1-17			3:1-17	
3:10-11				319
3:16	Al 13:20			
1 JOHN 1:1			1:1	
1:9		76:41		
2:1,7-8,15-16,24			2:1,7-8,15-16,24	
2:1		110:4		
2:2	2N 9:21	76:41		
3:2-3	Moro 7:48	35:21; 130:1		64
3:6,8-9,16,18,21			3:6,8-9,16,18,21	
4:1				161, 202, 203
4:1-3				213
4:3,12			4:3,12	
5:13,18			5:13,18	
2 JOHN		25:3		
3 JOHN	no commentary			
JUDE 1:1,11			1:1,11	
1:6		38:5		
1:9				208
1:14-15				170
1:23		36:6		
REVELATION				191
1:1				
1:1-20			1:1-20	
1:1-3				247, 289
1:6		76:56		318, 369, 370
1:8,11		45:7; 61:1; 63:60; 75:1; 84:120; 110:4		
1:14-15		110:23		
1:16		6:2; 11:2; 12:2; 14:2; 33:1		

BIBLE	BOOK OF MORMON	DOC. & COV.	JST	PofGP/TPJS
20				65
20:1,6			20:1,6	
20:1-3	1N 22:26	43:1-3; 88:110-111; 101:28		
20:3				13
20:5		88:101		
20:7-10		29:22; 88:113		
20:8				280
20:12-15	2N 9:10-13; 28:23	76:36-37; 128:6-7		
21:2				86
21:3				84
21:8		63:17; 76:103		
22:9			22:9	
22:17				82
22:18-19		20:35		

NOTES

1. *Discourses of Brigham Young*, comp. John A. Widtsoe (Salt Lake City: Deseret Book Co., 1925), p. 127.

2. *Teachings of the Prophet Joseph Smith*, comp. Joseph Fielding Smith (Salt Lake City: Deseret Book Co., 1974), p. 327; hereafter *TPJS*.

3. A compilation of Joseph Smith's doctrinal teachings on the Bible can be found in *TPJS*. The accompanying chart provides a key to those teachings.

4. *Discourses of Brigham Young*, p. 125.

5. For the complete list of changes, we are indebted to the excellent work of Robert J. Matthews, *"A Plainer Translation": Joseph Smith's Translation of the Bible—A History and Commentary* (Provo, UT: Brigham Young University Press, 1975), Appendix A, pp. 393–98. Additional explanations are given in the body of his book.

6. For a treatise on these Isaiah statements, see Monte S. Nyman, *Great Are the Words of Isaiah*, Appendixes C, D, and F. There are only sixty-six Doctrine and Covenants statements in Appendix D. Seven others have been found since this publication.

Modern Revelation: A Window to the Past

7

Joseph Fielding McConkie

In the category of theological irony, the dogma that one can love, reverence, understand, and faithfully follow Bible precepts while denying the spirit of revelation by which those precepts came certainly merits a prize. The loudest protests against modern prophecy are couched in claims of loyalty to Jesus and the Bible. Yet the Bible asserts that "the testimony of Jesus is the spirit of prophecy" (Revelation 19:10). It was Peter who said: "No prophecy of the scripture is of any private interpretation. For the prophecy came not in old time by the will of man [nor, may we add, did it come by the understanding of man]: but holy men of God spake as they were moved by the Holy Ghost." (2 Peter 1:20–21). Peter is simply saying that what comes from the Holy Ghost is to be interpreted by the Holy Ghost. In other words, that which comes by the spirit of revelation is to be interpreted and understood by the spirit of revelation.

Joseph Fielding McConkie is Associate Professor of Ancient Scripture at Brigham Young University.

The Spirit of Prophecy and Scripture

To reject the spirit of revelation is not only to forfeit that which the Spirit would have revealed; it is also to lose the understanding of all that the Spirit *has* revealed. The Lord explained the principle to Nephi thus: "Unto him that receiveth I will give more; and from them that shall say, We have enough, from them shall be taken away even that which they have" (2 Nephi 28:30). A theology that seals the heavens to those of our day also has the effect of sealing from any meaningful understanding the scriptural records in our possession. Conversely, that same spirit which opens the heavens in our day breathes the breath of life and understanding into the inspired writings of the past. A people without the power to pen scripture are also without the power to understand scripture.

Those in the meridian of time who rejected the spirit which testified that Jesus was the Christ also lost the spirit by which they could have seen and understood that everything within the Law of Moses was designed and ordained to point their attention to Christ and to prepare them to accept him. Conversely, those in Joseph Smith's day who had the faith to accept the Book of Mormon and its testimony of Christ were immediately rewarded with a revelation about Moses' day and the great revelatory experiences that were his (see Moses 1).[1]

It is characteristic of the spirit of revelation to constantly enlarge our understanding. In so doing, it is as natural for that spirit to reach to the past as it is to reach to the future. All things—past, present, and future—are as one with God (Moses 1:6; D&C 130:7). Surely it is no more difficult for God to draw upon the past than upon the future to illustrate his teachings. For instance, Christ frequently used the past to prophesy of the future. "As it was in the days of Noah, so it shall be also at the coming of the Son of Man," he declared, "for it shall be with them, as it was in the days which were before the flood; for until the day that Noah entered into the ark they were eating and drinking, marrying and giving in marriage; and knew not until the flood came, and took them all away; so shall also the coming of the Son of Man be" (Joseph Smith—Matthew 1:41–43). The disciples asked Christ "concerning the destruction of the temple, and the Jews" and what signs would precede his return and the "destruction of the wicked" (Joseph Smith—Matthew 1:4). His answer to the latter questions virtually repeated his answer to their questions as to when the temple and the nation of the Jews would be destroyed. The destruction of the nation of Judah in the meridian of time was but the prophetic foreshadowing of the destruction awaiting the wicked in the last days.

The meridian destruction was a type, a shadow, a miniature replica of the events of the last days.

Our Kinship with the Past

No religion has a closer kinship with men and women of the past than that of the Latter-day Saints. It is fundamental to our theology that we cannot be saved without our kindred dead and that they cannot obtain an exaltation without us. Further, neither we nor the ancient Saints can be saved without the keys and authority that have been restored to us by the prophets who held that power and authority anciently. Ours is the dispensation of the fulness of times—it is a dispensation distinguished by the "whole and complete and perfect union, and welding together of dispensations, and keys, and powers, and glories . . . from the days of Adam even to the present time" (D&C 128:18). We profess the same faith, doctrines, priesthoods, and rituals enjoyed by the ancients whenever they were in possession of the fulness of the gospel.

The Old Testament concludes with the promise that in a future day Elijah will return and that his return will cause the hearts of the ancient fathers to turn to their children and the hearts of the children to turn to their fathers (see Malachi 4:5–6). Moroni gave Joseph Smith a more perfect rendering of this passage, explaining that the Lord would "plant in the hearts of the children the promises made to the fathers," and that the hearts of the children would "turn to their fathers" (D&C 2:2). The spirit of the restored gospel brings with it a strong feeling of kinship with the faithful of ages past. It seems probable that covenants were made before the foundations of the earth under which our ancestors agreed to do certain things that would bring blessings to us and that we in turn covenanted to do a labor by which the full blessings of salvation would be extended to them. When John the Baptist, the first of the ancients to restore authority in this dispensation, laid his hands upon the heads of Joseph Smith and Oliver Cowdery, his first words were, "Upon you my fellow servants"—in other words, my brethren in the cause of Christ and the battle for righteousness—"I confer the priesthood of Aaron" (D&C 13:1).

It is one thing to read the words of the prophets and quite another to be tutored by prophets. Who among the world's scholars can boast of having stood face to face with Adam, Enoch, Noah, a messenger from Abraham's dispensation, Moses, John the son of Zacharias, Peter, James, and John? While religious leaders were claiming that the heavens were sealed to them, Joseph Smith was being personally tutored by these ancient prophets, who laid their hands upon his head and conferred upon him the power, keys, and authority they held. Again, it is one thing to read of Christ and quite another to stand in his presence, as was the experience of Joseph Smith and as is promised to all faithful Saints (see D&C 93:1).

The Seer at Work

The primary role of a prophet is to preach by the spirit of revelation. As necessary and appropriate, under inspiration he may also foretell future events and reveal the past and the present. A seer, who is "a prophet also," is "greater than a prophet," we are told (Mosiah 8:15–17), but apart from the seer's ability to use "interpreters" the context of Ammon's statement lacks specific detail on the difference. Clearly the sense of the word *seer* is "a person who sees, particularly preternatural [that is, exceeding what is natural] sights," and it is this definition that Adam Clarke gives for the Hebrew word for *seer* as used in 1 Samuel 9:9—where the word *seer* is used in the Bible for the first time.[2]

The great modern seer is Joseph Smith, to whom visions and revelations came like a flood. While he made many prophecies of things to come, he manifested appreciably more to us about history past than about history future. Upon reflection, we realize that this is appropriate: first, because ours is a restored gospel—we claim keys, authority, and doctrines that were had by the ancients; and second, ours is the dispensation in which the promises to the ancient fathers are to find fulfillment.

A brief review of the revelations given to Joseph Smith establishes the point. As the work of the restoration begins, Moroni becomes the Prophet's first tutor. He labors to show the youthful Joseph how the events that are about to unfold constitute a fulfillment of the words of the prophets. In a detailed account of what Moroni told Joseph Smith, published in the *Messenger and Advocate*, the Church periodical in Kirtland, Oliver Cowdery cited over forty verses of scripture that Moroni quoted to Joseph from the Bible. His references from the Old Testament were taken from the books of Deuteronomy, Psalms, Isaiah, Jeremiah, Ezekiel, Joel, and Malachi. From the New Testament he quoted from the gospels of Matthew and John, Acts, 1 Corinthians, and 1 Thessalonians.[3] Indeed, ours is a day looked to by all the holy prophets since the world began (Acts 3:21; D&C 86:10), a day described by them in remarkable detail.

Though the Book of Mormon contains much that is prophetic, it deals more with history than with futurity. It is in the context of the history of the ancient inhabitants of this continent that the student of the Book of Mormon is taught the basic principles of the gospel.

With the understanding gained from his labors in translating the Book of Mormon, Joseph Smith was directed by the Lord to commence a translation of the Old and New Testaments. In the process, many revelations were granted. The most notable are as follows:

1. Moses 1, which is an account of Moses' being caught up into an exceedingly high mountain and seeing God face to face. It also relates the account of a confrontation Moses had with Satan, and contains brief extracts from a marvelous vision in which Moses was shown the earth and its inhabitants. Later chapters contain the Lord's account of the creation of this earth.

2. Doctrine and Covenants 7, which is the restoration of the content of a parchment written by John the Beloved. We learn from this revelation that John did not taste of death, but was allowed to live until the Second Coming.

3. Doctrine and Covenants 76. This section is "The Vision," the marvelous revelation in which Joseph Smith and Sidney Rigdon were allowed to see the Father and the Son seated upon their heavenly thrones, experience a flashback to the events of the pre-earth life, and then obtain a view of the celestial, terrestrial, and telestial kingdoms.

4. Doctrine and Covenants 77, which is the "key" to unlock the book of Revelation.

5. Doctrine and Covenants 132, a revealed explanation of the practice of plural marriage by the great patriarchs of the Old Testament, along with the announcement of the principle of eternal marriage.

These revelations, like so many others received by Joseph Smith, required that the prophetic gift be coupled with that of seership. This was also the case in the translation of the book of Abraham; as with the Book of Mormon plates, Joseph Smith did not give any explanation of the translation process used on the Egyptian papyrus. We are left with the simple announcement that he was a seer.

In his revelations Joseph Smith consistently unfolded the past. He was obviously doing so to enhance our understanding of the importance of present events and our knowledge and understanding of the future. Given all that was restored to us through Joseph Smith, we are well within the mark in saying that no prophet of whom we have record used the gift of seership to a greater degree than the Prophet Joseph Smith.

The Restoration of the Priesthood

As the flooding of the Nile covered the inhabitable part of Egypt with fertile soil, so the restoration of the priesthood brings a new depth of richness to our understanding of the nature of the Church in biblical times. First John came, declaring the Aaronic Priesthood. This priesthood, we learn from Joseph's revelation, was the authority by which baptisms were performed from the days of Aaron to the days of Christ. By the authority of the Aaronic Priesthood, the righteous from the time of Aaron to the days of John the Baptist had the authority to entertain angels and teach the preparatory gospel of repentance and faith in Christ (see Joseph Smith—History 1:69; D&C 84:26–27). There is no biblical evidence for such an assertion; the scholarly world has never supposed it, and the so-called Bible-believing world would reject it out of hand. Despite the fact that we have John's word for it and two independent revelations in the bargain, this fact remains little known, even among teachers in the Church today.

John could not have restored what he did not possess, any more than one can come back from where one has not been. Laying his hands on the heads of Joseph and Oliver, he said, "Upon you my fellow servants, in the name of Messiah, I confer the Priesthood of Aaron, which holds the keys of the ministering of angels, and of the gospel of repentance, and of baptism by immersion for the remission of sins; and this shall never again be taken from the earth until the sons of Levi do offer again an offering unto the Lord in righteousness" (Joseph Smith—History 1:69). Our revealed commentary explains that when the holy priesthood was taken from the earth, "the lesser priesthood continued, which priesthood holdeth the key of the ministering of angels and the preparatory gospel; which gospel is the gospel of repentance and of baptism, and the remission of sins, and the law of carnal commandments, which the Lord in his wrath caused to continue with the house of Aaron among the children of Israel until John" (D&C 84:26–27). Accepting Joseph Smith as a prophet, we can no more argue that "baptism by immersion" did not exist among the children of Israel than we can argue that "the law of carnal commandments" did not exist among them. Again we are told, "The power and authority of the lesser, or Aaronic Priesthood, is to hold the keys of the ministering of angels, and to administer in outward ordinances, the letter of the gospel, the baptism of repentance for the remission of sins, agreeable to the covenants and commandments" (D&C 107:20).

It is true that the word *baptism* is not found within the covers of the Old Testament. Yet did Nephi not tell us that many "plain and precious" parts would be taken from the Old World record "and also many covenants of the Lord" (1 Nephi 13:26)? The Book of Mormon, which is contemporary with much of the Old Testament, is replete with references to this sacred ordinance. It would be rather hard to imagine that Lehi and his family took the Melchizedek Priesthood with them to the New World but did not have a knowledge of the ordinance of baptism. It would be equally difficult to suppose that God had one system of salvation for those in the Old World and a completely different one for those in the New World. From Bible texts restored to Joseph Smith, we know that the principles of faith, repentance, and baptism were taught in the days of Adam. We read that the faithful of Adam's day were told that "this [was] the plan of salvation unto all men" (Moses 6:59–60, 62). Again, our revelation declares that those who take upon themselves the name of Christ in the waters of baptism "and endure in faith to the end should be saved" (D&C 20:25). Indeed, our whole system of temple work would be unnecessary if at any time baptism or any of the saving ordinances now performed in the temples were unnecessary.

In restoring his priesthood, John announced that he was acting under the direction of the presidency of the meridian Church (Joseph Smith—History 1:72). Peter was its president. The order in which John gives their names suggests that James was the first counselor and John the second. As to the priesthood they restored, we are told that it is the authority by which the gospel is administered, the mysteries of the kingdom restored, and God himself made manifest (see D&C 84:19). The revealed word states, "The power and authority of the higher, or Melchizedek Priesthood, is to hold the keys of all the spiritual blessings of the church—to have the privilege of receiving the mysteries of the kingdom of heaven, to have the heavens opened unto them, to commune with the general assembly and church of the Firstborn, and to enjoy the communion and presence of God the Father, and Jesus the mediator of the new covenant" (D&C 107:18–19).

This description of the priesthood constitutes a remarkable commentary on the spiritual activities of the ancients. We have the power and authority that they had, and it is their example to which we turn for direction and understanding. It is through Joseph's seeric gift that we know that those who held the priesthood anciently had "power, by faith, to break mountains, to divide the seas, to dry up waters, to turn them out of their course; to put at defiance the armies of nations, to divide the earth, to break every band, to stand in the presence of God; to do all things according to his will, according to his command, subdue principalities and powers; and this by the will of the Son of God which was from before the foundation of the world" (JST, Genesis 14:30–31).

Thus, it was by the power of the priesthood restored to Joseph Smith and Oliver Cowdery that Enoch caused the earth to tremble, mountains to flee, and rivers to turn out of their courses; that the cities of Enoch and Salem were translated; that Moses parted the

Red Sea, and brought water from a rock; that Elijah sealed the heavens for three-and-a-half years, and raised the dead; that Christ turned water to wine, fed the multitudes from a few fishes and loaves, stilled the storm, and brought the decaying body of Lazarus to life. By this authority sins were remitted, angels entertained, and men brought into the presence of God. Textbooks and universities, kings and congresses, armies and weapons are incapable of conveying such authority. Without the books of Moses and Abraham, the Nephite record, and the revelations in the Doctrine and Covenants, we would know little or nothing of such events. It is through these books that we are offered the visions of a seer and invited to perceive and know of the activities of our faithful kin in ages past.

The Doctrines of the Priesthood

In a series of great revelations, Joseph Smith was the major instrument for a partial fulfillment of Paul's prophecy about the dispensation of the fulness of times as a period in which all things would be gathered together in one (see Ephesians 1:10). Both the Doctrine and Covenants and the Book of Mormon attest that the Church the ancients had was to be restored (See D&C 84:2; 2 Nephi 9:2; 3 Nephi 21:22). The restoration of this ancient people to the lands of their inheritance is of no moment if they are not first brought to a knowledge of the saving truths of the gospel and membership in the Church and kingdom of God. The Lord has never granted any people a land of promise except as a symbol of the eternal promises that are given to those who keep the covenants they have made with him.

A land of promise is the rightful ultimate inheritance of the sanctified and of none else. It is the earthly symbol of the heavenly kingdom or the rest of the Lord. "Now this Moses plainly taught to the children of Israel in the wilderness, and sought diligently to sanctify his people that they might behold the face of God; but they hardened their hearts and could not endure his presence; therefore, the Lord in his wrath, for his anger was kindled against them, swore that they should not enter into his rest while in the wilderness, which rest is the fulness of his glory" (D&C 84:23–24). Since Israel spurned the fulness of priesthood blessings, the Lord took Moses and the holy priesthood from them. They were then given a lesser priesthood and a law of carnal commandments.

Having forfeited the Melchizedek Priesthood and those ordinances that would prepare them to stand in the presence of God, the children of Israel were to be confined to the privileges of the ministering of angels and a preparatory gospel. Before that day, membership in the Church (D&C 107:4) had surely included the fulness of temple blessings. Temples and the special endowment of knowledge and power granted therein have been enjoyed by the Saints of all ages. From the book of Abraham, Joseph Smith learned that sacred matters pertaining to the Holy Priesthood were revealed "to Adam in the Garden of Eden" and also to "Seth, Noah, Melchizedek, Abraham," and all others "to whom the Priesthood was revealed" (Abraham, facsimile 2, figure 3).

As to the government and organization of the Church, Joseph Smith said, "We believe in the same organization that existed in the Primitive Church, namely, apostles, prophets, pastors, teachers, evangelists, and so forth" (Articles of Faith 1:6). In restoring the Aaronic Priesthood, John the Baptist told Joseph Smith that "he acted under the direction of Peter, James and John, who held the keys of the Priesthood of Melchizedek" (Joseph Smith—History 1:72). In a revelation directing the organization of the First Presidency, we are told that the keys of this priesthood always belong to this quorum (D&C 81:2).

The extent of Joseph Smith's knowledge of the manner in which the Church was governed anciently was obviously attributable to the gift of seership. On one occasion, apparently concerned at the lack of attention and discipline exhibited by some of the brethren in their council meetings, Joseph described the proper spirit and nature of such councils. "In ancient days," he said, "councils were conducted with such strict propriety, that no one was allowed to whisper, be weary, leave the room, or get uneasy in the least, until the voice of the Lord, by revelation, or the voice of the council by the Spirit, was obtained, which has not been observed in this Church to the present time. It was understood in ancient days, that if one man could stay in council, another could; and if the president could spend his time, the members could also."[4] Similarly, commenting on Malachi's promise of Elijah's return, Joseph Smith said that Malachi "had his eye fixed on the restoration of the priesthood, the glories to be revealed in the last days, and in an especial manner this most glorious of all subjects belonging to the everlasting gospel, namely, the baptism for the dead" (D&C 128:17).

In ordaining his father, Joseph Smith, Sr., to the position of Patriarch to the Church, the Prophet Joseph explained much relative to the ancient order of the Church. These verses, now a part of Doctrine and Covenants 107, were revealed at that time: "Three years previous to the death of Adam, he called Seth, Enos, Cainan, Mahalaleel, Jared, Enoch, and Methuselah, who were all high priests, with the residue of his posterity who were righteous, into the valley of Adam-ondi-Ahman, and there bestowed upon them his last blessing. And the Lord appeared unto them, and they rose up and blessed Adam, and called him Michael, the prince, the archangel. And the Lord administered comfort unto Adam, and said unto him: I have set thee to be at the head; a multitude of nations shall come of thee, and thou art a prince over them forever.'' (D&C 107:53–55.)

Joseph promised the same blessing to his father, saying that he (Joseph Sr.) would be a prince over his posterity, that he would hold the keys of patriarchal blessings within the Church, and that he would yet sit in the general assembly of patriarchs spoken of by Daniel (see Daniel 7:9–13). ''And again, blessed is my father,'' said Joseph Smith, ''for the hand of the Lord shall be over him, and he shall be full of the Holy Ghost: for he shall predict whatsoever shall befall his posterity unto the latest generation.'' Thus the promise given to Adam was granted to Joseph Smith, Sr. (See D&C 107:56.) Further, Joseph Jr. promised his father that he would ''see the affliction of his children pass away, and their enemies under their feet.'' Joseph Smith, Sr., was likened to an olive tree whose branches were bowed down with much fruit. The blessing given by Jacob to his son Joseph (Genesis 49:22–26) was then placed on the head of the Prophet's brother Hyrum and through him to his posterity. He was to be blessed ''to the uttermost'' even that he might be ''a fruitful bough: he shall be as a fruitful bough, even a fruitful bough by a well whose branches run over the wall, and his seed shall abide in strength, and the arms of their hands shall be made strong by the hands of the mighty God of Jacob, and the God of his fathers: even the God of Abraham, Isaac and Jacob, shall help him and his seed after him; even the Almighty shall bless him with blessings of heaven above and his seed after him, and the blessings of the deep that lieth under: and his seed shall rise up and call him blessed.''[5]

This blessing provides an important commentary on the past, the present, and the future. It affirms that the blessing given by the ancient patriarch Jacob to his son Joseph was intended to be a prophetic window through which the destiny of Joseph's posterity could be seen. It assured that the Lord had not forgotten those promises and that they were about to be fulfilled. Finally, in it we see the ancient prophecy come full circle. The ancient Joseph's children were to be as branches that crossed over a well; now the latter-day children of Joseph were to return. We witness the fulfillment of this promise in two ways: first, in the descendants of Joseph (those of the tribes of Ephraim and Manasseh) going from the American continent throughout all the nations of the earth to gather Israel; and second, in the eventual return of a representative number from Joseph's tribes to claim their ancient promises in the land of Palestine.

That it was the destiny of the descendants of Joseph to do the work of the gathering of Israel in the last days was well known to the ancients. Such prophecies could only be fulfilled by those holding the same priesthood and keys by which Israel was gathered in ancient times. In some prophecies this is explicitly stated, in others it is alluded to or implied. For instance, Abraham was told that his righteous seed would be blessed with the priesthood and assume a ministry to declare the gospel of salvation among all nations. That the prophecy not be spiritualized away or otherwise misunderstood, the Lord specifically stated that this would be the "literal seed," or the seed of Abraham's "body" (Abraham 2:9–11). Then to Joseph Smith the Lord said, "Abraham received promises concerning his seed, and of the fruit of his loins—from whose loins ye are, namely my servant Joseph" (D&C 132:30). In like manner tens of thousands of others have had their lineage as descendants of Joseph, through either Ephraim or Manasseh, confirmed by the spirit of revelation. These modern Israelites have had the priesthood conferred upon them and have gone forth to search out their lost kindred. In his prophetic description of these things, Moses spoke of Ephraim and Manasseh pushing Israel together from the ends of the earth. He likened them to a bullock, having horns like a unicorn (Deuteronomy 33:17). His imagery is well chosen—the horn was a symbol of power and authority among the ancients, while the unicorn represented the "sword or the word of God."[6]

Conclusions

There is but one Church and kingdom of God and its principles are of necesssity everlastingly the same. God is not the author of confusion or uncertainty. The plan of salvation is not in flux. The principles of salvation as revealed in this dispensation are the same principles revealed to those of past dispensations. Our God is the God of Abraham, Isaac, and Jacob, and theirs was the God of Adam, Enoch, and Noah. The law of the gospel was "irrevocably decreed in heaven before the foundations of this world" (D&C 130:20). Birth does not change the law, death does not change it, nor is it modified for various nations and peoples. The Lord emphasized this point by asking rhetorically, "Will I appoint unto you, saith the Lord, except it be by law, even as I and my Father ordained unto you, before the world was?" (D&C 132:11).

As God is the same yesterday, today, and forever, so the principles of his gospel are the same yesterday, today, and forever. To know those principles in one age is to know them in all ages. To know those principles in this life is "to have so much the advantage in the world to come" (D&C 130:14), for the principles are the same. Thus, the restored gospel becomes the key by which we are to unlock the past. To fail to use the Book of Mormon prophets to understand the teachings of Old World prophets is to misunderstand the eternal nature of God and the gospel. To fail to use the revelations of the Doctrine and Covenants to interpret the teachings of the Old and New Testaments is to misunderstand the very nature of the Restoration. Our doctrines and our covenants were their doctrines and their covenants.

When Palestine was Christ's classroom, the Old Testament was his textbook. When the Americas were his classroom, we are told that he "expounded all the scriptures in one" (3 Nephi 23:14), adding both Old and New Testament writings to the Nephite canon (see 3 Nephi 12–14; 15:16–17; 24–25). Joseph Smith translated the Book of Mormon into the idiom of the King James Bible. The same language has also been used for all the revelations in the Doctrine and Covenants. Clearly, the intent is that they be woven together as one book.

In hundreds of instances the revelations in the Doctrine and Covenants pick up the language of the Bible writers—expanding, expounding, and explaining their meaning. These texts are as a window to past texts and restore to us many of the plain and precious things that have been lost from the ancient record. It would be foolish to study Isaiah without studying Nephi's commentary on his fellow prophet, the scores of corrections in the Isaiah text that the Book of Mormon preserves for us, and the questions and answers on Isaiah found in Doctrine and Covenants 113. Similarly, Joseph Smith gave us a revealed key for unlocking the book of Revelation (D&C 77), a revelation explaining the parable of the wheat and the tares (D&C 86), others explaining statements of Paul (D&C 74, 88), a marvelous revelation explaining John's statement that there would be two resurrections—one of the just and another of the unjust—and still another explaining how the Lord justified the ancient practice of plural marriage. Not only does the list go on, but Joseph Smith's successors in the Presidency of the Church have continued to record revelations which expand and unfold the meaning of Bible texts, doing so in the language of the King James Bible. Obvious illustrations include John Taylor's account of the martyrdom (D&C 135); Brigham Young's revelation on the order of the camps of Israel for the westward trek (D&C 136); and Joseph F. Smith's vision of the redemption of the dead (D&C 138), a commentary on Peter's statement that Christ preached to the spirits in prison (1 Peter 3:18–20).

Such is the providence of God, for all these revelations are to be expounded "in one." Nephi declared the principle thus: "Know ye not that the testimony of two nations is a witness unto you that I am

God, that I remember one nation like unto another? Wherefore, I speak the same words unto one nation like unto another. And when the two nations shall run together the testimony of the two nations shall run together also." (2 Nephi 29:8.) Similarly, Ezekiel spoke of the stick of Judah and the stick of Joseph becoming one in our hands (Ezekiel 37:19). Many years earlier the Lord had told Joseph of Egypt that these two records would "grow together," that they might confound false doctrines, end contentions, and thus establish peace (JST, Genesis 50:31; see also 2 Nephi 3:12).

By expounding the fulness of the standard works as one, we fulfill scripture, follow the example of Christ and the prophets, enhance our understanding, and increase our testimony of the restored gospel. In 1832 the Lord addressed the Saints' failure to do this, saying: "Your minds in times past have been darkened because of unbelief, and because you have treated lightly the things you have received—which vanity and unbelief have brought the whole church under condemnation. And this condemnation resteth upon the children of Zion, even all. And they shall remain under this condemnation until they repent and remember the new covenant, even the Book of Mormon and the former commandments which I have given them, not only to say, but to do according to that which I have written." (D&C 84:54–57.)

On the day the Church was organized, the Lord promised the Saints that if they would give heed to "all his words and commandments" which they would receive through the Prophet Joseph Smith, "the gates of hell" would not prevail against them, that God would "disperse the powers of darkness" from before them, and that he would "cause the heavens to shake" for their "good, and his name's glory" (D&C 21:4–6). Following the death of the Prophet, the Lord affirmed this promise to the Church. Those who faithfully accepted that which had been revealed "from the days of Adam to Abraham, from Abraham to Moses, from Moses to Jesus and his apostles, and from Jesus and his apostles to Joseph Smith," were assured that they would behold the glory of God (D&C 136:37). To that we add the ancient promise, "He that receiveth a prophet in the name of a prophet shall receive a prophet's reward" (Matthew 10:41).

NOTES

1. See also Joseph Smith, *History of the Church* 1:98.

2. Adam Clarke, *The Holy Bible with a Commentary and Critical Notes*, 6 vols. (Nashville: Abingdon, n.d.), 2:235.

3. Joseph Fielding McConkie, *His Name Shall Be Joseph* (Salt Lake City: Hawkes, 1980), p. 58.

4. *Teachings of the Prophet Joseph Smith*, comp. Joseph Fielding Smith (Salt Lake City, Utah: Deseret Book Co., 1977), p. 69.

5. Joseph Fielding Smith, *Life of Joseph F. Smith* (Salt Lake City, Utah: Deseret News Press, 1938), pp. 34–36.

6. J. E. Cirlot, *A Dictionary of Symbols* (New York: Philosophical Library, 1971), p. 357.

Joseph Smith and "Magic": Methodological Reflections on the Use of a Term

8

Stephen D. Ricks
Daniel C. Peterson

Few subjects have so riveted the attention of Latter-day Saints recently as the sale of forged documents purporting to deal with early Mormon history. Certain of these documents—such as the "White Salamander Letter"—portrayed early Mormon history in a very different light than did the traditional history, and raised uncomfortable questions about the influence on the young Joseph Smith of the "magical" elements in his environment. Many historians claim that even though the documents produced by Mark Hofmann are known to be forgeries, enough incontestably authentic materials remain to require a reassessment of the religious and "magical" impulses in the earliest period of Mormon history. Although "magic" has figured prominently in discussions of these materials, relatively little effort has been devoted to formulating a clear definition of the term. Considering the generally pejorative connotations associated with the word "magic" (especially where it is contrasted with "religion"), as well as its somewhat inconsistent use in religious studies, a study of the use of the term seems

---

Stephen D. Ricks is Associate Professor of Hebrew and Semitic Languages at Brigham Young University.

Daniel C. Peterson is Instructor of Hebrew and Semitic Languages at Brigham Young University.

warranted. In this paper, as a backdrop to considering its appropriateness with reference to the early years of Joseph Smith, we wish to consider the meaning and use of the term in the Old Testament, the New Testament, and early Christianity, and the significant shift in the meaning and use of the term during the Reformation.

Recent studies on magic have generally stressed its continuity, rather than cleavage, with religion. Activities have been defined as "magical" when goals sought are "attained through the management of supernatural powers in such a way that results are virtually guaranteed"; further, and equally important, "magic is defined as that form of religious deviance whereby individual or social goals are sought by means alternate to those normally sanctioned by the dominant religious institution."[1] According to such a definition of magic, which includes both the elements of the speaker or writer's perspective as well as the components of coerciveness and assured results, it is not merely the nature of the magical action but also the status of the actor vis-à-vis the speaker or writer that determines its character. In antiquity, magic was not regarded as a separate institution with a structure distinct from that of religion, but was, rather, a set of beliefs and practices that deviated sharply from the social norms of the dominant social group, and was thus considered antisocial, illegal, or unacceptable.[2] In the Old Testament, magic (as this and related words have been understood in the Hebrew and rendered in versions from the Septuagint to the most recent Jewish Publication Society translation)[3] is the activity of the "outsider", whether practiced by non-Israelites or by those who deviated from the Israelite norm and engaged in prohibited practices. Magic is also perceived as a form of subversion in ancient Israel, and is consequently severely punished, since it was viewed as undermining the religious basis of Jehovah's people. Similarly, as Jonathan Smith and Morton Smith have shown in the case of the Greco-Roman world—the world of the New Testament—magic and magical practices are quintessentially the activities of the outsider. According to Jonathan Smith, in the Greco-Roman world "magic was not different in essence from religion, but rather different with regard to social position. . . . The one universal characteristic of magic" is that "it is illegal, . . . and it carried the penalty of death or deportation."[4] In the same vein, Morton Smith notes, "In the Roman Empire, the practice of magic was a criminal offense (Paulus, *Sententiae* 5:23.14–18), and the 'magician' was therefore a term of abuse. It still is, but the connotation has changed: now it is primarily fraud; then it was social subversion."[5]

The biblical accounts that most lucidly show magicians as outsiders and refute a simple definition of magic as the employment of words and actions that function *ex opere operato* (i.e., have their desired effect merely by being performed or spoken) are the stories of Moses and Aaron and Pharaoh's wise men and magicians, Joseph and the wise men and magicians of Pharaoh, and Daniel and the Babylonian astrologers and wizards. According to the account in Exodus 7:9,[6] the Lord said to Moses and Aaron, "When Pharaoh speaks to you and says, 'Produce your marvel,' you shall say to Aaron, 'Take your rod and cast it down before Pharaoh.' It shall turn into a serpent" (Exodus 7:8–9). They came before the Pharaoh and did precisely that: Aaron cast down his rod in the presence of Pharaoh, and it turned into a serpent. The Pharaoh then summoned his own wise men and sorcerers, and the Egyptian magicians did the same thing with their spells (Exodus 7:11). Though the rods of the Egyptian magicians were able to become serpents, Aaron's rod swallowed all of their rods. The Egyptian wise men and sorcerers were further able to imitate Moses and Aaron in the turning of the bodies of water of Egypt into blood and in bringing frogs upon the land by their spells, but they failed in their efforts to produce lice; they were fully discomfited when the boils affected them as they did the other Egyptians, so that they were not even able to stand before Pharaoh.

As shown in Genesis 41, Pharaoh had dreams that left him troubled. He sent for his magicians and for his wise men to interpret his dreams for him. After Pharaoh had told them his dreams, the magicians and wise men said that they were not able to interpret them for him. At this point the chief cupbearer remembered Joseph, who was then called before Pharaoh and was able, through the gift of God (Genesis 41:16), to interpret Pharaoh's dreams to his satisfaction.

As recorded in Daniel 2, Nebuchadnezzar, like Pharaoh, had dreams that left his spirit agitated, whereupon he called his magicians, exorcists, sorcerers, and Chaldaeans to tell him what he had dreamed. They were threatened with death if they failed to produce for him both his dream and its interpretation, but they claimed that such a demand as the king was making of them had never been made of a magician, exorcist, or Chaldaean before: "The thing asked by the king is difficult; there is no one who can tell it to the king except the gods, whose abodes are not among mortals" (Daniel 2:11). Thereupon the king flew into a violent rage, and gave an order to kill all of the wise men of Babylon. However, Daniel, who would also have fallen under this death order, was able to interpret the dream through the power of the "God of heaven," thereby saving himself and the others from death.

Several significant features in these stories that are relevant to our subject are worth noting: (1) In each of these three instances, Israelites are pitted against practitioners of the religion of non-

Israelite "outsiders," and in each instance the superior power of God is shown. When the magicians and wise men of Pharaoh are not able to produce lice by their own spells, they exclaim to Pharaoh, "This is the finger of God" (Exodus 8:19). Daniel similarly emphasizes Israel's God as the source of his power and its superiority to the power of the wise men and magicians: "The mystery about which the king has inquired—wise men, exorcists, magicians, and diviners cannot tell to the king. But there is a God in heaven who reveals mysteries, and He has made known to King Nebuchadnezzar what is to be at the end of days" (Daniel 2:27–28). Further, (2) in the cases of Joseph and Daniel, there is no clear indication given of the specific manner in which they show themselves superior to the Egyptian and Babylonian magicians, except through prayer and the power of God. However, in the case of Moses and Aaron in Pharaoh's court, the action by which the effect was achieved was the same. In addition, the very word used here in the text for the Egyptian magicians—*ḥarṭom* (in the phrase "*ḥarṭummê miṣrayim*"—"the magicians of Egypt")—is borrowed from the Egyptian *ḥr tp*, "lector priest," one who, in Egyptian materials at least, is not generally associated with magic (for which the regular Egyptian word is *ḥk'*).[7] This suggests to me an implicit polemic in the text against all practitioners of Egyptian religion, with the hint that they are all magicians (because they are non-Yahwists).

Jacob Milgrom has pointed out that before the performance of each miracle, Moses is silent; Pharaoh's magicians, on the other hand, are only able to copy Aaron's actions "by their spells" (*bĕlahăṭêhem*—if we are to follow the rendering of the new Jewish Publication Society translation—rather than the more traditional translation, "by their secret arts").[8] By acting alone, and not speaking, Moses behaves in a manner that is distinct from that of the Egyptians (which is, by implication, "magical"). We find this position somewhat unsatisfying. As Milgrom himself notes, later Israelite prophets do not refrain from speaking while performing their wonders. Thus, Elijah said to King Ahab, "As the Lord, the God of Israel lives, whom I serve, there will be no dew nor rain in the next few years except at my word" (1 Kings 17:1). During his contest with the priests of Baal on Mount Carmel, Elijah both speaks and acts (1 Kings 18:16–46). Similarly, Elisha speaks and acts when miraculously providing oil for the widow (2 Kings 4:2–7). If the essence of magic is acting and speaking together when performing wonders, why are these prophets never referred to as "magicians" or "sorcerers" in the text of the Bible, despite its rich vocabulary for describing practitioners of such arts? Departing for a moment from Israelite religion, it should be noted that practitioners of numerous normative religious traditions, ancient and modern (e.g., Catholicism), include both words and actions in their rites. Similarly, Jesus performed many of his miracles by a combination of words and actions. By the definition of magic that Milgrom uses, do these traditions, and do Jesus' miracles also, become "magical"? That definition, based, as it is, upon notions that only gained wide currency during the Reformation, must be reassessed.[9] The decisive element in all of these accounts—of Elijah and Elisha, as well as Moses—is the Israelite, Yahwist context.[10]

Probably the best-known list of prohibited practices in the Pentateuch is found in Deuteronomy 18:10–11: "Let no one be found among you who consigns his son or daughter to the fire, or who is an augur, a soothsayer, a diviner, a sorcerer, one who casts spells, one who consults ghosts or familiar spirits, or one who makes inquiries of the dead." These activities are quintessentially the practices of the outsider, as the context of the list makes clear: not merely are they considered abhorrent practices when performed by Israelites, but their abhorrent nature is at least in part the result of their being observed by Israel's neighbors, as the wider context of the pericope shows. The verse immediately preceding the list of prohibited practices begins: "When you enter the land that the Lord your God is giving you, you shall not learn to imitate the abhorrent practices of those nations." Further, these practices of the people of the land form one of the grounds for their being dispossessed, as the passage following the list indicates: "For anyone who does such things is abhorrent to the Lord, and it is because of these abhorrent things that the Lord your God is dispossessing them before you. You must be wholehearted with the Lord your God. Those nations that you are about to dispossess do indeed resort to soothsayers and augurs; to you, however, the Lord your God has not assigned the like." (Deuteronomy 18:12–14.)

There are a score or so of words in the Hebrew Bible that refer to practices or practitioners of magic (as it is generally understood), falling roughly into the categories of magic in general or sorcery, divination, and astrology (these categories, it should be pointed out, have been devised by modern exegetes, not by the Israelites themselves: in none of these lists are these types of magical practices explicitly divided).[11] Roughly three-quarters of the occurrences of these words refer, explicitly or implicitly, to non-Israelite practitioners or activities. Indeed, some of the words are used exclusively of non-Israelites. The remainder of the occurrences refer to deviant Israelite practices or practitioners. In no instance that we have found are any of these used favorably of an Israelite practice.[12] Even in those instances where there is no strongly negative tinge to these words (e.g., Genesis 30:27, 44:5, 15; 1 Kings 20:33), they refer either to non-Israelites or to Israelites in a non-Israelite setting (e.g., Joseph in Egypt).

The three divinatory instruments that are regularly associated with the Israelite cultus—lots,[13] Urim and Thummim,[14] and ephod[15]—have a distinct vocabulary associated with them. Unlike any of the words mentioned above, these terms are used primarily in connection with Israelites, only occasionally of non-Israelites,[16] and almost invariably in a favorable context. Nowhere in the Hebrew Bible is there a description of the method by which these divinatory instruments are used. Thus, there is no way to test the divinatory methods used in connection with the lot, ephod, and Urim and Thummim against the traditional definition of magic or to determine formal differences in the method used by those who employed them and the techniques used by the *ôb, ḥōbēr,ˆyid'ōnî, menaḥḥēš, me'ōnēn*, and *qōsēm*—those practitioners associated with non-Israelite divination. The decisive testable difference between the two groups is their association with Israel's religion and cultus: the ephod, Urim and Thummim, and lots are acceptable because they are Israelite, while the others are rejected because they are not.

Accusations that Jesus was a magician are implicit in the New Testament and explicit in the writings of the early Church Fathers. This seems to be reflected particularly clearly in the "Beelzebub" passage recorded in Mark 3:20–26 (New International Version):

> Then Jesus entered a house, and again a crowd gathered, so that he and his disciples were not even able to eat. When his family heard about this, they went to take charge of him, for they said, "He is out of his mind."
>
> And the teachers of the law who came down from Jerusalem said, "He is possessed by Beelzebub! By the prince of demons he is driving out demons."
>
> So Jesus called them and spoke to them in parables: "How can Satan drive out Satan? If a kingdom is divided against itself, that kingdom cannot stand. If a house is divided against itself, that house cannot stand. And if Satan opposes himself and is divided, he cannot stand; his end has come."

From this passage it is apparent that Beelzebub is a name for Satan. The phrase "by the prince of demons" mentioned here probably refers to the charge of the use of demonic powers in order to achieve his miracles.[17] According to P. Samain, the accusation of using demonic powers to achieve miracles is tantamount to a charge of magic since, in a Jewish context, prophets and other holy men were thought to validate their missions by the performance of miracles, while those thought to be in league with Satan were also believed capable of performing wonders.[18] This passage serves as a response to such a charge by claiming that one is hardly likely to use "magic" (through the agency of demonic powers) in order to drive out demons.

The Gospel accounts of the temptation of Jesus may also be understood as showing Jesus rejecting conventional magical means to attain his goals. In this account, which is recorded in detail in Matthew and Luke, following his forty-day fast Jesus is tempted by the devil to turn a stone into bread, to leap from the pinnacle of the temple, and to fall down and worship him in return for all the kingdoms of the earth.[19] The temptation story is commonly interpreted as relating to the question of religious vs. political messianism. However, since turning stone into bread and flying through the air are commonly claimed by magicians, Samain suggests that the account of the temptations should also be understood as implying the refusal of Jesus to use magical powers to accomplish his goals.[20]

The charge that Jesus was a magician has been preserved outside the New Testament in both Jewish[21] and pagan traditions.[22] In the tractate Shabbat of the Babylonian Talmud the following note is recorded in the midst of a discussion on impurities: "Did not Ben Stada [i.e., Jesus] bring forth sorcery from Egypt by means of scratches on his flesh?"[23] The Church Fathers were keenly aware of the charge—made by Jew and Gentile alike—that Jesus was a magician.[24] In reply to this assertion, these early Christian writers made no effort to distinguish Jesus' actions from those of a wonder worker. Rather, they affirmed the divine source of his power and the prophetic predictions of his life and activities. It was a question, not of the form of the wonders, but of the relationship of the purported doer to the person speaking or writing. Thus, members of the Christian community saw Jesus as God-inspired, and therefore not a magician. Jews and pagans, on the other hand, who viewed the Christians as the "outsiders," viewed Jesus' miraculous acts as either fraudulent or demon-inspired, but in either case "magical." In effect, whether Jesus was viewed as a magician or not was almost solely dependent upon whether he was seen as an "insider" or an "outsider."

No one has more thoroughly documented the parallels between the activities of the wonder worker of the Greek world and Jesus' activities than Morton Smith in *Jesus the Magician*. Based solely on superficial similarities between the acts of these (generally gentile) wonder workers and Jesus, an objective observer would be compelled to apply, or withhold, the designation "magician" from both. But by his own definition, noted above, a subjective judgment is decisive in designating an individual as magician: magic, according to Smith, is a term of abuse, and is used of an "outsider" who is viewed as being particularly subversive.[25] Similarly, for the

Jewish contemporaries of Jesus who believed both genuine prophets as well as God's enemies were capable of working miracles, it is less the nature of the act than its source that determines whether it is miraculous. Colin Brown touches on the nub of the issue when he notes, in his review of *Jesus the Magician*, "Morton Smith's argument is an elaborate statement of the charge that, according to the Gospels, was brought against Jesus from the start, namely that his actions were evil, that he was demon-possessed and even in league with Satan. . . . Perhaps the greatest service that Smith's book can perform is to state forcibly the question, 'By what power did Jesus act?' "[26] Geza Vermes in his book, *Jesus the Jew*, is more to the point. He observes that "the representation of Jesus in the Gospels as a man whose supernatural abilities derived, not from secret powers, but from immediate contact with God, proves him to be a genuine charismatic, the true heir of an age-old prophetic religious line."[27]

The traditional view of the structural cleavage between magic and religion in Western scholarship is the result, in part at least, of the sharp Protestant reaction to certain Roman Catholic sacraments and other practices. This position is represented at least as early as 1395 by the Lollards in their "Twelve Conclusions":

> That exorcisms and hallowings, made in the Church, of wine, bread, and wax, water, salt and oil and incense, the stone of the altar, upon vestments, mitre, cross, and pilgrims' staves, be the very practice of necromancy, rather than of the holy theology. This conclusion is proved thus. For by such exorcisms creatures be charged to be of higher virtue than their own kind, and we see nothing of change in no such creature that is so charmed, but by false belief, the which is the devil's craft.[28]

According to the Lollard Walter Brute, the very procedures of the priests were modeled on those of the magician. Both thought their spells were more effective when pronounced in one place and at one time rather than another; both turned to the east to say them; and both thought that mere words could possess a magic virtue.[29] But if the Protestants criticized holy water and the consecration of church bells, they launched a veritable offensive against the central Catholic doctrine of the Mass. In the view of one Reformer, transubstantiation differs in no significant way from conjurations, "the pretense of a power, plainly magical, of changing the elements in such a sort as all the magicians of Pharaoh could never do, nor had the face to attempt the like, it being so beyond all credibility." John Calvin wrote that the Roman Catholics "pretend there is a magical force in the sacraments, independent of efficacious faith." According to Bishop Hooper, the rite of the Roman Mass was "nothing better to be esteemed than the verses of the sorcerer or enchanter . . . holy words murmured and spoken in secret."[30] The essential features of magic thus came to be understood as consisting of the automatic efficacy of ritual words (incantations) and procedures (magical operations). Based on this view of the automatic and immediate efficacy of ritual words, a different relationship to Deity (or deities) was posited: Magic was said to be manipulative and coercive, while religion (based on the Reformers' views of efficacious faith) was perceived as supplicative. It is probably not insignificant that the anthropologist Mary Douglas (herself a Roman Catholic) has noted that, by the application of a simple functional definition of magic, the more radical formulations of grace of fundamentalist and evangelical Protestants could also be termed "magical." Indeed, nearly every normative religious tradition has elements that could be construed as magical by such a definition.

Recent discussions of "magic" in the early years of Joseph Smith differ significantly in the amount of space devoted to defining magic, and to the element of perspective in determining the limits of magic. Ronald Walker, in his two papers that appeared in the Fall of 1984 number of *Brigham Young University Studies*, uses the word *magic* occasionally, noting that the nineteenth-century dichotomization of magic and religion has "failed to bear up under recent structural-functional or phenomenological analysis."[31] Richard Bushman, in *Joseph Smith and the Beginnings of Mormonism*, uses the term *magic* and *magician* occasionally.[32] Nowhere does he show he is defining "magic," but, given its frequent juxtaposition with the values of Enlightenment rationalism,[33] it appears that the "magician" was one who did not share the values of the Enlightenment. Richard L. Anderson, in his article, "The Mature Joseph Smith and Treasure Searching," cites the recent work by David Aune on magic in the Bible and in early Christianity, and uses various perceived structural-functional distinctions between magic and religion to argue against the appropriateness of the term *magic* with reference to Joseph Smith's treasure searching.[34] Marvin Hill, in "Money-Digging Folklore and the Beginnings of Mormonism: An Interpretive Suggestion," uses, in the course of a sixteen-page article (including footnotes) the term *magic* (in each case unadorned with any modifiers) a score of times. Nowhere that we can see has he attempted an explanation of what he means by the term, nor does he direct us to works that study the meaning of the word.[35] Alan Taylor, in his study, "Rediscovering the Context of Joseph Smith's Treasure Seeking," provides an extensive, if somewhat puzzling, definition of magic. In certain respects, his definition reflects the Reformation attempt to dichotomize religion and magic:

> Magic is a particular way of looking at the universe. Magic perceives the supernatural as inseparably interwoven with the material world while the pure "religion" of definition divorces the two, separating them into distinct dimensions. Magic detects supernatural entities throughout our natural environment, intermediaries between man and God, spirits both good and evil that can hurt or help men and women both materially and spiritually. To minimize harm and secure benefit, people who believe they dwell in a magical cosmos practice rituals intended to influence the spiritual beings, the supernatural entities. In contrast, abstract "religion" strips the natural environment of its spirits and relocates God's divine power to a distant sphere.[36]

In many respects, this view of God's divine power being located in a distant sphere parallels the normative Christian doctrine of God, and reflects the view of Enlightenment rationalism's disdain for an immanent Deity. However, in practice every normative religious tradition assumes the possibility that the Divine may in fact be influenced. Further, nearly every religious tradition (not least primitive Christianity)[37] recognizes a world of demons and spirits intermediary between the worlds of deity and man. Recognizing that, Taylor continues:

> The sharp distinction between "magic" and "religion" seems clear and straightforward, but anthropologists and religious historians have repeatedly discovered that magic and religion have at most times and in most places been interwoven. Few people anywhere have ever possessed a religious faith shorn of hope that through its pursuit they could manipulate the supernatural for protection and benefit in this life as well as the next. Moreover, our century's neat distinction between magic and religion is laden with the value judgment that magic is superstitious, deluded, and irrational, if not downright evil, while religion is the lofty, abstract expression of our highest ideals.[38]

The implications of this position are significant. In the first part of his discussion of magic, Taylor allows for a dichotomy between magic and religion. However, in the second part he appears to be admitting that such distinctions between magic and religion are ideologically driven, pejorative, and necessarily used to describe "outsiders," i.e., others than oneself. It is the sort of value-laden term that might have been used by the intelligentsia of Joseph Smith's day about treasure searching. Taylor describes this Enlightenment elite as "utterly self-confident in their superior rationality and access to urban ideas. [T]he village elites disdained rural folk notions as ignorant, if not vicious, superstitions that obstructed commercial and moral 'improvement.' "[39] Given Taylor's recognition that the term *magic* is inevitably value-sensitive and potentially pejorative, and that the dichotomy with magic that his position implied would not bear scrutiny, one might have expected that he would refrain from using it thereafter in his article, or would at least have explained that he was using it from the perspective of the Enlightenment rationalists (which, of course, might be co-extensive with his own view). However, he does none of these things: he uses the terms *folk magic* and *magic* several times thereafter and provides no further explanation.

"An Open Letter to our Family and Friends," recently written by two former members of the Church, presents a particularly puzzling picture of Joseph Smith and "magic."[40] The authors deny categorically the existence of magic in the biblical tradition.[41] Following *Webster's*, the authors define the word *occult* as "certain alleged mystic arts, such as magic, alchemy, astrology, etc.," and the word *magic* as "the use of charms, spells, and rituals in seeking or pretending to cause or control events, or govern certain natural or supernatural forces; sorcery; witchcraft."[42] They further cite the definition of "magic" from the *New Standard Bible Dictionary*:

> Magic . . . properly has to do with the use of objects or actions to produce, through infuence over the spirits or jinn, the physical results contrary to the natural order. . . . Magic or sorcery was an effort to determine fate, not so much by foretelling as by working out the destiny by means of charms, or spells, or potions, or the use of objects which in themselves are supposed to possess power, or into which the sorcerer himself has infused efficacy.[43]

The definitions in *Webster's* are sufficiently broad and ambiguous that the ritual acts of nearly any religious tradition could be construed as "occult" or "magical." According to the definition in the *New Standard Bible Dictionary*, magic seeks to achieve "results contrary to the natural order." But how is it possible to determine whether an action is "contrary to the natural order" except on the basis of *a priori* assumptions about the character of the natural order, i.e., assumptions that are extrinsic to the act itself?[44]

As we consider the specific details that the authors cite as forays of Joseph or of his family into what they term "magic" and the "occult,"[45] we are struck by the similarities between certain biblical accounts and the alleged activities of Joseph, his family, and his associates. In the Bible, the rod of Aaron is an instrument for manifesting God's power; the Urim and Thummim, lots, and the ephod are means for making known his will. At another time a prophet might be called upon to use his God-endowed powers to help to find a lost animal. Similarly, the "rod of Aaron" or the "rod of nature" was used by Joseph and his associates to determine God's will; the seerstone might also be used to establish God's will, to aid in the translation of an unknown foreign language, or to find lost objects. It is irrelevant, in our view, whether the instruments mentioned in the Bible and the ones used by Joseph and his associates were exactly the same. Indeed, it is not possible to determine their similarity or identity, since the biblical accounts do not provide us with sufficient information about these objects to allow us to reconstruct them with certainty.[46] What is essential in each instance is the use of some instrument to determine God's will, or to make his power manifest.

In the final analysis the designation "magic" or "occult" in the Bible or in the lives of Joseph or his associates has less to do with the nature of the act or acts—which, based on the instances they cite and their commentary on them, seem to exercise the authors so much—but the power by which those acts are performed. There is no clear indication that Joseph, his family, or any others associated with him, believed that the "rod of nature," the seerstone, or any other object they might have used operated except through the power of God. The revelation to Oliver Cowdery in April 1829, in both its original and edited forms, make this manifest (changes in more recent editions are indicated in parentheses):

> Now this is not all (thy gift); for you have another gift, which is the gift of working with the rod (which is the gift of Aaron); behold, it has told you many things; behold, there is no other power, save (the power of) God, that can cause this rod of nature (gift of Aaron to be with you), to work in your hands (and you shall hold it in your hands and do marvelous works; and no power shall be able to take it away out of your hands), for it is the work of God.[47]

We affirm our belief in Moses and Aaron as prophet and spokesman chosen by God, who made plain God's power through the rod; and in Joseph, Oliver, and many others, who through the "rod of Aaron" were enabled to know God's will. Similarly, we accept Samuel as prophet and judge, who was able to find things hidden; so too, we believe in and accept the gifts of Joseph, who was known, from an early age, to have the gift of seeing. Just as we accept as divinely authorized the use of lots, the ephod, and the Urim and Thummim in the Bible to determine God's will, we accept, too, Joseph's use of the Nephite interpreters and the seerstone to know what could not be determined by merely human power. We see magic or the occult in none of these instances. We do not presume to dictate what means of determining God's will are acceptable for a prophet to use, so long as the origin of that inspiration is God. The authors' thesis notwithstanding, it appears to us that they see "magic" in Joseph's activities because they reject him as a prophet, rather than rejecting him as a prophet because they object to his alleged involvement in the "occult."

Haralds Biezais, in his study on the relationship between religion and magic, denies any formal distinction between the two, claiming that all such presumed differences are ideologically motivated.[48] This observation, even if somewhat too starkly stated, contains a fundamentally important insight: where on the religion-magic continuum religion ends and magic begins depends upon the stance of the person speaking or writing. To the extent that elements of social and religious deviance may be described as "magic" and distinguished from "religion," we find useful Goode's nuanced continuum of "nondichotomous differences" between religion and magic:[49]

Magic	*Religion*
Manipulative attitude	Supplicative, propitiatory, or cajoling attitude
Professional-client relationship	Shepherd-flock or prophet-follower relationship
Individual goals	Group goals
Activities more likely to be private and individual	Activities more likely to be carried out by groups
In case of failure, substitution or introduction of other techniques	Substitution rarer
Lesser degree of emotion, even impersonality	More emotion, possibly awe or worship
Practitioner decides whether the activity is to be carried out	Practitioner may decide when, but is less likely to decide whether, the activity is to be carried out
Activities used instrumentally, for specific goals, which can be directed in favor of or against almost anyone	Activities sometimes used for goals, but also viewed as ends in themselves

Based on these "nondichotomous" differences between magic and religion, which Goode views as being on a continuum, he makes the following additional observations:

1. Magical activities are likely to absorb less of the available resources of the society than do religious activities.
2. Magical acts and practices provide less direction to the major institutions (e.g., political decisions) than religious acts.
3. If practitioners of magic and of religious acts form separate groups in the society, the religious practitioners will have greater prestige.
4. The accoutrements of magical activities are more likely to be viewed as personal property, and are not likely to be counted among the property or treasures of the society.

5. Members of the society have a more continuous relationship with supernatural forces through religion than through magic.

6. Children are less likely to observe or participate in magical activities than in religious activities.

7. It is more likely that magical activities will be paid for than a religious activity, which is frequently paid for by a tax on everyone.

Though not explicitly stated by Goode, many of these differences and concomitant hypotheses reflect the antisocial, deviant, illegal, "outsider" nature of magical activities. Further, Goode's model of continuity between magic and religion underscores the subjective nature of the distinction between the two. Depending upon one's perspective, actions may be deemed deeply religious or thoroughly magical (thus the rite of the Mass, the casting of lots, or the miracles of Jesus). Morton Smith's choice of a title for his book *Jesus the Magician* (or, conversely, a hypothetical book entitled *Jesus the Miracle Worker*) says as much about the book's author as it does about the activities of the person whom it purports to describe.

In the Bible's case, the major factor dividing acts that might be termed "magical" from those which might be termed "religious" is the power by which an action is performed. Acts performed by the power of God are, in the view of the writers of the Bible, by that very fact nonmagical, even where they may be formally indistinguishable from those that are depicted as magical. Activities are "magical" because they are perceived as objectionable, not objectionable because "magical." The Reformation definition of magic represents, in essence, the crystallization of strong Protestant objections to certain Catholic practices.[50] Similarly, the designation of Joseph Smith's treasure seeking as "magical" seems to be hardly more than the concretization of the distaste for the supernatural by contemporary Enlightenment rationalists, who had "drained Christianity of its belief in the miraculous."[51] So far as we are aware, Joseph himself never described these practices as "magic," although, even if he had, it might have been for the same reason that groups often ultimately accept the designations of outsiders—the terms Yankee, Christian, and Mormon, for instance, were first used by hostile outsiders—even where these designations were originally intended as terms of abuse.[52] *Magic* as a descriptive term for practices reflected in the Bible, or in any other religious tradition, retains some usefulness, but it should be employed in a more carefully reticulated fashion than has generally been the case in the past, taking into consideration its subjective nature and its potentially pejorative connotations, while also retaining a sensitivity to the internal categories of the persons involved in these activities, as well as an awareness of our own presuppositions in applying the term. Perhaps, however, in the light of the longstanding negative connotations with which the term *magic* is (perhaps inextricably) fraught, and given the potential for continued misunderstanding where the term is not hedged about by further definitions and modifications, a less value-laden term (e.g., "popular religion" or "folk religion") ought to be employed instead.

To the extent that treasure seeking was practiced by Joseph Smith, it was, as Alan Taylor notes, a "deeply spiritual" exercise,[53] and was viewed as being done by the power of God. There is no clear evidence that would indicate that the Smiths saw themselves as engaging in this practice through any other agency than that of God. Joseph was believed to possess a gift through which he could improve the straitened circumstances of his family. It is a token of his spiritual maturing that he could come to recognize that this gift was given to him for other, far greater purposes than merely to find earthly treasures.

NOTES

1. D. E. Aune, "Magic in Early Christianity," in Wolfgang Haase, ed., *Aufstieg und Niedergang der Römischen Welt* (Berlin: Walter de Gruyter, 1980), 2:23:2, p. 1515. In a similar vein, see Haralds Biezais, *Von der Wesensidentität der Magie und Religion*, in *Acta Academiae Aboensis, Series A: Humaniora* 55:3(1978); note the comment of Jorunn Jacobsen Buckley in the *Abstracts: American Academy of Religion/Society of Biblical Literature Annual Meeting 1986* (Decatur, GA: Scholars Press, 1986), 53, concerning a Mandaean document that "lends itself well to defend the thesis that there is no difference between 'religion' and 'magic'—this distinction is a scholarly evaluative fiction." Among the more recent literature that maintains a solely or primarily structural distinction between "religion" and "magic," see Stephen Benko, "Magic," in Paul J. Achtemeier, ed., *Harper's Bible Dictionary* (San Francisco: Harper and Row, 1985), 594–96; Piera Arata Mantovani, "La magia nei testi preesilici dell'Antico Testamento," *Henoch* 3(1981): 1–21; J. B. Segal, "Popular Religion in Ancient Israel," *Journal of Jewish Studies* 27(1976): 6–7. Among the older works, see, e.g., Arvid Kapelrud, "The Interrelationship Between Religion and Magic in Hittite Religion," *Numen* 6(1959): 32–50; A. Lods, "Le rôle des idées magiques dans la mentalité israélite," in *Old Testament Essays: Papers Read Before the Society for Old Testament Study* (London: Charles Griffin and Company, 1927), 55–76; A. Lods, "Magie hébraïque et magie cananéenne," *Revue d'Histoire et de Philosophie Religieuses* 7(1927): 1–16.

2. David E. Aune, "Magic; Magician," in Geoffrey W. Bromiley, ed., *The International Standard Bible Encyclopedia* (Grand Rapids, MI: W. B. Eerdmans, 1986),3:213.

3. The matter of the translation and subsequent interpretation of words traditionally rendered as magical is an important one that should not be overlooked in investigations of magic, since the choice of words used in a translation reflects a whole host of *a priori* assumptions made by the writer or translator.

4. Jonathan Z. Smith, "Good News Is No News: Aretalogy and Gospel," in *Map Is Not Territory* (Leiden: Brill, 1978), 163; cf. Jules Maurice, "La terreur de la magie au IV. siècle," *Comptes rendus de l'Academie des Inscriptions et Belles-Lettres* (1926): 188. While agreeing with Smith's statement in principle, we are inclined to see certain other "nondichotomous" differences between magic and religion (such as those noted by Goode below) besides the antisocial character of magic.

5. Morton Smith, *Clement of Alexandria and a Secret Gospel of Mark* (Cambridge, MA: Harvard University Press, 1973), 163. In the light of this statement, it is significant—and telling—that one of Smith's subsequent books is entitled *Jesus the Magician.*

6. This and other Bible translations in this chapter are the authors'.

7. Adolf Erman and Hermann Grapow, *Ägyptisch-Deutsches Wörterbuch*, 6 vols. (Leipzig: J. Hinrichs, 1929), 3:177.

8. Jacob Milgrom, "Magic, Monotheism, and the Sin of Moses," in H. B. Huffmon, F. A. Spina, A. R. W. Green, eds., *The Quest for the Kingdom of God: Studies in Honor of George E. Mendenhall* (Winona Lake, IN: Eisenbrauns, 1983), 251–65.

9. Aune, "Magic," 213.

10. We readily concede that Moses may be shown as refraining from speaking in order to distinguish him from the "magicians" and "sorcerers" in Pharaoh's court, but question whether these Egyptians are thus described because they speak when performing their acts rather than because they are non-Israelites and non-Yahwists.

11. These categorical distinctions are to be found in G. André, "*kāšap*," in G. Johannes Botterweck, Helmer Ringgren, and Heinz-Joseph Fabry, eds., *Theologisches Wörterbuch zum Alten Testament* (Stuttgart: W. Kohlhammer Verlag, 1984), 4:379.

12. In Isaiah 3:2, the "augur" (*qôsēm*) is mentioned together with warrior, priest, and king; in Micah 3:6, 7, 11, the "augur" (*qôsēm*) is mentioned together with the prophet. If there is no explicit disapproval of the diviner in either of these passages, neither is there anything like approval: both passages occur in oracles of doom prophesied against all of these persons.

13. Leviticus 16:8; Numbers 26:55; Joshua 7:14, 14:2; 1 Samuel 10:16–26; 14:42; Daniel 12:13; Joel 1:3; Psalm 22:18; Proverbs 18:18; 1 Chronicles 24:5; 25:8; 26:13. The *pûr*, explicitly identified with the lot (*gôrāl*) in Esther 3:7, was used by Haman to determine the month and day on which to carry out the pogrom against the Jews.

14. Exodus 28:30; Leviticus 8:8; Numbers 27:21; Deuteronomy 33:8; 1 Samuel 14:41; 28:6; Nehemiah 7:65.

15. 1 Samuel 23:9–12; 30:7–8.

16. E.g., Jonah 1:7; Obadiah 11; Nahum 3:10.

17. Matthew 12:24; Mark 3:22; Luke 11:15.

18. P. Samain, "L'accusation de magie contre le Christ dans les Évangiles," *Ephemerides Theologicae Lovanienses* 15(1938):455.

19. Matthew 4:1–11; Luke 4:1–13.

20. Op. cit., 489; cf. Aune, "Magic in Early Christianity," 1540–41.

21. T. B. Sanhedrin 43a; J. Klausner, *Jesus of Nazareth* (New York: Macmillan, 1925), 18–47; H. L. Strack, *Jesus, die Häretiker und die Christen nach den ältesten jüdischen Angaben* (Leipzig: Hinrichs, 1910); H. L. Strack and P. Billerbeck, *Kommentar zum Neuen Testament aus Talmud und Midrasch* (Munich: Beck, 1926), 1: 38, 84, 631. H. van der Loos, *The Miracles of Jesus* (Leiden: Brill, 1965), 156–75; Samuel Krauss, "Jesus," in I. Singer, ed., *The Jewish Encyclopedia*, 12 vols. (New York: Funk and Wagnalls, 1904), 7:170–73.

22. These accusations are preserved particularly clearly in Origen's *Contra Celsum*, a tract written in response to a variety of charges against Jesus and the Christians by the pagan Celsus.

23. TB Sabbath 104b. H. Freedman, who translated and annotated the tractate Sabbath in I. Epstein, ed., *The Babylonian Talmud* (London: Soncino, 1938), 2.1:504, fn. 2, adds the following passage from the unexpurgated version of TB Sabbath: "Was he then the son of Stada—surely he was the son of Pandira?—Said R. Hisda: the husband was Stada, the paramour was Pandira. But the husband was Pappos b. Judah?—His mother was Stada. But his mother was Miriam the hairdresser?—It is as we say in Pumbeditha: This one has been unfaithful to (lit. "turned away from"—*satah da*) her husband." It is generally agreed that this passage refers to Jesus; thus R. Travers Herford, *Christianity in Talmud and Midrash* (Clifton, NJ: Reference Book Publishers, 1966), 35–41, 54–56; Smith, *Jesus the Magician*, 47, 178.

24. Jewish charges that Jesus was a magician: Arnobius, *Against the Heathen* 1.44; Irenaeus, *Against Heresies* 32:3; Justin Martyr, *First Apology* 30; Lactantius, *Divine Institutions* 4.15.1, 5.3; Origen, *Contra Celsum* 1.28. Pagan charges that Jesus was a magician: Origen, *Contra Celsum* 1.6, 38, 68; 2.9, 14, 16, 48, 49; 6.77.

25. See note 5.

26. Colin Brown, *Miracles and the Critical Mind* (Grand Rapids, MI: Eerdmans, 1983), 276.

27. Geza Vermes, *Jesus the Jew: A Historian's Reading of the Gospels* (London: Collins, 1973), 69, cited in Brown, *Miracles*, 276–77.

28. Cited by H. S. Cronin in "The Twelve Conclusions of the Lollards," *English Historical Review* 22(1907): 298.

29. Cited in John Foxe, *The Acts and Monuments of Matters Most Special and Memorable* (London: Adam Islip, Foelix Kingston and Robert Young, 1632), 3:179–80.

30. Quoted in Keith Thomas, *Religion and the Decline of Magic* (New York: Charles Scribner's Sons, 1971), 53.

31. Ronald W. Walker, "The Persisting Idea of American Treasure Hunting," *Brigham Young University Studies* 24:4(1984): 435; his other article in the same issue is "Joseph Smith: The Palmyra Seer," 461–72.

32. Richard Bushman, *Joseph Smith and the Beginnings of Mormonism* (Urbana, IL: University of Illinois Press, 1984), 7, 70–72, 79–80, 184.

33. E.g., ibid., 184: Joseph "prized the Urim and Thummim and the seerstone, never repudiating them even when the major charge against him was that he used magic to find buried money. His world was not created by Enlightenment rationalism with its deathly aversion to superstition." But by using the terms *magic* and *superstition* Bushman himself appears to be conceding the premises of Enlightenment rationalism.

34. Richard L. Anderson, "The Mature Joseph Smith and Treasure Searching," *Brigham Young University Studies* 24:4(1984): 534–35.

35. Marvin S. Hill, "Money-Digging Folklore and the Beginnings of Mormonism: An Interpretive Suggestion," *Brigham Young University Studies* 24:4(1984): 473–88.

36. Alan Taylor, "Rediscovering the Context of Joseph Smith's Treasure Seeking," *Dialogue* 19:4(1986): 19.

37. See, e.g., Walter Wink, *Naming the Powers* (Philadelphia: Fortress Press, 1985), for a study of the extent of the belief in the New Testament of such spiritual powers.

38. Taylor, "Rediscovering," 19.

39. Ibid., 21.

40. J. A. C. and LeAnn Redford, "An Open Letter to Our Family and Friends," unpublished letter, 1985, 1–17; fns. 1–18. Since the Redfords themselves describe this as an "open letter," we have not felt it inappropriate to discuss it here.

41. Redford and Redford, "An Open Letter," fn. 16.

42. *Webster's New American Dictionary of the American Language*, 2nd Collegiate ed. (New York: Simon and Schuster, 1980): 984, 850.

43. "Magic and Divination," in M. W. Jacobus, E. E. Nourse, and A. C. Zenos, eds., *A New Bible Dictionary* (New York: Funk and Wagnalls, 1926): 537–38.

44. Given Elder Bruce R. McConkie's strong and repeated affirmation of faith in the divine origins of Joseph Smith's work, it strikes us as somewhat ludicrous to use his definition of the occult and magic as evidence against Joseph, as do the Redfords in "An Open Letter," p. 12. Whatever the intent of Elder McConkie's definitions, they were certainly not meant to include the activities of Joseph, his family, or his associates.

45. It is remarkable how many of the examples that the Redfords cite do not explicitly concern Joseph, but mention his father, his mother, or the family generally. Such evidence is, in our view, of only secondary value in establishing Joseph's own involvement in these activities.

46. We are, of course, aware that the term *Urim and Thummim* is not used in the Book of Mormon, and does not seem to have been used to refer to Joseph's means of translating until after 1830.

47. D&C 8:6–8, cited in Redford and Redford, "An Open Letter," 5–6. The changes in subsequent editions may, in our view, be the result of a growing awareness of the Restoration's affinities to previous dispensations, reflected in the wording of the revelations themselves, and have nothing to do with a sense of embarrassment about such objects as the "rod of Aaron."

48. Biezais, *Wesensidentität*, p. 30.

49. William J. Goode, "Magic and Religion: A Continuum," *Ethnos* 14(1949): 172–82; Goode, *Religion among the Primitives* (Glencoe, IL: Free

Press, 1951), 50–55; and, most recently, Goode, "Comment on 'Malinowski's Magic: The Riddle of the Empty Cell,' " *Current Anthropology* 17:4(December 1976):677.

50. Thomas, *Decline of Magic*, 51–77.

51. Bushman, *Joseph Smith*, 7.

52. Hans-Dieter Betz, "The Formation of Authoritative Tradition in the Greek Magical Papyri," in Ben F. Meyer and E. P. Sanders, eds., *Jewish and Christian Self-Definition*, 3 vols. (Philadelphia: Fortress Press, 1982), 161–70, notes that "magician" was occasionally (though not frequently) used as a self-designation in the Greek Magical Papyri.

53. Taylor, "Rediscovering," p. 27.

"Not As the World Giveth . . .": Mormonism and Popular Psychology

9

Daniel K Judd

A few years ago while reading a magazine, I came across a cartoon that pictured a Catholic priest seated in the confessional giving counsel to a parishioner. On the shelves behind the priest and in his lap and hands were many of the "self-help" books we find in the psychology section of most bookstores. On a bottom shelf of the confessional booth rested the Bible . . . covered with cobwebs. The caption of the cartoon read: "Not to worry, my son. Get off your guilt trip and take the road less traveled. The good book says you're OK. All you need is to pull your own strings, focus on your erroneous zones, take control of your life, and self-actualize yourself so you can achieve your greatest potential . . . and you'll be just fine."[1]

Being both a religious educator and a psychologist by training, I found a special interest in this cartoon. While at first it brought a chuckle, I have since realized the cartoon's message may not be so comical. The priest had forsaken the wisdom of the Bible for the wisdom of popular psychology. He was teaching "for doctrines the commandments of men" (Joseph Smith—History 1:19), not those

---

Daniel K Judd is LDS Church Educational System Coordinator in East Lansing, Michigan.

of God. In the time since I first read the cartoon, I have reflected upon my experience with psychology and religion and learned what I believe to be some important lessons. This article is an attempt to share some of the areas of concern I have identified relative to the influence psychology is having on our religious beliefs and everyday lives.

Psychology and Religion

A noted psychologist has written the following concerning religion: "[Religion] is in many respects equivalent to irrational thinking and emotional disturbance. . . . The elegant therapeutic solution to emotional problems is to be quite unreligious . . . the less religious they are, the more emotionally healthy they will be."[2] Notice how similar this statement is to the words of Korihor, a Book of Mormon anti-Christ: "Ye look forward and say that ye see a remission of your sins. But behold, it is the effect of a *frenzied mind*; and this derangement of your minds comes because of the traditions of your fathers, which lead you away into a belief of things which are not so." (Alma 30:16, italics added.)

This alleged relationship between religion and mental illness was taught by Korihor in his day, is taught by many popular psychologists in our day, and was even taught by some in the early days of our Church.

The Mental Health of Mormons

In 1860 Dr. Robert Bartholow, the assistant surgeon of the United States Army, reported on his visit with the Mormons by writing that the Mormons have "an expression of compounded sensuality, cunning, suspicion, and a smirking self-conceit."[3] In 1858 a writer from *Harper's Weekly* offered the observation that the Mormon way of life turned women into "haggard, weary, slatternly women, with lackluster eyes and wan, shapeless faces, hanging listlessly over their gates, or sitting idly in the sunlight, perhaps nursing their yelling babies—all such women looking alike depressed, degraded, miserable, hopeless, soulless."[4]

While Mormons, both men and women, have been and continue to be seen by many as maladjusted, it may be surprising to some to find that research studies conducted by social scientists do not support this idea. Evidence supports the conviction that living the teachings of Mormonism actually helps one to live a happier life. Mormons as a whole are reported to have happy marriages, affectionate families, and low incidence of mental illness. Not one study has linked Mormonism and mental illness.[5]

A few years ago I conducted a study, administering a well-respected psychological test to members of several different religious groups. All of the groups investigated (LDS, Seventh-Day Adventists, Hari Krishna, and Bahai) tested "normal." It was exciting for me to note that of all the groups tested, the Mormons showed the least evidence of emotional problems.[6] Many, however, would have us believe differently. Examples of this are the many articles and television and radio programs concerning Mormon women and depression. Researchers report, however, that there is no difference between the prevalence of depression among Mormon women and that of non-Mormon women. Rather, Mormon women who were more active in their religion were found to be less depressed than the less-than-active Mormon women or the non-Mormon women. Specifically, this study reported that those women who frequently attended their church meetings and the temple were less depressed than those who did not attend frequently. Those who prayed frequently were less depressed than those who did not. Also, those who had three or more children were less depressed than those who had two or one.[7]

Why, then, do some individuals continue to lament that the Church has a "negative influence" on its members' mental health?

Inevitably there are exceptions, sometimes extreme ones. What causes a Church member or former member to lose his sense of reality to the extreme of committing a crime, even a hideous one, in response to an alleged "revelation from God"? Perhaps reading Korihor's own explanation to Alma as to why he did what he did may give us some answers:

> But behold, the devil hath deceived me; for he appeared unto me in the *form of an angel*, and said unto me: *Go and reclaim this people*, for they have all gone astray after an unknown God. And he said unto me: There is no God; yea, and he taught me that which I should say. And I have taught his words . . . because they were *pleasing unto the carnal mind*; and I taught them, even until I had much *success*, insomuch that I verily believed that they were true; and for this cause I withstood the truth, even until I have brought this great curse upon me. (Alma 30:53; italics added.)

Korihor reported that the devil appeared to him "in the form of an angel"; Satan can appear to do that which is good to lead us to do evil. Korihor's motives were based on the deceptively good notion that he was to "reclaim this people, for they have all gone astray." How often people attempt to persuade us to do wrong by letting us know of their "honorable" intentions to help us with our ills. Korihor's teachings were "pleasing to the carnal mind"; he successfully taught people doctrines they wanted to hear to soothe their consciences (see also 2 Timothy 4:3). The teachings of Korihor are as common today as they were two thousand years ago. We, however, can know good from evil by measuring that which we see, hear, or feel against the standard of the gospel. In addition to the words of living prophets of God, the Lord has given us the Book of Mormon—to aid us in dispelling the false teachings that are so evident in our world today. Let us now examine more of Korihor's doctrines as they relate to that which is being taught presently.

Sin and Guilt

Korihor taught "whatsoever a man did was no crime" (Alma 30:17). While there are many ideas being taught in our society today concerning guilt and sin, one can usually categorize them under one of two general views:

One view is that our sin and guilt are caused by the influence of our environment. Such factors as parents, society, genetic makeup, and "low self-esteem" are said to determine how we think, feel, and behave. We are taught by some that religious values are outmoded; beliefs in such teachings as sin and guilt need to be given up, since they only bring us unhappiness.

The gospel view is that while our environment may tend to influence us for evil (see Exodus 34:7), sin is something we alone are responsible for, and guilt is rightly experienced as we take responsibility for going against our conscience. Alma's counsel to his wayward son Corianton was to "let your sins trouble you, with that trouble which shall bring you down unto repentance" (Alma 42:29). It is only through accepting the responsibility for sin and resolving guilt through repentance that we can achieve the peace for which we are searching. Alma's experience testifies of the importance of resolving sin and guilt through repentance:

> And now, for three days and for three nights was I racked, even with the pains of a damned soul. And it came to pass that as I was thus racked with torment, while I was harrowed up by the memory of my many sins, behold I remembered also to have heard my father prophesy unto the people concerning the coming of one Jesus Christ, a Son of God, to atone for the sins of the world. Now, as my mind caught hold upon this thought, I cried within my heart: O Jesus, thou Son of God, have mercy on me, who am in the gall of bitterness, and am encircled about by the everlasting chains of death. And now, behold, when I thought this, I could remember my pains no more; yea, I was harrowed up by the memory of my sins no more. And oh, what joy, and what marvelous light I did behold; yea, my soul was filled with joy as exceeding as was my pain! (Alma 36:16–20.)

Guilt is to our spirit what pain is to our body. Guilt can be helpful as it can serve as a warning sign that something is amiss in our lives and needs correcting. The Apostle Paul taught this concerning guilt:

"Now I rejoice, not that ye were made sorry, but that ye sorrowed to repentance: for ye were made sorry after a godly manner, that ye might receive damage by us in nothing. For godly sorrow worketh repentance to salvation not to be repented of: but the *sorrow of the world worketh death.*" (2 Corinthians 7:9–10; italics added.) This "sorrow of the world" is what we feel when we are not honestly sorry for what we did, but rather we are sorry we were caught doing it. Sorrow of the world may be the price we pay so we can continue to sin. Sorrow of the world may be experienced when we are not successful in living up to the world's expectations for us, as opposed to our own and God's. Guilt not acted on with repentance can lead to depression and spiritual death. In Moroni we read, "And if ye have no hope ye must needs be in despair; and despair cometh because of iniquity" (Moroni 10:22).

While we bring upon ourselves most of the guilt we experience, some guilt, especially in children, can come about because of a parent's sins. The following story illustrates how "the sins of the fathers are visited upon the heads of the children" (Exodus 34:7):

> [A] young girl, when only five or six years of age, had gone walking with her younger brother. A short distance from their home was a deep gravel pit, which had filled up with water after heavy rains of a few days previous. Inquisitive, as most youngsters are, they walked to the edge of the gravel pit. The side caved in, they both fell into the pool, and her little brother was drowned. Hysterically, she ran home to her mother and father. In a moment of great anxiety, *the father told her that if she had been doing what she should have been doing, this accident would not have happened*. To the mind of this small girl was communicated the feeling that she had caused the death of her brother.[8]

Her "guilt" was not the result of her sin, but of the sin of her father, who blamed her for something she really was not responsible for.

Unrighteous Feelings

Guilt and many other negative emotions, such as irritation, bitterness, pride, lust, self-pity, depression, anxiety, boredom, anger, etc., are almost always feelings we create as opposed to feelings we are caused to feel by our circumstances. These negative emotions can serve as justification for not doing what we know is right. All of us have had the experience of initially knowing something is right and yet rationalizing ourselves into not doing it. Or we know something is wrong and yet we do it anyway. Why do we do such things? Perhaps one individual's story can give us a clue:

> Not long ago I moved into a ward where I found the Gospel Doctrine class to be extremely boring. It was obvious the teacher was ill prepared and unable to conduct the class in a meaningful manner. I found

myself resenting the fact that it was time for Sunday School . . . what a waste of valuable time! However, after the first fifteen minutes of class it wasn't so bad as I would begin to feel the heaviness of sleep come over me. I soon found that if I got there early I could sit on the back row and not be detected. If I wasn't particularly tired, I also found it to be kind of fun to count all the mistakes he made.

This individual was surprised when he learned, however, that his emotions (boredom) and even his physical sensations (sleepiness) were, in this case, things he was doing to give him an excuse for not taking part in class. He didn't do these things maliciously—he thought what he was doing was the only way he could think, feel, and behave; but he was mistaken. He had bought into one of the most common and yet false teachings of our society: *the idea that we are not responsible for our emotions*. His story continues:

After being taught that my boredom and sleepiness were actually excuses I was responsible for, I resisted. After all, this "teacher" (loose usage of the term) was really pitiful. How could I be expected to learn a thing from him?"

The next time he went to class, however, he began to see his teacher differently:

I soon realized that this guy [teacher] was really struggling. He may not be such a great teacher, but then I wasn't being such a great student either! I decided I would read my assignment for class the next Sunday. When I got there I participated and felt a lot better about my being there and even about him as a teacher.

Several months later this person was in a position where he was asked to give some counsel concerning the effectiveness of the Gospel Doctrine teacher. With love and not hypocrisy he suggested the teacher be replaced. He did not merely "whitewash" all that the teacher was doing and feign a "positive mental attitude" about the situation; he did what he felt was right—out of love.

Many people consider much of what they "should" do as an irritation. This may be reading to the children at night, doing home/visiting teaching, going to the temple, paying tithing, reading scriptures, visiting with someone who is lonely, attending church, etc. Their irritation is their justification for either not doing what they should or not putting their hearts into it. A friend of mine, in a private interview with a member of the Quorum of the Twelve, was counseled, "The day that obedience became a *quest* and not an *irritation* was the day I gained power."[9] The Lord requires us to serve him with a willing "heart" as well as "might, mind, and strength" (D&C 4:2; see also D&C 64:34).

Self-Deception

While most of us can identify with being bored or irritated, maybe an even more poignant example of being responsible for our emotions can be found in the following account:

> I know a young man who has been mistreated and victimized, both physically and emotionally, in his family. He is so bitter about the lifestyle of his parents and the love deficit he experienced in his childhood home that he is emotionally distraught. He will not give up his blaming. He wants to take them by the shoulders and shake them until they admit that they ruined his life. He would like to scream from the rooftops, "Look at them. Isn't that a catastrophe? They're not even human." He never received "parental validation," and he hates them; he hates himself. He spends so much time and energy with these emotions that he can't get his life together. He wants *revenge*, and his life revolves around this intense desire. He says, "They did it. Why should I forgive them?"[10]

This young man is *not* merely "making up" his feelings; he has deceived himself into believing, feeling, and behaving as though his parents are completely responsible for the way he feels. The truth is that, even though his parents may have sinned against him, he is the one responsible for his own sin—in this case, his feelings of hate. "If we say that we have no sin, we *deceive ourselves*, and the truth is not in us" (1 John 1:8, italics added). While traditional psychology may teach that this young man's emotions are justified by his parent's ill treatment and he either needs to "vent" his hate or "control" it, the gospel of Jesus Christ teaches the following: "Wherefore, I say unto you, that ye ought to forgive one another; for he that forgiveth not his brother his trespasses standeth condemned before the Lord; for there remaineth in him the *greater sin*. I, the Lord, will forgive whom I will forgive, but of you it is required to forgive all men." (D&C 64:9–10; italics added.)

Peace is not found in the worldly doctrines of "venting" or in "controlling," but in "giving up" the emotion through repentance and forgiveness. The source of this young man's problems is not that his parents, unfortunately, sinned against him, but that he is continuing to harbor bad feelings toward them. The simple fact is that by virtue of the miracle of the atonement of Jesus Christ this young man can repent, forgive, and be free of hate regardless of what his circumstances are. The Savior has already "suffered these things for all, that they might not suffer if they would repent; but if they would not repent they must suffer even as I" (D&C 19:16–17). The following story is of a woman who found peace through repenting and forgiving:

> Margaret asked to attend one of my seminars. She had been in counseling or therapy continuously for fourteen years, chronically depressed and almost non-functional. She blamed her inability to get on in life on her mother—though she would go for long periods without allowing herself to think of her mother (which is obviously an accusing thing to do, since it's a way of saying, "You're despicable to think about, you upset me too much"). At any one time, she said, she had at most one friend, toward whom she would behave so possessively that after a few months the friend could not tolerate her any more and would then leave her alone. Her lips trembled when she talked and were pinched in when she didn't; and almost always her eyes were downcast. I found it hard to pity her because she was obviously spending a lot of pity on herself already. In private I learned that her mother had molested and abused her frequently when she was a child and, as she thought, ruined her life.
>
> The seminar extended over the Christmas and New Year's holidays. When we reconvened on January 10, Margaret was the only participant not present. We started anyway, and about twenty minutes into the session a woman whom I did not recognize entered the room and took a seat at one of the tables where the participants were sitting. As I usually do in situations like this, because I don't like to have interruptions when everyone seems to be concentrating well, I let the discussion continue; another woman was recounting an experience she had. After a few minutes I realized with a shock who this mystery woman was . . . Margaret. Simultaneously, I noticed, others were doing the same. Margaret's face was relaxed, and there was a natural dignity in her bearing which was completely absent before. And when she spoke, as she did presently, her lips did not tremble. The self-pity was gone. To me, her countenance seemed to be illuminated.
>
> Margaret asked to speak, and told us she had taken the train over the holiday to see her mother, whom she had freely forgiven. She told her mother that she wanted more than anything else for her to have some peace before she died. So, she said, she was asking her mother's forgiveness for the hatred she had borne toward her through so many years. She said in the days since she returned she has often had tender feelings toward her mother, and has called and written to her.
>
> I have heard from Margaret periodically in the ensuing years. Her "cure" was far from instant, but that visit to her mother was a turning point. After about a year in which things gradually improved in her relationships with roommates, her fear of being betrayed by them finally disappeared. She has been able to hold [a] job successfully. Each time I hear from her she seems to be doing a little better.[11]

While I am well acquainted with the arguments of many that the gospel solution is "too simplistic" for complex problems, I believe that our desire for complexity can be a part of our self-deception. Elder Neal A. Maxwell has written, "We like intellectual embroidery. We like complexity because it gives us an excuse for failure . . . [it provides] more and more refuges for those who don't want to comply; . . . thereby [increasing] the number of excuses people can make for failure to comply.''[12]

While it is probably true that the majority of us will experience these negative emotions on a daily basis, an interesting scriptural comparison illustrates the fact that we are not justified in having them. In Matthew 5:22 we read: ''But I say unto you, That whosoever is angry with his brother *without a cause* shall be in danger of the judgment'' (italics added). But in the Joseph Smith Translation of the Bible (Matthew 5:24) and the Book of Mormon (3 Nephi 12:22) we read the corrected version: ''But I say unto you, that whosoever is angry with his brother shall be in danger of his judgment.'' The phrase *without a cause* is not included in the JST and the Nephite account, showing that anger is not justified by a ''cause'' of any kind. This does *not* mean that we should ''suppress'' or ''control'' our anger, either. It means that we need to ''give it up'' by repenting. Brigham Young taught the following:

> Suppose, when you arrive home from this meeting, you find your neighbors have killed your horses and destroyed your property, how would you feel? You would feel like taking instant vengeance on the perpetrator of the deed. But it would be wrong for you to encourage the least particle of feeling to arise in your bosom like anger or revenge, or like taking judgment into your own hands until the Lord Almighty shall say, ''Judgment is yours, and for you to execute.''
>
> Thought originated with our individual being, which is organized to be as independent as any being in eternity. When you go home, and learn that your neighbors have committed some depredation on your property, or in your family, and anger arises in your bosom, then consider, and know that it arises in yourselves. . . . If you are injured by a neighbor, the first thought of the unregenerate heart is for God to damn the person who has hurt you. . . . But dismiss any spirit that would prompt you to injure any creature that the Lord has made, give it no place, encourage it not, and it will not stay where you are.[13]

Some may say, ''But, don't the scriptures indicate the Savior became angry on occasion?'' The difference between the anger most of us experience and the anger the scriptures attribute to the Savior is recorded in the New Testament, ''And when he had looked round about on them with anger, *being grieved for the hardness of their hearts*, he saith unto the man, Stretch forth thine hand. And he stretched it out: and his hand was restored whole as the other'' (Mark 3:5; italics added). The ''anger'' Jesus felt arose because the Jews were hurting *themselves* and *others* through their hypocrisy; he was sad that they would not repent. Our anger, on the other hand, is generally *self*-concerned. *We* take offense and feel that *we* have been wronged.

The teaching that we ought to ''let all . . . anger . . . be put away from you, with all malice: And be ye kind one to another, tenderhearted, forgiving one another" (Ephesians 4:31–32) is very different from the teachings of many of the popular psychologies of our day. They teach us that anger is justified by its mere existence and that we should use it as a tool to get what we want out of life. Many popular psychologists and psychiatrists advocate the idea that suppressing anger is the cause and expressing it is the cure of many if not all of our physical and emotional problems.[14]

Self-Esteem, Self-Actualization, and Sanctification

Another area where we may be mingling our religious beliefs with the "doctrines of men" is in our focus on "self." It is quite common for us to hear/see such words as self-esteem, self-concept, self-awareness, and self-actualization used in the context of a sacrament meeting talk, a Sunday School lesson, or even in some lesson preparation materials, but I have yet to find them in scripture. Is it possible that these seemingly "important" concepts represent the philosophies of men and not of God? Many well-meaning teachers, counselors, and writers tell us that the way to total happiness is to focus on self. The scriptures, however, counsel against this preoccupation with self: "For whosoever will save his life shall lose it; but whosoever shall lose his life for my sake and the gospel's, the same shall save it" (Mark 8:35). The following true story illustrates that peace is experienced in loving other people and not being focused on our own selfishness:

> For 35 years or so I muddled through life with many long periods of depression and few times of good spirituality. I read many books on psychology, hoping to gain insight into my life. Finally, a year ago I was given the profound insight that my *blaming* others was the major cause of my feelings of inadequacy, inferiority, and general inability to deal with people effectively. I was also made aware that betrayal of my conscience was the main cause of my general unhappiness in life. I had never known or understood these ideas before. I had always pursued the premise that "I must be loved," and in that pursuit I blamed and accused others and betrayed myself. I also had ignored the love that many others, including God, had given me. I had been living in a "false reality." Now I was presented with the truth: that I was a valuable, capable person who was free to accomplish good things, but I was required to forgive others and not use anything they did as an excuse to behave badly. My new objectives in life are to love others, be kind and patient with myself, avoid all blaming, and do all the good things in life that I can. I now feel basically free and peaceful, and when negative feelings come, I reorient myself to the truth that in *loving others* we find peace and happiness!

Positive Mental Attitude Is Not Enough

Another example of man's focus on "self" is the aphorism we often hear in church or seminary that tells us that "whatever we believe we can achieve." The idea has a "form of godliness," but it denies "the power thereof." (2 Timothy 3:5.) Might we be leaving out something, or, more accurately, some One?

The Savior taught us that positive mental attitude is insufficient when he said: "Which of you by taking thought can add one cubit unto his stature?" (Matthew 6:27.) Korihor taught that man's own strength is sufficient: "Every man fared in this life according to the management of the creature; therefore every man prospered according to *his* genius, and . . . every man conquered according to *his* strength" (Alma 30:17; italics added).

In the Book of Mormon we are taught that our own physical and mental abilities are only a fraction of what is necessary, for we are *saved by grace*, "after all that we can do" (2 Nephi 25:23). We also read that being "meek and lowly of heart"—in addition to our "good works"—will enable us to live in personal peace:

> Preach unto them repentance, and faith on the Lord Jesus Christ; teach them to humble themselves and to be meek and lowly in heart; teach them to withstand every temptation of the devil, with their faith on the Lord Jesus Christ.
>
> Teach them to never be weary of good works, *but to be meek and lowly of heart; for such shall find rest to their souls.*
>
> Yea, and cry unto God for all thy support; yea, let all thy doings be unto the Lord, and whithersoever thou goest let it be in the Lord; yea, let thy thoughts be directed unto the Lord; yea, let the affections of thy heart be placed upon the Lord forever.
>
> Counsel with the Lord in all thy doings, and he will direct thee for good. (Alma 37:33–34, 36–37; italics added.)

While it is certainly important for us to understand that God does not "command in all things" (D&C 58:26) and that we must do "many things of . . . [our] own free will" (D&C 58:26–27) to solve our own problems and be self-reliant, we should not seek to do so to the exclusion of our relationship with our Father in Heaven. We need to recognize the source from which our blessings come: "And in nothing doth man offend God, or against none is his wrath kindled, save those who confess not his hand in all things, and obey not his commandments" (D&C 59:21).

Conclusion

The peace and happiness mankind is seeking can only be found in living the gospel of Jesus Christ. While many of the philosophies of men have "a form of godliness," we often find that they "deny the power thereof" (Joseph Smith—History 1:19). In Proverbs we read, "Whoso boasteth himself of a false gift is like clouds and wind without rain" (Proverbs 25:14).

Elder Boyd K. Packer has said: "True doctrine, understood, changes attitudes and behavior. The study of the doctrines of the gospel will improve behavior quicker than a study of behavior will improve behavior. Preoccupation with unworthy behavior can lead to unworthy behavior."[15]

The restoration of the gospel in these the latter days has provided us with all that is essential for both our temporal and our eternal salvation. The Savior taught us that his peace cannot be found by following the philosophies of men: "Peace I leave with you, my peace I give unto you: not as the world giveth, give I unto you. Let not your heart be troubled, neither let it be afraid." (John 14:27.)

NOTES

1. Mary Chambers, *His* Magazine, December 1984, p. 12.

2. Albert Ellis in *Journal of Consulting and Clinical Psychology*, 1980, vol. 48(5), pp. 635–39.

3. L. Bush as cited in L. A. Moench, "Mormon Forms of Psychopathology," *The Journal of the Association of Mormon Counselors and Psychotherapists*, March 1985, p. 61.

4. G. L. Bunker and D. Bitton, as cited in Moench, "Mormon Forms of Psychopathology," p. 62.

5. See D. K Judd, "Religiosity and Mental Health: A Literature Review 1928–1985," Unpublished master's thesis, Brigham Young University, 1985, Provo, Utah.

6. See D. K Judd, "Religious Affiliation and Mental Health," *Journal of the Association of Mormon Counselors and Psychotherapists*, vol. 12, no. 2.

7. See D. Spendlove, D. West, and W. Stanish, "Risk Factors in the Prevalence of Depression in Mormon Women, *Social Science and Medicine*, vol. 18(6), 1984, pp. 491–95.

8. See A. L. Thornock, "Handling Guilt Feeling," *Book of Mormon Symposium*, 19–21 August 1982, Brigham Young University, Provo, Utah, p. 87; italics added.

9. C. T. Warner, "Repenting of Unrighteous Feelings," Devotional address given at Ricks College, Rexburg, Idaho, 1 March 1983, p. 12.

10. As told by D. Rasmussen in the *Newsletter of the Association of Mormon Counselors and Psychotherapists*, Summer 1984, p. 1.

11. A slightly different version of that appearing in C. T. Warner's "What We Are," *BYU Studies*, vol. 26, no. 1 (Winter 1986), p. 61.

12. Neal A. Maxwell, *Things As They Really Are* (Salt Lake City: Deseret Book Co., 1978), p. 101.

13. *Journal of Discourses* 2:134–35.

14. For a detailed critique of these theories, see Carol Tavris, *Anger: The Misunderstood Emotion* (New York: Simon and Schuster, 1982), and Robert C. Solomon, *The Passions* (Garden City, New York: Doubleday, Anchor Press, 1976).

15. Boyd K. Packer, Conference Report, October 1986, p. 20.

Is Mormonism Christian? An Investigation of Definitions

10

Daniel C. Peterson
Stephen D. Ricks

Since the very inception of The Church of Jesus Christ of Latter-day Saints, there have been some who have denied that it is Christian. Within the past several years this tendency has become quite noticeable in certain circles. In response to this claim, articles have been written[1] and general conference addresses have been devoted to a reaffirmation of our deep and abiding commitment to Christ.[2] Given the importance of the question, it would be profitable to investigate the basis for the claim that Latter-day Saints are not Christian. At root, this involves determining how the earliest Christians—those of the New Testament period and the immediately succeeding generations—viewed and defined themselves, and what they believed.

Does the New Testament Define "Christianity"?

An explicit treatment of the word *Christian* is totally lacking in the gospel accounts. Indeed, the word appears only three times in

---

Daniel C. Peterson is Instructor of Hebrew and Semitic Languages at Brigham Young University.
Stephen D. Ricks is Associate Professor of Hebrew and Semitic Languages at Brigham Young University.

the whole New Testament, and never in the mouth of Christ himself. Further, the word *Christianity* is completely absent from the New Testament.

In Acts 11:26 we are told that "the disciples were called Christians first in Antioch." Here, the use of the passive construction "were called Christians" strongly suggests that the term was first used, not by Christians, but by non-Christians (similarly, the names "Yankee" and "Mormon" were first used by outsiders). It was probably modeled on such words as *Herodian* and *Caesarian*, already in circulation at that time, and means nothing more complicated than "Christ's people" or, perhaps, "partisans of Christ." It is important to note that the Christian congregation at Antioch represented a wide range of backgrounds and included Jews as well as non-Jews, and believers in this Christian congregation displayed the whole spectrum of attitudes toward the Jewish law.

At Acts 26:28 Agrippa II made his famous reply to Paul, after the Apostle had related to Agrippa and Festus the story of his conversion: "Almost thou persuadest me to be a Christian." The doctrinal content of Paul's speech is not great: Paul bore witness that Jesus had been foretold by the Jewish prophets, that he suffered and rose from the dead, and that it is through him that forgiveness may be obtained. Paul described Christ's mission as that of summoning people to "repent and turn to God, and do works meet for repentance" (Acts 26:20). The scriptural account gives no indication that Paul attempted to suggest to Agrippa that belief in these basic doctrines did not represent the essence of "Christianity."

1 Peter 4:16 is the last instance of the appearance of the word in the New Testament. Yet this verse is virtually without doctrinal content, merely assuring the believer that he need not worry if he suffer as a "Christian." Persecution is here contrasted with suffering "as a murderer, or as a thief, or as an evildoer." Even here, perhaps, we are to think of "Christian" as a term used by persecuting outsiders, just as "murderer," "thief," and "evildoer" might be judgments rendered by a Roman court.

In each of the three instances where the term *Christian* is used in the New Testament, it appears to originate from someone outside of the community of Christians themselves. In particular, in neither of the passages in Acts where the word is found is it used by Paul himself, but by non-Christians. In the case of 1 Peter, it is used, as we have noted above, parallel to legal terms, and may have derived from current Roman (i.e., non-Christian) legal usage. In those instances where it is used, the beliefs of the Christians that are implied—that Christ suffered and died, that through him we may obtain forgiveness of our own sins—are a far cry from the theological reasons commonly given for denying that Latter-day Saints are

Christians. Several of the more common reasons will be listed and discussed below.

Do Denials That Latter-day Saints Are Christians Find Support in the Early Church?

As we have seen, the term *Christian* began its career among outsiders, "more as an insult than as a title of honor."[3] The great Roman historian, Tacitus, for example, is able to describe how Nero's persecuting zeal fell upon "a class of men, loathed for their vices, whom the crowd styled Christians."[4] Indeed, it was not until the second century that Christians began using the designation themselves.[5] By February of 156, Polycarp could boldly declare to the Roman proconsul, just prior to his martyrdom, "I am a Christian."[6]

What did the early Christians mean by their use of the term? Ignatius, in his *Epistle to the Romans*,[7] addresses his cobelievers with regard to his impending martyrdom: "Only pray for me for strength, both inward and outward, that I may not merely speak, but also have the will, that I may not only be called a Christian, but may also be found to be one." He got his wish, and was thrown to the beasts at Rome under Trajan, ca. A.D. 108. Plainly, to Ignatius, who was—significantly[8]—the third bishop of Antioch, being a Christian depended at least partially upon behavioral criteria.[9] "A Christian . . . gives his time to God," he writes to Polycarp. "This is the work of God."[10] On several occasions he calls us to be "imitators of God."[11] On another occasion he exhorts the Magnesians, "Let us learn to lead Christian lives."[12] Ignatius is faithful, in other words, to an important part of the heritage of his church in Antioch, reiterating the ethical emphasis of the Gospel of Matthew—which very likely was written there only a few decades earlier.[13]

Outsiders, too, sometimes noticed the great emphasis given by Christians to moral behavior. Writing some time between A.D. 97 and A.D. 109, Pliny the Younger describes a regular "ceremony" practiced in the early Church: Christians, he tells the Emperor Trajan, "bind themselves by oath . . . to abstain from theft, robbery, and adultery, to commit no breach of trust and not to deny a deposit when called upon to restore it."[14]

In his *Epistle to the Ephesians*, Ignatius appears to presume yet another sense of the term *Christian*, an ecclesiastical one, when he writes of "the Christians of Ephesus, who . . . were ever of one mind with the Apostles."[15] This is consistent with his *Epistle to the Magnesians*, where he declares that "we should be really Christians, not merely have the name."[16] And how do we do so? The burden of this epistle is that we must be subject to the authority of the bishop, who presides "in the place of God."[17]

It cannot, of course, be denied that, for Ignatius, being a Christian involves more than simply mere behavior and obedience to priesthood authority. He gives us a few theological guidelines to follow. He is the first writer known to have used the term *Christianity*, which he explicitly contrasts with "Judaism."[18] Much like Paul before Agrippa, he bears witness of Christ's birth, death, and resurrection. Against the Docetics, who teach of Jesus that "his suffering was only a semblance," Ignatius affirms that the Savior "was truly born, both ate and drank . . . [and] was truly crucified."[19] "I beseech you therefore," he writes to the Trallians, "live only on Christian fare, and refrain from strange food, which is heresy."[20] Here, at last, we seem to have a doctrinal criterion for what is and what is not Christian.

In answer to the implicit question of how one is to distinguish truth from heresy, Ignatius immediately falls back on lines of priesthood authority.[21] "This will be possible for you," he declares, "if you are not puffed up, and are inseparable from God, from Jesus Christ and from the bishop and ordinances of the Apostles. He who is within the sanctuary is pure, but he who is without the sanctuary is not pure, that is to say, whoever does anything apart from the bishop and the presbytery and the deacons is not pure in his conscience."[22] And as for the "strange food" of the heretics, which Ignatius contrasts with "Christian fare," is it not reasonable to see in that an allusion by the bishop of Antioch to eucharistic service conducted by invalid authority? "Let no one," he admonishes the Smyrnaeans, "do any of the things appertaining to the Church without the bishop. Let that be considered a valid Eucharist which is celebrated by the bishop, or by one whom he appoints."[23]

"Let no one be deceived," Ignatius warns the Smyrnaeans. Even the heavenly hosts are subject to judgment. Thereupon Ignatius applies his ethical standard to the heretics: "Mark those who have strange opinions concerning the grace of Jesus Christ which has come to us, and see how contrary they are to the mind of God. For love they have no care, none for the widow, none for the orphan, none for the distressed, none for the afflicted, none for the prisoner, or for him released from prison, none for the hungry or thirsty."[24] They have, in other words, forgotten what the epistle of James (1:27) describes as "pure religion and undefiled." Statements by Jesus himself are relevant to the question at issue: "By this shall all men know that ye are my disciples [*mathetai*], if ye have love one to another." For Ignatius, notes Walter Grundmann, "*Christianismos* simply means discipleship." It is "being a Christian as expressed in life-style."[25] This ethical view of Christianity is not unique to

Ignatius, either. The early–second-century Shepherd of Hermas, one of the "Apostolic Fathers," views Christianity as "above all, a series of precepts that must be followed."[26]

As is implied in the assertion that "the disciples were called Christians first in Antioch," the original word applied to the followers of Jesus was "disciples."[27] It was, states Grundmann, "obviously the term which the original believers used for themselves."[28] K. H. Rengstorf argues that the Greek *mathetes*, "disciple," is merely a translation of the Hebrew *talmud*, and that it derives from the common name which Palestinian Christians used in self-description. It gave way to the term *Christian* only as the Church became more and more Hellenized.[29]

What did the earliest followers of Jesus understand by "discipleship"? Rengstorf sees three—largely behavioral—elements: (1) commitment to the person of Jesus; (2) obedience to Jesus; and (3) obligation to suffer with Jesus.[30] "Then said Jesus to those Jews which believed on him, If ye continue in my word, then are ye my disciples indeed" (John 8:31).[31] Commenting on this verse, Bruce Vawter remarks, "Merely to be receptive to the word is not enough; one must also take it in and act on it constantly. Then alone can one be a true disciple of the Lord."[32] The following verse continues: "This is my Father's glory, that you may bear fruit in plenty and so be my disciples" (John 15:8 NEB).[33]

Being a disciple of Jesus was not an easy thing. "Those who responded," writes Frederick Sontag, "left their family, friends and conventional religious practices to follow an itinerant preaching, healing ministry which was at the time subject to danger. To follow Jesus meant to abandon convention and to join a religious cult of the day. . . . Thus, the most obvious definition for 'Christian' would be: 'One called to follow Jesus no matter what danger or ostracism is involved.' "[34]

It appears that there are few if any guidelines to be found in the New Testament or in earliest Christianity for ruling on who is, and who is not, Christian. And apart from a condemnation of docetism, there are no doctrinal criteria given whatsoever. There is, furthermore, sufficient ambiguity in the records left behind by the earliest Christians that the question of just which doctrine and what practice is authentically "primitive" has historically remained very much open. In late antiquity, each Christian sect claimed apostolicity.[35] Among nineteenth-century American Protestants "each church conceived of itself as conforming more closely to the primitive church than any of its rivals."[36] Why should it be so difficult to get a fix on the pure Christianity of the earliest believers? Modern biblical and patristic scholarship would reply that this is because there never was a golden age of unambiguous and unanimously held Christian truth. "The fact is," says Loraine Boettner, "that [the Church fathers] scarcely agree on any doctrine, and even contradict themselves as they change their minds and affirm what they had previously denied."[37]

Terms like *orthodoxy* and *heresy* seem increasingly—to modern objective scholarship—to be mere self-congratulatory epithets worked up by the victors in the dogmatic skirmishes of Christian history.[38] In earliest Christianity, the two are often impossible to distinguish, at least without the benefit of hindsight. In many areas, the "heretics" were the established church, while the "orthodox" were the damnable minority. And this is not merely the case in later "apostate" centuries. The New Testament itself contains conflicting perspectives and positions that resist even the most determined harmonizer.

Can the Councils and Creeds Be Used to Banish Mormonism from Christendom?

Latter-day Saints make no secret of having sources of authority beyond the Bible. Their opponents, on the other hand, like to think that they represent pure biblical Christianity, arrayed against Mormonism, which is "decadent" and "syncretistic" (because Latter-day Saints accept sources of authority outside of the Bible). Yet this is highly implausible on the face of it. Besides this, we have already shown that the Bible offers no real reason to deny that Mormonism is Christian. So anti-Mormons have recourse—overtly or, as is more often the case, covertly—to doctrinal principles that are, at the very best, doubtfully present in primitive Christianity, most often deriving from the creeds.

The great creeds and the ecumenical councils of mainstream Christendom—while they can clearly be used to demonstrate that Mormonism is out of step with the evolution of "historic Christianity"—furnish very weak grounds upon which to deny that Mormons are Christian. This is so for at least three reasons: (1) the creeds are themselves innovative, and of a nature foreign to the earliest period of Christianity; (2) the creeds are not inclusive of all those groups generally viewed as Christian; and (3) the ecumenical councils that generated the creeds have never been viewed as consigning to "non-Christianity" those whom they anathematized.[39]

According to Edwin Hatch, in his magisterial study *The Influence of Greek Ideas on Christianity*:

> It is impossible for anyone, whether he be a student of history or no, to fail to notice a difference in both form and content between the Sermon on the Mount and the Nicene Creed. The Sermon on the Mount is the

> promulgation of a new law of conduct; it assumes beliefs rather than formulates them; the theological conceptions which underlie it belong to the ethical rather than the speculative side of theology; metaphysics are wholly absent. The Nicene Creed is a statement partly of historical facts and partly of dogmatic inferences; the metaphysical terms which it contains would probably have been unintelligible to the first disciples; ethics have no place in it. The one belongs to a world of Syrian peasants, the other to a world of Greek philosophers.
>
> The contrast is patent. If anyone thinks that it is sufficiently explained by saying that the one is a sermon and the other a creed, let it be pointed out in reply that the question why an ethical sermon stood in the forefront of the teaching of Jesus Christ, and a metaphysical creed in the forefront of the Christianity of the fourth century, is a problem which claims investigation.[40]

Of course, certain creed-like passages can be located in the New Testament, although not of the metaphysical type popular in succeeding centuries. Both Protestant and Catholic scholars recognize 1 Corinthians 15:1–11, for example, as a very early Christian creedal statement.[41] It is quite similar to Paul's statement before Agrippa. Latter-day Saints accept it fully—and in a much more literal way than liberal Protestants. However, this makes little or no difference in the eyes of some of their critics, who still claim that Latter-day Saints are not Christians.

After a survey of the various creeds and councils, Einar Molland concludes that the Lord's Prayer is "the one creed of all branches of Christendom."[42] All other creeds exclude one denomination or other that is universally recognized to be Christian. Acceptance of the Lord's Prayer, Molland implies, is good demonstration of one's Christianity. While Mormons do not use the Lord's Prayer liturgically—they have very little liturgy to speak of—they certainly accept it. Indeed, 3 Nephi 13:9–13 has the resurrected Christ teach that prayer in the New World.[43]

J. O. Sanders identifies Christianity with the so-called Apostles' Creed.[44] But is this acceptable as a basic definition of what a Christian believes? According to Einar Molland, "If we take the recognition and use of the Apostles' Creed as our test, both the Orthodox Church and a number of Protestant Communions will fall outside the limits of Christendom, which would be absurd."[45] While Latter-day Saints do not use this creed, they do—as some non-Mormons have observed—accept its principles.[46]

Some conservative bishops, even among those who were committed to the doctrinal position taken by the Council of Nicea, were very much worried by the fact that, in it, a word utterly foreign to the scriptures—*homousios*—was proclaimed the dogmatic standard for the church.[47] This consideration ought to, but does not, give pause to those who would make of the Nicene Creed—or any of its Hellenistic cousins—the *sine qua non* of Christianity. In any event, the Nicene Creed is not accepted even by all those churches universally recognized as Christian.[48]

In 431 the Council of Ephesus condemned Nestorius and his followers. Yet the Nestorians are invariably described as Christians.[49] The verdict of that council is now generally recognized to have been unjust.[50] Further, the Monophysites were condemned at the Council of Chalcedon in A.D. 451. Yet they—and their numbers include the Coptic, Armenian, Ethiopian, and Jacobite churches—are invariably described as Christian.[51] Is there any authority anywhere who would dispute the claim of, say, the Coptic Church, to the title "Christian"? The idea is preposterous. Is this merely a matter of some bloodless modern "tolerance"? Clearly, no. In 531 that great persecutor of the Monophysites, the Emperor Justinian, sent envoys to the Monophysite Negus of Ethiopia, requesting, "by reason of our common faith," assistance in the war against the Sassanians.[52]

The Fifth Ecumenical Council, in A.D. 553, posthumously condemned Theodore of Mopsuestia, who had died in A.D. 428.[53] Norbert Brox characterizes the period of Theodore's excommunication in terms that could also be used to describe some brands of anti-Mormonism: "A nervous, polemical climate of polarization dominated the era, in which people positively waited for their enemies to commit dogmatic or political mistakes."[54] Still, he is invariably referred to as a Christian.[55]

A look at other major "heresies" discloses that they, too, are, in both specialist and common usage, referred to as Christian. The Montanists, for example, were a faction of the second and third centuries A.D. whose chief sin was admitting post-biblical revelation. Yet they are always called Christians.[56] Their most famous convert, the great Latin father, Tertullian, is described by one historian as "the first Protestant."[57] Similarly, Donatism, condemned as a heresy in A.D. 405, is considered to be Christian by the scholars who deal with it.[58] Authorities are not at all reluctant, in discussing what is perhaps the most radical complex of heresies ever to appear in Christendom, to speak of "Christian gnosticism."[59] Marcion and his followers are routinely called Christians.[60]

Never condemned were the "Christian Platonists of Alexandria"—who surely represent a melding of biblical doctrines with pagan influences, and who count among their number some of the most illustrious thinkers in the history of Christendom.[61] Even the Docetists, who seem to be the only group that might, on the basis of earliest Christian writings, justifiably be termed non-Christian, are not.[62] Nevertheless, it may be interesting to examine some of the specific standards that anti-Mormons claim to derive from the Bible, and by which they claim to be able to discern "true" Christians from false pretenders.

Specific Reasons Given for Denying That Latter-day Saints Are Christians

Claim 1: Because Latter-day Saints reject the traditional doctrine of the Trinity, they are not Christian.

The first Article of Faith of The Church of Jesus Christ of Latter-day Saints is "We believe in God, the Eternal Father, and in his son Jesus Christ, and in the Holy Ghost." This is a straightforward statement of belief in the Trinity. However, the key to understanding the claim is the phrase "traditional doctrine of the Trinity." The specific form of trinitarian belief that those making this claim insist on is usually reflected in the creedal formulations of the fourth and fifth centuries, the most famous of which is the Nicene Creed. These creeds were themselves the product of centuries-long debates about the nature of the Godhead. To be sure, these debates and the resulting creeds are utterly irrelevant to Mormon theology, which does not share their Hellenistic metaphysical presuppositions. But it is also highly questionable whether these creeds reflect the thinking or beliefs of the New Testament Church. "The exact theological definition of the doctrine of the Trinity," notes the Protestant Bible commentator J. R. Dummelow, "was the result of a long process of development, which was not complete until the fifth century, or maybe even later."[63] And as Bill Forrest aptly remarks, "To insist that a belief in the Trinity is requisite to being Christian, is to acknowledge that for centuries after the New Testament was completed thousands of Jesus' followers were in fact not really 'Christian.' "[64] Certainly the way in which the doctrine of the Godhead was taught by Joseph Smith that pierces through the centuries-old debates on the subject must be among his greatest theological insights.

Claim 2: Because Latter-day Saints believe that human beings can become like God, they are not Christian.

Yet even a cursory glance at early Christian thought reveals that a similar idea—known in Greek as *theosis* or *theopoiesis*—is to be found virtually everywhere, from the New Testament through the Church Fathers.[65] According to an ancient formula, "God became man that man might become God."[66] Early Christians "were invited to 'study' to become gods" (note the plural and its polytheistic implications).[67] The notion is also characteristic of the Church Fathers Irenaeus (second century A.D.) and Clement of Alexandria (third century A.D.).[68] It is fundamental to Athanasius (fourth century A.D.).[69] Indeed, so pervasive was it in the fourth century that it was also held by Athanasius' archenemies, the Arians.[70] Athanasius opposed the Arians because he feared that, in their belief, Christ's deity was not sufficiently robust to sustain redemption as deification.[71]

Though the idea of human deification waned in the Western church in the Middle Ages, it remained very much alive in the Eastern Orthodox faith.[72] Indeed, as Jaroslav Pelikan notes, "the chief idea of St. Maximus, as of all of Eastern theology, [was] the idea of deification."[73] However, echoes of it are still found in the work of modern writers in the West.[74] Thus, for instance, C. S. Lewis's writings are full of the language of human deification.[75]

Related to the claim that Latter-day Saints are not Christians because they believe that man may become as God is the assertion that the Latter-day Saints do not view Jesus as uniquely divine. Such an assertion is fundamentally misleading. The phrase, "only begotten Son," for example, occurs with its variants at least ten times in the Book of Mormon, fourteen times in the Doctrine and Covenants, and nineteen times in the Pearl of Great Price. Surely this by itself should suffice to demonstrate the uniqueness of Jesus in Latter-day Saint scripture and theology. However, Mormons will confess to taking seriously such passages as Psalm 82:6, John 10:33–36, and Philippians 2:5–6, where a plurality of gods and the possibility of becoming God's equal are mentioned. Is this truly a closed question? After all, the Origenist monks at Jerusalem divided, in the fourth century, over this very question, "whether all men would finally become like Christ or whether Christ was really a different creature."[76]

Claim 3: Because Latter-day Saints practice baptism for the dead they are not Christian.

This argument, however, presumes that it has been definitively established that the meaning of 1 Corinthians 15:29 has nothing to do with an early Christian practice of baptism for the dead. It also ignores the fact that such groups as the Montanists—who are universally recognized as Christians—practiced a similar rite.[77] As Hugh Nibley has shown in great detail, many of the Church Fathers understood this verse literally, even when they did not always know what to make of it.[78] But it is not only the Latter-day Saint practice of vicarious baptism that is a point of disagreement. Mormon temple ritual in general is a source of contention, because the alleged "secrecy" surrounding it is "un-Christian." But the New Testament scholar Joachim Jeremias has shown that "the desire to keep the most sacred things from profanation"—a concern shared by the Latter-day Saints—is widely found in the New Testament and in the early Christian community.[79] Indeed, Jeremias argues that this was the very motive that led the writer of the Gospel of John consciously to omit an account of the Lord's Supper, "because he did not want to reveal the sacred formula to the general public."[80] The second-century Church father Ignatius of Antioch was also known to have held "secret" doctrines.[81] Tertullian (second century A.D.) takes the heretics to task because they provide access to their services to everyone without distinction.[82] As a result, says Tertullian, the demeanor of these heretics becomes frivolous, merely human, without seriousness and without authority.[83] The pagan critic Celsus probably referred to Christianity as a "secret system of belief" because access to the various ordinances of the Church—baptism and the sacrament of the Lord's supper, for example—were available to the initiated only. In his response to Celsus, Origen (third century A.D.) readily admits that there are both practices as well as doctrines that are not available to everyone, but he argues that this is not unique to Christianity.[84] As late as the fourth century, efforts were being made to return to an earlier Christian tradition of preserving certain doctrines and practices for the initiated only.[85]

Claim 4: Because Latter-day Saints do not believe in the doctrine of creation ex nihilo *they are not Christian.*

Latter-day Saints certainly do not adhere to the doctrine of creation *ex nihilo* (a Latin phrase meaning "from nothing"), which implicitly denies that matter existed before the Creation. "Yet medieval Jewish thinkers . . . held that the account of creation in Genesis could be interpreted to mean that God created from pre-existing formless matter, and ancient Jewish texts state that he did so."[86] This is precisely the doctrine taught by Mormon texts such as Abraham 3:24–4:1. It is highly doubtful that the doctrine of *ex nihilo* creation is to be found in Genesis or anywhere else in the Old Testament.[87] There is good reason to believe that the doctrine was "far from being commonly accepted" by the classical rabbis.[88] "We have to wait until the second half of the second century to find unambiguous Christian statements of creation *ex nihilo*."[89] The fact is that among rabbinic Jews of the ancient and medieval periods, and among Christian Fathers of the second century, there were those who affirmed a creation from pre-existent matter.[90] Should

Mormons be driven from Christianity over a doctrine so ambiguously attested in the earliest Church?

Claim 5: Because Latter-day Saints do not accept the Bible as their sole authority in faith and doctrine, but claim other sources, they are not Christian.

Of course, Latter-day Saints do accept as scriptural certain writings—the Book of Mormon, the Doctrine and Covenants, and the Pearl of Great Price—in addition to the Bible. But the whole question of canon—which writings are sacred, inspired, and normative—has always been a complicated one in the history of Christianity. It is quite difficult, in the earliest period of the Christian church, to see a distinction being made between canonical and noncanonical writings.[91] For example, the epistle of Jude draws heavily on noncanonical books such as *1 Enoch* and *The Assumption of Moses*. Indeed, as E. Isaac says of *1 Enoch*, "it influenced Matthew, Luke, John, Acts, Romans, 1 and 2 Corinthians, Ephesians, Colossians, 1 and 2 Thessalonians, 1 Timothy, Hebrews, 1 John, Jude (which quotes it directly), and Revelation (with numerous points of contact). There is little doubt that *1 Enoch* was influential in molding New Testament doctrines concerning the nature of the Messiah, the Son of Man, the messianic kingdom, demonology, the future, resurrection, the final judgment, the whole eschatological theater, and symbolism."[92]

The so-called Muratorian Fragment, dating from the late second century A.D., shows that at least some Christians of the period accepted the *Apocalypse of Peter.* Clement of Alexandria, writing around A.D. 200, seems to have admitted a New Testament canon of some thirty books, including the *Epistle of Barnabas* and the *Epistle of Clement*, and the *Preaching of Peter*. Origen recognized *Barnabas* and the *Shepherd of Hermas.*[93]

Even in more recent times, the question of canon has not been unanimously resolved. Among Reformation figures the question of canon was not entirely settled. Martin Luther characterized the epistle of James as "an epistle of straw"[94]—largely because, it needs to be pointed out, it seemed to disagree with his teachings of justification by faith alone. Luther also "mistrusted" the book of Revelation.[95] Roman Catholics and the Orthodox churches tend to accept the Apocrypha as canonical. In fact, Eastern Orthodoxy has never really settled the question of the canon—which is, of course, rather odd if that question is all-important. It has been pointed out that the Church has priority, both logically and historically, over the Bible—that is, a group of believers existed before a certain body of texts (in this case, the books of the Old and the New Testaments) were declared canonical.[96]

Claim 6: Because Latter-day Saints believe that the Bible contains errors they are not Christian.

This claim is a flagrant oversimplification. The current controversy over the question of biblical inerrancy makes it abundantly clear that even conservative Protestants are not at one on this issue.

Claim 7: Because Latter-day Saints deny the doctrine of original sin they are not Christian.

Why single out the Mormons? "In the history of the church, fierce controversy has raged about the doctrine of original sin."[97] Yet, as we have already seen, their Christianity is not denied. In fact, the notion of original sin as it is usually understood today is distinctly late, evolving out of the controversies of the fourth and fifth centuries. Tertullian (second century), who was very concerned with the idea of sin, knows nothing of the doctrine of original sin. The Greek Fathers, for example, show little or no interest in it. It was not clearly enunciated until Augustine (fourth-fifth century) needed it in his battle with the Pelagians, who denied the doctrine, and it came to be associated with the Council of Carthage in A.D. 418.[98]

By Augustine's time, the idea that some single great sin lay behind the visible decay of Roman society was common to both pagans and Christians.[99] Augustine, indeed, may have been more inclined toward it because of his Manichaean past, which he never entirely outgrew.[100] But, as Norbert Brox points out, "properly considered, Pelagian theology was the traditional one, especially in Rome. But the Africans, under the theological leadership of Augustine, managed to make their charge of heresy stick within the church, thereby establishing the Augustinian theology of grace as the basis of the Western tradition."[101] Some modern scholars now raise the issue of whether Augustine, and not Pelagius, was the archheretic.[102]

Claim 8: Because Latter-day Saints reject the doctrine of salvation by grace alone, or solafidianism, which is the core of Christianity, they are not Christian.[103]

Perhaps the most succinct statement of Latter-day Saint understanding of the relation between grace and works is to be found in 2 Nephi 25:23: "It is by grace that we are saved, after all we can do." This idea is sometimes termed synergism.[104] "Implicit in solafidianism," notes F. R. Harm, "is the doctrine of divine monergism, which declares that man's salvation is totally dependent upon God's activity and is in no way conditioned by the action of man."[105] It should be pointed out that solafidianism—the doctrine of salvation through faith alone—is not a biblical, but a distinctly Reformation doctrine: there are no instances in the text of the New Testament of the phrase "grace alone" or "faith alone."[106] The prominent philosopher-theologian Frederick Sontag argues eloquently that Jesus himself was interested not in words, and not even in theological dogma, but in action. For the Jesus of Matthew, he says, "action is more important than definition."[107] Richard Lloyd Anderson, in his study, *Understanding Paul*, shows that, even in the epistles that contain Paul's major treatments of the doctrine of grace (in particular, Romans and Ephesians), there is a balancing element of works as well.[108] Other New Testament writers, most notably James, make it clear that saving faith can only be recognized through works: "Faith, if it hath not works, is dead, being alone" (James 2:17).

The generations immediately following the New Testament period also recognized the need for both grace and works for salvation.[109] According to the illustrious Werner Jaeger, "The oldest datable literary document of Christian religion soon after the time of the apostles is the letter of Clement of Rome to the Corinthians, written in the last decade of the first century." In it, "the special emphasis is on good works, as it is in the Epistle of James, which may belong to the same time and is so clearly polemical against Paul."[110] The famous *Didache, The Teaching of the Twelve Apostles,* which dates back to before A.D. 70, is conspicuous for its "moralism" and "legalism."[111] The second century *Shepherd of Hermas* contains twelve commandments. There "are a summary of the duties of a Christian, and *Hermas* affirms that in obeying them there is eternal life." Indeed, summarizes J. L. Gonzales, according to the *Shepherd of Hermas* "it is possible to do more than the commandment requires, and thus to attain a greater glory."[112] Ignatius of Antioch downplays Jesus as a redeemer from sin in order to emphasize Jesus as a "revealer of God." In fact, in the epistles of Ignatius the word *sin* appears only once. On the other hand, he could advise Polycarp: "Let your works be your deposits, that you may receive the back-pay due to you."[113] "The Biblical doctrine of divine grace, God's favour shown to sinful humanity," writes F. F. Bruce, "so clearly (as we might think) expounded in the teaching of Christ and the writings of Paul, seems almost in the post-apostolic age, to reappear only with Augustine. Certainly the majority of Christian writers who flourished between the apostles and Augustine do not seem to have grasped what Paul was really getting at . . . Marcion has been called the only one of these writers who understood Paul."[114] But other observers, including Edwin Hatch, have identified the trend in nearly an opposite manner. To them, a growing emphasis on doctrine, on orthodoxy, came to supplant the ethical focus of earliest Christianity.[115]

Likewise, "Eastern Orthodox Christians emphasize a unity of faith and works. For the Orthodox, being conformed to the image of Christ . . . includes a response of our faith *and* works."[116] In the fourth century, at least one prominent Christian bishop was teaching the necessity of rituals. "If any man receive not Baptism," wrote Cyril of Jerusalem, "he hath not salvation."[117] Intriguingly, too, he writes of an ordinance called "anointing," or "chrism." "Having been counted worthy of this Holy Chrism, ye are called Christians. . . . For before you were deemed worthy of this grace, ye had properly no right to this title."[118]

Certain Protestant writers, sensing the danger that a "grace alone" position could become "cheap grace" (to borrow an expression from the German Protestant theologian Dietrich Bonhoeffer) or "a theologically thin, no-sweat Christianity,"[119] have adopted positions that recognize that works also play a vital role in salvation.[120] In any event, it hardly seems justifiable to exclude the Latter-day Saints from Christianity because they reject the doctrine of grace alone.

Conclusion

Believing members of The Church of Jesus Christ of Latter-day Saints easily meet the minimal definition of a Christian implicit in the New Testament: we believe that Christ's coming was foretold by ancient prophets, that he suffered for our transgressions, that he was put to death but that he rose from the dead, that it is through him that forgiveness of sins may be obtained, and we look forward to his coming again in glory. As we have seen above, most of the reasons given to exclude Latter-day Saints from being Christians are the result of doctrinal positions reflective more of creeds formulated in the fourth and fifth centuries or tenets developed during the Reformation than of the New Testament. If it were asserted (as it has been) that Latter-day Saints are not Christians because they do not subscribe to the creeds, Latter-day Saints might naturally respond that whether a person is Christian or not ought to be determined more by his or her adherence to the beliefs and practices of the "primitive" (i.e., New Testament) Church than to doctrines formulated centuries after the Apostles. If the same claims against the Christianity of members of The Church of Jesus Christ of Latter-day Saints were made against members of other churches as well, only a small percentage (probably less than ten percent) of adherents of churches traditionally regarded as Christian could still be called "Christians." To a large extent, those stating that Latter-day

Saints are not Christians mean, at root, that we do not believe as they do, which is a different matter entirely. If we hear the charge being made that Latter-day Saints are not Christians, we should first ask, "What does the person making this claim mean by the word *Christian*?" Only then can we begin to discover the meaning of the statement.

A definition of Christianity that would, we believe, exclude no denominations that desire the name is a belief in Jesus as a uniquely normative person. But, rather than attempting to establish a standard of what a Christian is, it is perhaps best to take the person claiming to be a Christian at his word and to let the Lord judge. As Augustine once said, in fundamentals we agree, in other things diversity, but in all things charity.

NOTES

1. Jack Weyland, "I Have a Question: When Nonmembers Say We're Not Christians, What Is the Best Way to Respond?" *Ensign*, January 1985, pp. 43–45.

2. For example, the October 1986 general conference address of President Gordon B. Hinckley, "The Father, Son, and Holy Ghost," *Ensign*, November 1986, pp. 49–51.

3. H. Küng, *Christ Sein* (Munich: Deutscher Taschenbuch Verlag, 1980), 135: "eher ein Schimpfname als ein Ehrenname."

4. Tacitus, *Annal* 15:44—*quos per flagitia invisos vulgus Christianos appellabat.*

5. F. F. Bruce, *New Testament History* (Garden City, NY: Doubleday and Company, 1972), 268. Clearly, by the time of the correspondence between Pliny and Trajan, i.e., between A.D. 97 and A.D. 109, the term *Christian* was both well known and held in contempt.

6. Ignatius, *The Martyrdom of Polycarp* 10:1; cf. 12:1–2. F. D. Gealy, "Christianity," in G. A. Buttrick, ed., *The Interpreter's Dictionary of the Bible*, 4 vols. (Nashville: Abingdon Press, 1962), 1:562, agrees that it is in the second century that the term *Christian* came into "common use" among the followers of Jesus themselves.

7. Ignatius, *Epistle to the Romans*, 3:2.

8. J. P. Meier, "Part One: Antioch," in R. E. Brown and J. P. Meier, *Antioch and Rome* (New York: Paulist Press, 1983), 35, thinks so. See also J. L. Gonzales, *A History of Christian Thought*, 3 vols. (Nashville: Abingdon Press, 1970) 1:76 n. 56; Walter Grundmann, "*chrio* etc.," in Gerhard Kittel and Gerhard Friedrich, eds., *Theological Dictionary of the New Testament*, trans. Geoffrey Bromiley, 10 vols. (Grand Rapids, MI: Eerdmans, 1974), 9:576.

9. In a similar situation, *Martyrdom of Polycarp*, 3:2, speaks of "the nobility of the God-loving and God-fearing people of the Christians." Aristides, a Greek Christian apologist of the early second century A.D., empha-

sized the Christians' mutual love and "superior customs." "Because of this [public-relations–style] manner of presenting Christianity, Aristides says little about the beliefs" of the Church; see Gonzales, *History of Christian Thought*, 1:102. A virtually identical charge is routinely made against the Mormons. The great German theologians and historians of doctrine, Albrecht Ritschl and his student Adolf von Harnack, *Das Wesen des Christentums* (Leipzig: J. C. Hinrichs, 1901), held that ethics and morals were the essence of Christianity—not dogma.

10. Ignatius, *Epistle to Polycarp*, 8:3.

11. See, for example, Ignatius, *Epistle to the Ephesians*, 1:1; *Epistle to the Trallians*, 1:1; *Epistle to the Philadelphians*, 7:2; cf. Ignatius, *Romans* 6:3.

12. Ignatius, *Epistle to the Magnesians*, 10:1.

13. See Meier, "Antioch," 81.

14. Pliny, *Epistulae*, 96.

15. Ignatius, *Ephesians*, 11:2.

16. *Magnesians*, 4.

17. *Magnesians*, 6:1; cf. 2:1, 7:1, and especially 13:2.

18. *Magnesians*, 10:3; *Philadelphians*, 6:1; cf. Ignatius, *Romans* 3:3; see also Grundmann, "*chrio*," 576. *Ibid.*, 537 sees the term *Christian* as having arisen with the realization that the followers of Jesus now constituted a group distinct from the Jews.

19. *Trallians*, 9–11; cf. *Epistle to the Smyrnaeans*, 2, 5–7. Compare, in the New Testament itself, 1 John 4:2–3. Docetism was a real threat in Antioch to the form of Christianity advocated by Ignatius; see J. P. Meier, "Antioch," 75.

20. *Trallians*, 6:1.

21. Ignatius's view of "priesthood" is not altogether unlike that of the Latter-day Saints, who do not accept the notion that priest and prophet are naturally opposed. Writes J. P. Meier, "Antioch," 76–77: "Ignatius does not view his office as un-charismatic. Rather, in Ignatius we find a peculiar fusion of office and charism, perhaps because Ignatius has come forth from the college of prophets and teachers and still considers himself very much a man of the Spirit. . . . To sum up, then: the presiding teacher-prophet at Antioch became the one bishop, the other teachers and prophets became the college of elders."

22. *Trallians*, 7:1–2.

23. *Smyrnaeans*, 8:1. Docetists proper tended to ignore the eucharist, presumably because they denied the incarnation; see *Smyrnaeans*, 7:1. The word *strange* in Lake's translation of *Trallians* 6:1 renders the Greek *allotrios.* This can also mean "belonging to another," "alien," "hostile," "enemy," or, as a substantive, "other people's property." See Walter Bauer, *A Greek-English Lexicon of the New Testament and Other Early Christian Literature*, trans. and ed. William F. Arndt and F. Wilbur Gingrich (Chicago: University of Chicago Press, 1957), 40. There may also be a possible reference to idol offerings, as at Acts 15:20, 29; 21:25; 1 Corinthians 8:4.

24. *Smyrnaeans*, 6:1–2.

25. Grundmann, "*chrio*," 576 (we have transliterated the Greek of the original).

26. J. L. Gonzales, *History of Christian Thought*, 1:89.

27. This did not forbid the use of other titles. See K. H. Rengstorf, "*manthano*," in Kittel and Friedrich, eds., *Theological Dictionary of the New Testament*, 4:457.

28. See Grundmann, "*chrio*," 536. Pierson Parker, "Disciple," in G. A. Buttrick, ed., *Interpreter's Dictionary*, 1:845, surveying the gospels and Acts, calls "disciple" "the most frequent and general term for believers in Christ."

29. Rengstorf, "*manthano*," 458–59. Irenaeus (d. ca. A.D. 202), notes Pierson Parker, "Disciple," 845, "used 'disciple' as equivalent to 'Christian.' "

30. A notable fact is that the word "disciple" [*mathetes*] occurs about 260 times in the Gospels and in Acts, yet is utterly absent from the rest of the New Testament; see Rengstorf, "*manthano*," 441.

31. This is a "classic passage" on the subject; thus Rengstorf, "*manthano*," 458.

32. In R. E. Brown, Joseph Fitzmyer, and Roland E. Murphy, eds., *The Jerome Bible Commentary* (Englewood Cliffs, NJ: Prentice-Hall, Inc., 1968), 63:111. Likewise R. Russell, "St John," in R. C. Fuller, Leonard Johnston, and Conleth Kearns, *A New Catholic Commentary on Holy Scripture* (Nashville and New York: Thomas Nelson, 1975), 810h.

33. The New English Bible is slightly clearer here than the King James Version.

34. F. Sontag, "The Once and Future Christian," *International Journal for Philosophy of Religion* 19(1986): 113.

35. N. Brox, *Kirchengeschichte des Altertums* (Düsseldorf: Patmos, 1984), 149.

36. K. J. Hansen, *Mormonism and the American Experience* (Chicago: University of Chicago Press, 1981), 56.

37. L. Boettner, *Roman Catholicism* (Phillipsburg, NJ: The Presbyterian and Reformed Publishing Company, 1986), 78; cf. 41.

38. Such a view represents a significant shift in interpretation, but reflects the trend set by the groundbreaking work of Walter Bauer, *Orthodoxy and Heresy in Earliest Christianity* (Philadelphia: Fortress Press, 1971); cf., for example, Robert Wilken, "Diversity and Unity in Early Christianity," *The Second Century* 1:2(1981): 101–10.

39. See *ibid.*, 170, 183–84, on the problematic character of conciliar authority.

40. E. Hatch, *The Influence of Greek Ideas on Christianity* (Glocester, MA: Peter Smith, 1970), 1. Latter-day Saints, adherents of an essentially creedless church, access to whose temples depends upon ethical worthiness far more than upon doctrinal purity, would tend to see the change as merely further evidence of the Great Apostasy.

41. D. F. Payne, "Jude," in F. F. Bruce, ed., *The International Bible Commentary*, rev. ed. (Grand Rapids, MI: Zondervan Publishing House, 1986), 1591.

42. E. Molland, *Christendom* (New York: Philosophical Library, 1959), 360.

43. *Ibid.*, 360. Still—strangely—Molland denies that Latter-day Saints are Christian.

44. J. O. Sanders, *Cults & Isms: Ancient and Modern*, rev. and enlarged ed. (Grand Rapids, MI: Zondervan Publishing House, 1962), 15; cf. K. Boa, *Cults, World Religions, and You* (Wheaton, IL: Victor Books, 1984), 67. The received text of this creed probably dates back to no earlier than the sixth century.

45. Molland, *Christendom*, 355.

46. See Elmer T. Clark, "Latter-day Saints," in V. Ferm, ed., *An Encyclopedia of Religion* (New York: Philosophical Library, 1945), 432; R. C. Broderick, *The Catholic Encyclopedia* (Nashville and New York: Thomas Nelson Publishers, 1976), 401. Mormons would weigh carefully the phrase *ton sullepthenta ek pneumatos hagiou / qui conceptus est de Spiritu Sancto*, the translation of which is sometimes questionable. They are concerned to affirm the divine fatherhood of the Father.

47. Brox, *Kirchengeschichte*, 179.

48. Molland, *Christendom*, 356–57.

49. F. L. Cross and E. A. Livingstone, eds., *The Oxford Dictionary of the Christian Church*, 2nd ed. (Oxford: Oxford University Press), 962; S. G. F. Brandon, "Neoplatonism," in S. G. F. Brandon, ed., *A Dictionary of Comparative Religion* (New York: Charles Scribner's Sons, 1970), 468.

50. As by Brox, *Kirchengeschichte*, 161–62.

51. C. E. Farah, *Islam: Beliefs and Observances* (Woodbury, NY: Barron's Educational Series, 1968), 20, speaks of "Christian Abyssinia," while on p. 30 he implicitly so labels the Jacobites. Speaking specifically of the Ethiopians and the Arab Ghassanids, F. E. Peters explicitly calls Monophysites "Christians" at least a score of times. Monophysitism is implicitly identified as Christian by Cross and Livingstone, *Dictionary of the Christian Church*, 932; S. G. F. Brandon, "Monophysitism," in Brandon, ed., *Dictionary of Comparative Religion*, 450. Similar references—these have been found largely at random—could be multiplied indefinitely.

52. F. E. Peters, *Allah's Commonwealth* (New York: Simon and Schuster, 1973), 25.

53. N. Brox, *Kirchengeschichte*, 186.

54. *Ibid.* (Translation ours.)

55. J. C. Brauer, *The Westminster Dictionary of Church History* (Philadelphia: The Westminster Press, 1971), 814–15.

56. On the Montanists, see P. Johnson, *A History of Christianity* (New York: Atheneum, 1983), 71. They are implicitly identified as Christians in *ibid.*, 85–86; Cross and Livingstone, *Dictionary of the Christian Church*, 934. The label is explicitly given to them by Clarence T. Craig, "Montanism," in Ferm, ed., *Encyclopedia of Religion*, 505, and by the *Oxford English Dictionary.*

57. P. Johnson, *History of Christianity*, 50.

58. Herman Hausheer, "Donatism," in Ferm, *Encyclopedia of Religion*, 233; P. Johnson, *History of Christianity*, 83–85; C. T. Manschreck, *A History of Christianity in the World*, 2nd ed. (Englewood Cliffs, NJ: Prentice-Hall, 1985), 59; implicitly, D. W. Treadgold, *A History of Christianity* (Belmont, MA: Nordland Publishing Company, 1979), 71.

59. Examples of this or similar phrasing include R. E. Brown, Joseph A. Fitzmyer, and Roland E. Murphy, eds. *The Jerome Bible Commentary* (Englewood Cliffs, NJ: Prentice-Hall, 1968), 60:3; J. M. Robinson, *The Nag*

Hammadi Library (San Francisco: Harper & Row, 1978), 4; H. Jonas, *The Gnostic Religion*, 2nd ed. (Boston: Beacon Press, 1963), 124; K. Rudolph, *Gnosis: The Nature and History of Gnosticism*, tr. Robert McLachlan Wilson (San Francisco: Harper & Row, 1983), 118; E. Pagels, *The Gnostic Gospels* (New York: Random House, 1981), xxxvii; M. W. Meyer, *The Secret Teachings of Jesus: Four Gnostic Gospels* (New York: Random House, 1986), xvii. The astute reader will recognize that this list reads like a partial "Who's Who" of authorities on gnosticism. Cf. Cross and Livingstone, *Dictionary of the Christian Church*, 1423, who clearly imply Valentinian gnosticism to be Christian, and Johnson, *History of Christianity*, 45, who explicitly says that the Valentinians were "quite inside Christianity." C. T. Manschreck, 30, identifies both Valentinus and Basilides as Christians. If Brox, *Kirchengeschichte*, 139, really denies the Christianity of the Gnostics—he is ambiguous—he is distinctly in the minority.

60. As by Manschreck, *History of Christianity*, 31. Johnson, *History of Christianity*, 46–48, implicitly so recognizes Marcion.

61. See Brox, *Kirchengeschichte*, 160. A classic book on the subject bears the title, *The Christian Platonists of Alexandria*.

62. Johnson, *History of Christianity*, 45, 89, implicitly identifies them as Christians.

63. Cited by Bill Forrest in "Are Mormons Christians?" (Mormon Miscellaneous Response Series) (Salt Lake City: Mormon Miscellaneous, n.d.)

64. *Ibid.*

65. See, for example, the index entries in Jaroslav Pelikan, *The Emergence of the Catholic Tradition (100–600): The Christian Tradition*, vol. 1 (Chicago: University of Chicago Press, 1971) and Pelikan, *The Spirit of Eastern Christendom (600–1700): The Christian Tradition*, vol. 2 (Chicago: University of Chicago Press, 1974) under "Salvation—defined as deification," as well as the appropriate index entry in A. Nygren, *Agape and Eros*, trans. Philip S. Watson (Chicago: University of Chicago Press, 1982); refer also to K. E. Norman, "Divinization: The Forgotten Teaching of Early Christianity," *Sunstone* 1(Winter 1975): 14–19, and Norman, "Deification: The Content of Athanasian Soteriology," Ph.D. dissertation, Duke University, 1980; Seely J. Beggiani, *Early Syriac Theology* (Lanham, MD: University Press of America, 1983), 73–78, on the Syriac tradition.

66. See P. Barlow, "Unorthodox Orthodoxy: The Idea of Deification in Christian History," *Sunstone* 8:5 (September/October 1983): 17.

67. *Ibid.*, 16.

68. G. W. Butterworth, "The Deification of Man in Clement of Alexandria," *Journal of Theological Studies* 17(1916): 157–69; A. Nygren, *Agape and Eros*, 356.

69. K. E. Norman, "Deification"; cf. Manschreck, *History of Christianity*, 62; Treadgold, *History of Christianity*, 57. Boettner, *Roman Catholicism*, 82, acknowledges Athanasius as "the champion of orthodoxy at the Council of Nicea."

70. A. Nygren, *Agape and Eros*, 428, note 3. And the Arians, as we have seen above, are routinely described as being Christians.

71. H. F. Davis, I. Thomas, and J. Crehan, eds., *A Catholic Dictionary of Theology* (New York: Nelson, 1971), 3:382; Brox, *Kirchengeschichte*, 189.

72. G. I. Mantzarides, *The Deification of Man: Saint Gregory Palamas and Orthodox Tradition*, trans. Liadain Sherrard (Crestwood, NY: St. Vladimir's Seminary Press, 1984), deals particularly with St. Gregory Palamas, but is useful for the Orthodox tradition generally. We are under no illusions that such figures as Athanasius and the Byzantine fathers, given their very different metaphysical presuppositions, understood *theosis* in the same way as do the Latter-day Saints. We do suspect, however, that the views of the Greeks represent the Hellenization of an earlier doctrine—which was perhaps much closer to Mormon belief.

73. J. Pelikan, *Spirit of Eastern Christendom*, 10, citing S. L. Epifanovic. Cf. A. Nygren, *Agape and Eros*, 428, note 3.

74. Apparently even Martin Luther was capable of speaking of "the deification of human nature," although in what sense or context we are unable to say. See Jack R. Pressau, *I'm Saved, You're Saved . . . Maybe* (Atlanta: John Knox, 1977), 57; A. Nygren, *Agape and Eros*, 734. P. Barlow, "Unorthodox Orthodoxy," 14–15, offers evidence that other post-Reformation theologians espoused a belief in deification. It is certain that the ancient doctrine had undergone massive dislocations by the time it reached the sixteenth century. It had already been "spiritualized" by the time of Pseudo-Dionysius; see A. Nygren, *ibid.*, 584ff.

75. See, for example, Lewis, *A Grief Observed* (New York: Bantam Books, 1963), 84–85; idem, *The World's Last Night and Other Essays* (New York: Harcourt Brace Jovanovich, 1960), 9; idem, *Mere Christianity* (New York: Macmillan Company, 1960), 138–40, 174, 187. Note that the bulk of the references above are to a book entitled *Mere Christianity*; this demonstrates the centrality of the concept in Lewis's thought. Cf. also Barlow, "Unorthodox Orthodoxy," 13–14.

76. C. T. Manschreck, *History of Christianity*, 52.

77. Samuel M. Gilimour, "Baptism for the Dead," in Ferm, ed., *Encyclopedia of Religion*, 54. The Marcionites, also invariably referred to as Christians, observed the practice as well. The practice was condemned in A.D. 393, by the Council of Hippo, which certainly implies that it was still a live issue in the late fourth century of the Christian era.

78. Hugh W. Nibley, "Baptism for the Dead in Ancient Times," *Improvement Era* 51:12 (December 1948): 786–88, 836; 52:1(January 1949): 24–26, 60; 52:2(February 1949): 90–91, 109–10, 112, 52:3(March 1949): 146–48, 180–83; 52:4(April 1949): 212–14.

79. Joachim Jeremias, *The Eucharistic Words of Jesus* (New York: Charles Scribner's Sons, 1966), 130.

80. *Ibid.*, 125, 136–37.

81. Ignatius, *Trallians*, 5; cf. Gilbert W. Scharffs, *The Truth About "The Godmakers"* (Salt Lake City: Publishers Press, 1986), 200–202. *Magnesians*, 1:2, and *Romans*, 6:2, may possibly contain very weak allusions to a doctrine resembling eternal progression.

82. Tertullianus, *Apologia*, 7–8. Initiates of mystery religions were also under a strict rule of secrecy, and Tertullian likened Christianity to the mystery religions in this respect.

83. Tertullianus, *De praescriptionibus adversus haereticos*, 41.

84. Origen, *Contra Celsum*, 1:7.

85. Norbert Brox, *Kirchengeschichte*, 134.

86. J. A. Goldstein, "The Origins of the Doctrine of Creation Ex Nihilo," *Journal of Jewish Studies* 35:2 (1984): 127.

87. B. W. Anderson, "Creation," in G. A. Buttrick, ed., *Interpreter's Dictionary of the Bible*, 4 vols. (Nashville: Abingdon, 1953), 1:728.

88. D. Winston, "Creation Ex Nihilo Revisited: A Reply to Jonathan Goldstein," *Journal of Jewish Studies* 37:1(1986): 91.

89. J. A. Goldstein, "Creation Ex Nihilo," 132. *Ibid.*, 133, thinks that he has found an "unequivocal" Jewish insistence on *ex nihilo* creation in Rabban Gamaliel II, "at the latest early in the second century C.E." But see the reply by Winston.

90. Goldstein, "Creation Ex Nihilo," 135.

91. On this, and on Orthodox and Roman views, see, generally, the interesting article on "Apocrypha," in Buttrick, ed., *Interpreter's Dictionary*, 1:161–69.

92. E. Isaac, "1 (Ethiopic Apocalypse of) Enoch," in J. H. Charlesworth, *The Old Testament Pseudepigrapha*, 2 vols. (Garden City, NY: Doubleday and Company, 1983), 1:10.

93. C. T. Manschreck, *History of Christianity*, 33.

94. See H. Holzapfel, *Die Sekten in Deutschland* (Regensburg: Verlag Josef Koesel & Friedrich Pustet A.G., 1925), 27; R. Bainton, *Here I Stand: A Life of Martin Luther* (Nashville: Abingdon-Cokesbury Press, 1950), 177, 331–32; T. Carson, "James," in F. F. Bruce, ed., *International Bible Commentary*, p. 1536; see Max Lackmann, *Sola Fide: Eine exegetische Studie über Jakobus 2 zur reformatorischen Rechtferigungslehre* (Gütersloh: C. Bertelsmann Verlag, 1949), for the definitive study of Luther's interpretation of this passage.

95. Bainton, *Here I Stand*, 332.

96. H. Holzapfel, *Die Sekten in Deutschland*, 20, 23–37. Johnson, *History of Christianity*, 22, supports the view that the canonical gospels are "products of the early Church."

97. E. F. Harrison, G. W. Bromiley, and C. F. H. Henry, eds., *Baker's Dictionary of Theology* (Grand Rapids, MI: Baker Book House, 1960), 488.

98. K. Rahner, "Original Sin," in Rahner et al., eds., *Sacramentum Mundi: An Encyclopedia of Theology*, 6 vols. (London: Burns and Oates, 1969), 4:329; Cross and Livingstone, *Dictionary of the Christian Church*, 1011.

99. P. Brown, *Augustine of Hippo* (Berkeley and Los Angeles: University of California Press, 1969), 388.

100. He was often accused, even after his conversion, of being still a Manichaean, rather than a Christian. See P. Brown, *ibid.*, 203–4, 370–71, 386, 393–94.

101. N. Brox, *Kirchengeschichte*, 141 (translation ours). Note that Prof. Brox specifies that, even triumphant, Augustine's innovation became only the "basis of the *Western* tradition" (italics added).

102. See W. E. Phipps, "The Heresiarch: Pelagius or Augustine?" *Anglican Theological Review* 62(1980): 124–33. Latter-day Saints' views would be closer to the Rabbis'—who, after all, spent a great deal of time in meditation upon the text of Genesis—than to Mani. S. G. F. Brandon, "Original Sin," in Brandon, ed., *Dictionary of Comparative Religion*, 481, summarizes: "Jewish Rabbinic thought traced man's tendency to actual sin to Adam's Fall, and explained death thereby."

103. Bill Forrest's pamphlet, "Are Mormons Christians?" contains a brief summary of the claim, and a concise but effective reply. See also G. W. Scharffs, *The Truth About "The Godmakers"* (Salt Lake City: Publishers Press, 1986), 18–19, 21–22, 39, 96, 191–95, 198–200, 241–42, 275. J. R. Pressau, *I'm Saved, You're Saved*, 1, is also apt here: "It is a scandal that the widest credibility gap among Christians is caused by the many meanings of this central doctrine of 'the faith which was once for all delivered to the saints.' It's ironic that the salvation understanding gap generates so much condescension and pride from some Christians and so much suspicion and ill will from others when *both* were exhorted to 'love one another.' "

104. Roman Catholicism is described by Van A. Harvey, *A Handbook of Theological Terms* (London: George Allen & Unwin, 1966), 199, as a subtle and nuanced synergism. Thus one of the canons at the Council of Trent specifically repudiates the notion of grace alone: "If anyone saith that justifying faith is nothing else but confidence in the divine mercy which remits sin for Christ's sake alone; or, that this confidence alone is that whereby we are justified, let him be anathema" (Session VI, Canon 12), cited in Boettner, *Roman Catholicism*, 261. For a good summary of the Catholic position, see J. Pohle, "Grace," in Charles G. Herbermann, et al., eds., *The Catholic Encyclopedia*, 16 vols. (New York: Robert Appleton Company, 1909), 6:689–714. As pointed out in Brauer, *Dictionary of Church History*, 799–800, even Luther's close associate Philip Melanchthon, disturbed by some of the implications of Luther's extreme grace-alone position, flirted with a doctrine of synergism.

105. F. R. Harm, "Solafidianism," in W. A. Elwell, ed., *Evangelical Dictionary of Theology* (Grand Rapids, MI: Baker Book House, 1984), 1032. Etymologically, *mon-ergism* conveys the idea of "working alone," while *synergism* denotes "working together." Both terms are, of course, derived from Greek.

106. Sometime between November 1512 and July 1513, after an intense preoccupation with Paul's teaching in Romans 1:17, Martin Luther came to his doctrine of *sola gratia* ("by grace alone"), but, tellingly, the phrase itself is missing from the passage. See, however, the intriguing article of John Dillenberger, "Grace and Works in Martin Luther and Joseph Smith," in Truman G. Madsen, eds., *Reflections on Mormonism: Judaeo-Christian Parallels* (Provo, UT: Brigham Young University Religious Studies Center, 1980), 175–86, in which he argues that there is more of works in Martin Luther, and more of grace in Joseph Smith, than is generally realized.

107. See F. Sontag, "The Once and Future Christian," 116–18.

108. Richard L. Anderson, *Understanding Paul* (Salt Lake City: Deseret Book Co., 1983), 185–86, 272–76; cf. 355–62.

109. Gonzales, *History of Christian Thought*, 1:94–96.

110. W. Jaeger, *Early Christianity and Greek Paideia* (Cambridge: Harvard University Press, 1961), 12, 15–16.

111. Gonzales, *History of Christian Thought*, 1:69.

112. *Ibid.*, 89.

113. Ignatius, *Epistle to Polycarp*, 6:2.

114. F. F. Bruce, *The Spreading Flame* (Grand Rapids, MI: Wm. B. Eerd-

mans Publishing Company, 1979), 334. Marcion was a second-century Gnostic Christian who distinguished between the God of the Old Testament—a mere demiurge—and the God of the New Testament, whom he termed "the Father." Thus, he rejected the Old Testament utterly, as well as any New Testament writings too much "tainted" with Old Testament ideas. He produced a canon of scripture—the first—which recognized no apostle of Jesus except Paul. The others were considered falsifiers of the gospel. It is tempting to see in Marcion the first Protestant.

115. See Hatch, *Influence of Greek Ideas*, 1; Cf. N. Brox, *Kirchengeschichte*, 138.

116. W. G. Rusch, "Getting to Know the Orthodox," *The Lutheran* (2 April 1986): 12 (italics added). This view is reminiscent of the Book of Mormon, at 2 Nephi 25:23, Moroni 10:32.

117. Cyril of Jerusalem, *Catechetical Lectures*, 3:10.

118. Cyril of Jerusalem, *Catechetical Lectures*, 21:5. On the anointing, see 1 John 2:20, 27.

119. Pressau, *I'm Saved, You're Saved*, 38.

120. See, for example, J. Macquarrie, *An Existentialist Theology* (Harmondsworth, GB: Penguin Books, 1973), 144–49, for a Protestant view in the tradition of Rudolf Bultmann. And, indeed, an article by K. R. Snodgrass, "Justification by Grace—to the Doer: An Analysis of Romans 2 in the Theology of Paul," *New Testament Studies* 32(1986): 72–93, argues for an interpretation of Paul himself which is quite close to the Mormon stance.

Biblical Criticism and the Four Gospels: A Critical Look

11

Robert L. Millet

For centuries men have been concerned with the meaning and historical reliability of valuable texts. In particular, treasured works and collections like the Bible have been the center of attention of persons with both sacred and secular motives and outlooks. *Biblical Criticism* is the science and methodology associated with taking a critical (close and precise) look at the holy scriptures. In its purest sense, biblical criticism is an attempt not to criticize the Bible (in the sense of denigrating or creating doubts) but to analyze it and to become more familiar with its content and formation. One scriptural scholar pointed out that "a proper biblical criticism . . . does not mean criticizing the Word of God, but trying to understand the Word of God and how it has been given to man."[1] Sir Frederic Kenyon noted that "there is nothing that need disturb or unsettle us in the idea that [God] has . . . imposed on us the responsibility of using the intellectual faculties with which He has endowed us in the study of the records in which the history of the chosen Hebrew people and of the foundation of the Christian Church have come down to us." Further, "these intellectual faculties may lead us

---

Robert L. Millet is Associate Professor of Ancient Scripture at Brigham Young University.

astray, just as we may go astray in far more important matters of faith and conduct; but it is a poor faith which does not believe that the Holy Spirit will, if we trust Him, ultimately lead us to the truth."[2]

"To Latter-day Saints," Elder John A. Widtsoe observed, "there can be no objection to the careful and critical study of the scriptures, ancient or modern, provided only that it be an honest study—a search for truth."

> The Prophet Joseph Smith voiced the attitude of the Church at a time when modern higher criticism was in its infancy. "We believe the Bible to be the word of God as far as it is translated correctly." This article of our faith is really a challenge to search the scriptures critically. Moreover, the Church had just been established, when Joseph Smith under divine direction, set about to revise or explain the incorrect or obscure passages of the Bible. The work then done is a powerful evidence of the inspiration that guided the Prophet.

"Whether under a special call of God," Elder Widtsoe concluded, "or impelled by personal desire, there can be no objection to the critical study of the Bible."[3]

We need not, however, accept the proposition, Kenyon pointed out, "that every result which every new critic proclaims is to be accepted forthwith as truth."

> It is only to say that it is not to be condemned forthwith without examination because it offends our present opinions and beliefs. The history of Biblical criticism, as of the criticism of all ancient history and literature, is full of erroneous views, confidently proclaimed, eagerly accepted by those who wish to appear in the vanguard of advance, and then disproved or allowed gradually to sink into obscurity. The way to counter the results of research which are distasteful to us is more research; and it is surely a healthier faith to believe that truth is great and will prevail than to hide one's head, ostrich-like, in the sand.[4]

Though questions of authorship and authority of scriptural books have been raised for millennia,[5] most critical inquiry into the origins of the New Testament belongs to the nineteenth and twentieth centuries. Obviously, not all biblical critics are motivated by the same interests or feel a commitment to values beyond their training or discipline. Unfortunately, many with linguistic and literary skills have taken positions regarding the New Testament which tend (directly or indirectly) to cast doubt upon accepted and traditional religious concepts: revelation, miracles, and a belief in the overall hand of Deity in the formation and preservation of the scriptures. In doing so, they have made the work of their "believing" colleagues much more difficult; the field of biblical criticism has come to be viewed with suspicion and disdain by many who could benefit from some of the findings in this area. It would appear that here, as in all serious studies, identifying one's presuppositions —recognizing, where possible, from the beginning, a scholar's orientation—is crucial. Donald Guthrie has noted that "there is a decided difference between a scholar who accepts the divine origin of Scripture and inquires into its historical and literary origins and a scholar who begins his critical inquiries with the assumption that there is nothing unique about the text and who claims the right to examine it as he would any other book. The former is not simply submitting the text to the bar of his own reason to establish its validity, but assumes that the text will authenticate itself when subject to reverent examination. His stance of faith and his critical inquiry in no way invalidate each other."[6]

Historical Criticism

One approach to a study of the New Testament is what is known in German as *Religionsgeschichte*, a history of religions approach. Here scholars have sought, for example, to examine the influence of contemporary religious ideas on early Christian texts—the supposed influence of the Essenes on John or Jesus, the impact of the Greek mystery religions on Christian ordinances or ritual, or the supposed pervasive influence of the Gnostics on Paul's letters.[7] One obvious presupposition of this perspective is that an event or a movement is largely (if not completely) a product of its surroundings, the result of precipitating factors in the environment.

Though it is certainly valuable to be able to look critically at the setting—for nothing takes shape in an intellectual or religious vacuum—and though it is true that many elements impinge upon a moment in history, we need not suppose a causal connection between any two factors in an environment. Simply because A precedes B, we need not conclude that A caused B, we need not be guilty of the logical fallacy of *post hoc ergo propter hoc*. Nor need we conclude that because A and B coexist they are necessarily related. Thus one of the flaws in the reasoning of some historical critics is an over-reliance upon a linear view of history, an acceptance of the principle that phenomena evolve from previously existing circumstances. Such is certainly not the case in all situations; many events or movements in history were more revolutionary than evolutionary.[8]

Another "history of religions" approach to the Gospels consists in stressing similarities between the Gospels and other contemporary documents, and in so doing minimizing the uniquenesss of the canonical books.[9] But what is it that one has established when one demonstrates that the idea of a "virgin birth" was known to the Greeks; that many Greeks accepted the idea of a God-man; that the crux of many of Jesus' sayings is to be found among Jewish rabbis before the first century A.D.; or that the concepts of martyrdom and ascension into heaven were not new to the world of Jesus of Nazareth? Latter-day Saints are blessed with an understanding of the plan of salvation that informs our thinking regarding antiquity. We know that Christ's eternal gospel has been preached from the beginning, and that Christian prophets have taught Christian doctrine and administered Christian ordinances since the days of Adam.[10] Should we be surprised that elements of that doctrine or semblances of the ordinances or ritual (albeit in fragmentary and even apostate form) should be found in cultures throughout the world?[11]

A more radical approach to historical criticism is that which virtually denies the historicity of foundational events in Christianity. For example, it became somewhat fashionable among some theologians of the twentieth century—caught up in the spirit of existential thought—to begin making reference to the "Christ event" as a "faith event"; to deny the importance of the literal bodily resurrection of Jesus Christ; and to assume that the response of the Christian communities was far more important than a single supernatural event which has occasioned the celebration of Easter ever since. Resurrection is a symbolic experience, they might be heard to say, a personal encounter with a spiritual renewal or rebirth. This line of reasoning would proceed as follows: Whether Jesus of Nazareth actually came forth from a tomb in Jerusalem—rose from the dead—is immaterial; what matters is that the Christians thought he did. It is that "Christ event," defined as what the church believed about Christ and not what really happened, in which the followers of the Nazarene have put their faith.

Alma explained that to have faith is to hope for something which is unseen *but which is true*, i.e., that really happened (Alma 32:21).[12] Strictly speaking, one can never have saving faith in someone or something which is not or never was! One non-LDS theologian has observed:

> There is an excellent objective ground to which to tie the religion that Jesus sets forth. Final validation of this can only come experientially [as we Latter-day Saints would say, by personal revelation]. But *it is desperately important not to put ourselves in such a position that the event-nature of the resurrection depends wholly upon "the faith." It's the other way around. The faith has its starting point in the event*, the objective event, and only by the appropriation of this objective event do we discover the final validity of it. . . .
>
> *The Christian faith is built upon Gospel that is "good news," and there is no news, good or bad, of something that didn't happen*. I personally am much

> disturbed by certain contemporary movements in theology which seem to imply that we can have the faith regardless of whether anything happened or not. I believe absolutely that the whole Christian faith is premised upon the fact that at a certain point of time under Pontius Pilate a certain man died and was buried and three days later rose from the dead. *If in some way you could demonstrate to me that Jesus never lived, died, or rose again, then I would have to say I have no right to my faith.*[13]

In short, the authenticity of an event is inextricably tied to its historicity; one's subjective testimony of a religious phenomenon is directly related to an objective and discernible occasion.

Textual Criticism

One of the major reasons for the variety of Bibles today is that the different versions are not necessarily translated from the same manuscripts. Unfortunately, today there are no original manuscripts of the New Testament, only copies of copies of copies. Scribal errors came early in the process of transmission; even careful scribes were prone to the mistakes associated with human limitations (eyes, ears, physical strength, and faulty judgment).[14] When an error in copying went undetected, it was preserved in successive copies. Through comparing variant readings and grouping together documents with similar readings, manuscript or "textual families" became apparent, each family of manuscripts possessing certain distinct characteristics in common. One of the major reasons why various English editions of today's Bible differ is that they represent translations of different textual families.

"Textual criticism, commonly known in the past as 'lower' criticism in contrast to the so-called 'higher' (historical and literary) criticism, is the science that compares all known manuscripts of a given work in an effort to trace the history of variations within the text so as to discover its original form."[15] The method of textual criticism, observed Bruce Metzger, "involves two main processes, recension and emendation. Recension is the selection, after examination of all available material, of the most trustworthy evidence on which to base a text. Emendation is the attempt to eliminate the errors which are found even in the best manuscripts."[16] Some of the principles or criteria for choosing among readings (and scholars would disagree as to the relative weighting of each of these factors) are as follows:

1. The earliest manuscript is likely to be the most correct.
2. The shorter reading is to be preferred to the longer.
3. The text supported by the most authorities (manuscripts and early quotations) is likely to be the most nearly correct.

4. The manuscripts with the widest geographical distribution are preferred.[17]

Textual criticism, a science dedicated to the discovery of the oldest and most accurate and authentic manuscripts (and thus the most ancient messages), has certainly proven to be one of the most valuable approaches to a study of the New Testament. There are, however, some precautions which must be taken by Latter-day Saints who are sincerely intent on discovering things as they were in antiquity.

First of all, the Book of Mormon is a powerful witness that the world has never had a complete Bible, that plain and precious truths were taken away or kept back from the Old and New Testaments long before the time of their compilation and canonization (see 1 Nephi 13:20–40). "The problem which lies before the textual critic," Kenyon observed, "is now becoming clear. The original manuscripts of the Bible, written by the authors of the various books, have long ago disappeared."[18]

Textual variants occur in many ways, both the unplanned and the planned ones. The unplanned—errors of the hand, the eye, the ear, and of judgment—will probably not occur in the same place in each copy. Such errors are dealt with without extreme difficulty; they may be corrected through a comparison with other copies. "It is the planned changes," Robert J. Matthews has noted, "that are the most damaging." These come about

> when the copyist or the translator begins to think for himself and deliberately makes his copy differ from the written document. In this manner, substantial changes may occur in a very short time and can result in added material or in the loss of material. Even these changes could be corrected if one had the original to refer to for comparison, but if the master copy is unavailable, the corrupted texts perpetuate the errors. All subsequent copies made from the altered text will bear the same shortcomings because there is no master copy or archetype with which to correct it. . . .
>
> As we read the words of the angel [in 1 Nephi 13], we discover that the world never has had a complete Bible, for it was massively, even cataclysmically, corrupted *before* it was distributed. If this is true, and since the originals disappeared early from the scene (thus preventing a correction from that source), what does this passage from Nephi mean to us about Bible textual criticism? . . .
>
> The great scholars, employing the science of textual criticism, seem to be effectively correcting the errors made by the carelessness and weakness of man. By extensively searching the available manuscripts, such as the Vaticanus, Sinaiticus, Alexandrinus, and lesser fragments, the text of the Bible may yet be recovered to the condition it was in *after* it was cataclysmically corrupted as spoken in 1 Nephi.

"It appears to me," Matthews concludes, "that the world has mistakenly identified the text of the second or third generation as being the same as the original. . . . Thus the great manuscripts so highly regarded are indeed precious for their antiquity and beauty, but they represent the depleted text and not the original. The plain and precious missing parts have not yet been made known through manuscripts and scholars, but are available only through the Book of Mormon, the Joseph Smith Translation, and modern revelation through the instrumentality of a prophet (see 1 Nephi 13:39–40, "other books")."[19]

Source Criticism

A close comparative study of the Synoptic Gospels (Matthew, Mark, and Luke, literally those which take a "similar look" at Christ) is most revealing. We find, for example, that essentially 606 of the 661 verses of Mark appear in Matthew and that 380 of Mark's verses reappear with only slight alteration in Luke. From another perspective, of the 1,068 verses of Matthew, about 500 contain material also found in Mark; of the 1,149 verses in Luke, about 380 are paralleled in Mark. There are only 31 verses in Mark not found in Matthew or Luke; only 7 percent of the Gospel of Mark is exclusive.[20]

What is one to make of such statistics? What *is* the chronological and literary relationship between the Synoptic Gospels? The issues underlying the relationships between these three Gospels constitute what biblical critics have come to denote the "Synoptic Problem." Since the nineteenth century many scholars have concluded that the solution of the Synoptic Problem was to be found by stressing the priority of Mark, the shortest of the Gospels. The general consensus has been that Mark was the first Gospel written and that Matthew and Luke drew upon Mark in preparing their own.[21] This approach, known as the "Markan Hypothesis," or the "Two-Document Hypothesis," contends that Matthew relied upon Mark, upon a "sayings source" or collection of sayings by Jesus (known as the Q Document, from the German word *Quelle*, "source"), and added his own peculiar style, perspective, and experiences (called M) in preparing the Gospel which we know as Matthew. Luke relied upon Mark, upon Q, and provided his own unique perspective (called L). In short, the Two-Document Hypothesis for the composition of Matthew and Luke is as follows:

Matthew = Mark + Q + M
Luke = Mark + Q + L

The Two-Document Hypothesis has been accepted by most of the New Testament scholarly world since the last century. The discovery of Gnostic Christian materials in the Nag Hammadi Library in Upper Egypt some forty years ago revealed, among other important things, a collection of 114 sayings, known as the "Gospel According to Thomas," which many scholars felt to be supportive of the proposition that "Jesus-sayings" (like Q) were afloat for many years before the formation of the canonical Gospels.[22] Others have wondered whether the reverse was not true: perhaps documents like the Gospel of Thomas simply drew upon or copied from older materials, like the Gospel of Matthew.[23]

Though it is a common presupposition of some biblical critics to prefer the shortest document as the oldest (thus assuming that the longer ones evidence embellishments and additions), Latter-day Saints should take seriously Nephi's vision of the corruption of the biblical texts in this regard. Is it not just as reasonable to suppose that Mark, having before him the longer Matthew or the longer Luke, chose to prepare an abbreviated Gospel, placing less stress upon sermons and parables and more stress upon the movements and actions of our Lord?[24]

William R. Farmer, for example, has argued for the primacy of Matthew, an approach which goes a long way toward eliminating the need for a hypothetical sayings source. Some of Farmer's suggestions as to the inadequacy of the Two-Document Hypothesis to resolve the Synoptic Problem include the following: (1) the failure of the Markan Hypothesis to account for Mark's selection of items "in relation to Matthew and Luke from the presumably rich storehouse of tradition available to him"; (2) another "inadequacy . . . is that it requires us to believe that Matthew and Luke are independent of one another." This does not explain the "numerous agreements between Matthew and Luke where they are supposed to be independently copying Mark"; in a related manner, "there are at least twenty topics that Matthew and Luke have in common. These cannot be explained through a dependence upon Mark, because Mark does not contain several of these topics. For example, Mark does not have birth narratives, a genealogy, a temptation story, the Sermon on the Mount, or large collections of parables," all of which are found throughout Matthew and Luke; (3) all the church fathers who mention the sequence of the Gospels indicate that Matthew was written first. "The earliest statement regarding sequence was made by Clement of Alexandria who indicates that both Matthew and Luke were written before Mark"; and finally, (4) there is the question of the relation between the historical spread and development of the Christian Church and the formation of the Gospels:

> Let us put the matter another way. Jesus and his disciples were Jews living in Palestine. In due time the community that began with Jesus and his disciples spread out into the Mediterranean world. As the extra-Palestinian expansion of the community took place, more and more gentiles sought membership in it until finally it developed into a community that was predominantly gentile.
>
> How does this affect our view of the Gospels? All would agree, of course, that Matthew is the most Jewish Gospel in the canon. It is also the Gospel that best reflects the Palestinian origins of the Christian church. Luke too is very Jewish, but there are many passages where, by comparison, this Gospel is better adapted for use by gentiles outside of Palestine. While unmistakably retaining traditions of Jewish and Palestinian origin, Mark is the best adapted of the three for gentile readers who are not acquainted with Palestinian culture. Thus, in terms of historical development, we can begin easily enough with Matthew and go on to Luke and/or Mark. But historically speaking, it is difficult to reverse the process and to place Matthew after either one or both of the others.[25]

The above is not presented to denigrate in any way the Two-Document Hypothesis as a heuristic device, but rather to suggest other alternatives.[26] It may well be that the Gospel of John, long believed to be the latest of the Gospels, took shape much earlier than we had supposed; perhaps, as some contend, it is the earliest! The discovery of the Dead Sea Scrolls has certainly shown the Gospel of John to be as "Jewish" in content as the other Gospels.[27]

Form Criticism

Form criticism is that science which attempts to identify the origins of literary materials in the Gospels. This method assumes that oral traditions in different *forms*—stories and sayings—were woven together by the Gospel writers to produce a more complete written tradition about Jesus and the events of his life.[28] According to Norman Perrin, some of the principles and presuppositions of the discipline are as follows:

> (1) The Gospels as we now have them are not single creations out of a whole cloth but consist of collections of material, the final selection and arrangement of which we owe to the evangelists [Gospel writers] themselves. Mark is here the primary influence; he created the literary form "Gospel" and Matthew and Luke both follow him and use his material.
>
> (2) The material now presented in the Gospels has a previous history of use in the church, largely a history of oral transmission. It circulated in the church in the form of individual units or small collections of related material and in this form it served definite functions in the life and worship of the church, in preaching and apologetic, in exhortation and instruction.

> (3) The smallest units of tradition, the individual story, saying, dialogue, etc., have definite forms which can be defined and studied. Each of these forms served a definite function in a concrete situation in the life of the early church. This situation is what is referred to as the *Sitz im Leben* ["setting in life" or "situation in life"] of the material.

In short, "the main purpose for the creation, the circulation, and the use of these forms was not to preserve the history of Jesus, but to strengthen the life of the church. Thus these forms reflect the concern of the church, and both the form and content have been influenced by the faith and theology of the church, as well as by her situation and practice."[29]

A serious student of the New Testament must feel some sense of gratitude for the focus which form criticism has given to the importance of oral transmission. There can be no doubt but that much good has come to the world as a result of a closer look at this almost neglected dimension of literary development. Acceptance of Christ and his gospel was accomplished first through the power of verbal human testimony. Much of the earliest scripture in the meridian dispensation (as perhaps in all dispensations) existed in an oral and unrecorded form.[30] The *kerygma* or proclamation of the gospel, the *logia* (sayings of Christ), and the *agrapha* (unwritten things) circulated as the witness of the Apostles spread from Jerusalem to the ends of the known world.

Though such form critics as Martin Dibelius and Rudolph Bultmann would suggest an evolutionary development in the Gospels from an oral stage to written document,[31] such need not to have been the case. Surely these oral testimonies spread at the same time that written documents were being prepared and circulated concerning the works and words of the Master.[32] In our own day genuine faith-promoting stories circulate in the Church orally at the same time that written accounts of the events are readily available. It does not require a severe stretch of the imagination to suppose that in the first-century Church written documents recounting many of the events of the life of Jesus were contemporaneous with the Saints' reminiscences and personal oral testimonies of the same. The manner in which oral traditions were valued is highlighted, for example, in a statement by Papias, bishop of Hierapolis in Asia Minor (ca. A.D. 130–140). "I will not hesitate to set down for you," he noted, "alongside my interpretations all that I ever learned well from the elders and remembered well, guaranteeing their truth. . . . If ever a person came my way who had been a companion of the elders, *I would inquire about the sayings of the elders*—what was said by Andrew, or by Peter, or by Philip, or by Thomas or James, or by John or Matthew or any other of the Lord's disciples." And then

Papias added: "For *I did not suppose that what I could get from books was of such great value to me as the utterances of a living and abiding voice.*"[33]

Not all biblical scholars are as enamored with form critical assumptions or methods as was once the case. That is, "one can be just as skeptical of form criticism as form criticism is of the Gospels," Richard L. Anderson observed. "Investigating how the Gospel accounts have changed begs the question of *whether* they have changed. The Gospels present parallel stories of Jesus' life with occasional contradictions in details, but each Gospel represents a rich supplement to the information on the life of Jesus available in any other Gospel." Further,

> Form criticism assumes a creativity on the part of the early Christian community different from the "continuity of revelation" creativity I [propose]; it is, instead, "invention" creativity—the assumption that the early Christian community adapted these stories to their preaching needs at any given time. . . .
>
> In my view, form criticism is . . . badly out-of-date in its assumption that there was a period of oral transmission of the stories of Jesus. The recovery of hundreds of fragments and of books from Qumran shows an intense religious creativity accompanied by an equally intense fanaticism for the writing of commentaries and handbooks of community living. The Qumran community is, of course, a slightly pre-Christian reformation movement of Judaism. Just the other side of the first century we have the letters of the apostolic fathers, the orthodox bishops of the early second century. We also have the fertile inventions of Gnostic dissidents which developed and continued a tradition from the same time period.
>
> We also have twenty-one letters of the New Testament, proving the capability and inevitability of writing output in the earliest Christian Church. With such impressive evidence of writing among Jewish reformists, orthodox Christians, and sectarian Christians, why should one assume a period of oral transmission divorced from the stability of written records?[34]

Martin Hengel has questioned the fundamental presupposition of form criticism—the circulation of individual units of Christian tradition prior to the writing of the documents.

> The idea cherished by form critics for decades, of individual traditions completely detached and in "free circulation" as isolated units, is just as unrealistic as the attempt to write a life of Jesus. It is based on a very schematic conception of oral tradition. The earliest stage was not the isolated individual tradition, but the elemental wealth of impressions called forth by the meteoric appearance of Jesus. Then, still during Jesus' life-time, there began a process of collection which at the same time meant selection and restriction. It should also be noted that in terms of antiquity the period of time between the start of the tradi-

> tion and the composition of our gospels was relatively short, and lasted only between thirty and sixty years. . . . There is also the fact that oral tradition in primitive Christianity was not at everyone's disposal in the same way; still less was it the result of the anonymous, creative productive force of some "Palestinian" or "Hellenistic" communities which cannot be defined more closely than that, and which shaped these traditions in accordance with their particular "needs." It is in fact amazing how few signs the synoptic gospels show of the "needs" of the communities as we know them from the letters of the New Testament. Often we are virtually forced to read these needs into the synoptic texts. . . . The basic stimulus towards the rise of the Jesus tradition was the man Jesus, in his proclamation, his behaviour and his actions. Anyone who posits a "community construction" must go on to give time, place, and reasons. However, in essentials we know far less about the "communities" which are said to have given rise to such traditions in an unbridled way than we do about Jesus himself. They often seem to be modern fabrications rather than historical realities.[35]

Form criticism, in the words of F. F. Bruce, has made a singular contribution: we now know "no matter how far back we may press our researches into the roots of the gospel story, no matter how we classify the gospel material, we never arrive at a non-supernatural Jesus."[36]

Redaction Criticism

Redaction criticism of the Gospels is a sub-discipline of biblical study which focuses attention upon the role of the Gospel writers as redactors or editors. In dealing with the Synoptic Gospels the redaction critic presupposes certain results from both source criticism (the Markan or Two-Document Hypothesis) and form criticism (the transmission of forms or units of tradition). This branch of study draws attention to the role of the Gospel writers in shaping and forming the Christian traditions into a document which would (1) meet the prevailing needs of the given Christian community; and (2) reflect the particular theological perspective of the Gospel writer. In regard to the latter function, Norman Perrin has written concerning the work of Matthew, Mark, and Luke in preparing the resurrection narratives: "The resurrection narratives are . . . literary expressions of the evangelists' understanding of what it means to say 'Jesus is risen.' They are narrative expressions of a distinctive theological viewpoint. . . . [The Gospel writer] intends to convince his readers that Jesus is the Messiah, that he is the Son of God, and that his life and fate have changed forever the possibilities for human life in the world. To this end he composes his narrative account of the sequence of events which began with the ministry of John the Baptist . . . and reached its climax in the women's discovery of the empty tomb." Perrin then makes this observation regarding the role of the Gospel writer: "He has taken traditional material circulating in the early Christian communities. . . . He has edited that material and composed it into a new whole—he may even have created some new narratives of his own on the basis of traditional sayings of Jesus and the interpretation of scripture—and everything that he has done, he has done in the service of his overriding conviction that he has a gospel to preach to his readers."[37]

There should be no doubt among Latter-day Saints that the canonical Gospels were compiled, composed, and written under the spirit of revelation. At the same time, we do not detract from the spiritual significance of the writers to suggest that Matthew, Mark, Luke, and John were also divinely directed *editors* as well as creative authors. Moses was a choice seer and a man open to the revelations of the Lord. He was also a gifted compiler and editor of earlier records.[38] Likewise, Mormon was an inspired author/editor whose "and thus we see" passages in the Nephite record help wondrously to demonstrate the wisdom of the ways of the Lord.

Like any other writer—inspired or uninspired—Matthew, Mark, Luke, and John had particular messages, styles, and points of view; a format characterizes their work which may be studied in light of some of their more evident literary characteristics. Their Gospels were certainly shaped by such factors as their own backgrounds and the intended audiences of the documents.[39] A recognition of these factors, however, need not lead us to interpretive extremes. Being a theologian does not preclude being a historian. "There is no reason . . . to suppose," writes one conservative scholar, "that theological interest must take precedence over historical validity." Further, "it is difficult to think of the narration of bare facts without some interpretation. But there is no reason to suppose that the interpretation made by each evangelist was his own creation."[40] Martin Hengel has suggested a much more reasonable setting and motivation for the preparation of the Gospels:

> When we inquire about the purposes of a New Testament author, we can never ignore the fact that such an author, who has a position within the Christian community and is at its service, does not seek primarily to display his theological individuality and originality, much less his rhetorical skill and historical learning. Keeping his own personality in the background, he works with existing traditions about the saving event which, while lying in the past, utterly governs the present of the community. Redaction-critical and structuralist approaches, so popular today, fail to do justice to this situation when in principle they ignore the question of the traditions standing behind the text and their historical basis, as being inessential and uninteresting. A text is never a completely isolated entity. We should therefore also guard against the temptation of a text fetishism. Precisely by isolating a "text in itself"

and giving it an absolute status, one ignores the historical reality which underlies it. Every text occurs in a particular "con-text" and as such serves to give an indication; it has the character of witness.[41]

Conclusion

There is much to be gained from a careful (critical) study of the Bible, and many of the approaches and findings of biblical critics should be of interest to Latter-day Saints who aspire to an understanding of the holy scriptures. Much of the research that has been done on the New Testament, for example, can be particularly valuable in understanding the formation, preservation, and inspiration surrounding the canonical Gospels. At the same time, Latter-day Saints would do well to ensure that theirs is a "critical" look at biblical critical presuppositions, methodologies, and conclusions; some things we simply need not swallow. A firm belief in prophecy, revelation, divine intervention, and absolute truths precludes an overwhelming and undiscriminating acceptance of many of the underlying principles of the science of biblical criticism.

"We have no right to take the theories of men," Elder Orson F. Whitney noted in 1915, "however scholarly, however learned, and set them up as a standard, and try to make the Gospel bow down to them; making of them an iron bedstead upon which God's truth, if not long enough, must be stretched out, or if too long, must be chopped off—anything to make it fit into the system of men's thoughts and theories! On the contrary," he instructed the Saints, "we should hold up the Gospel as the standard of truth, and measure thereby the theories and opinions of men."[42] What the world may view with an almost reverent attitude as established fact in these areas of study should be viewed by Latter-day Saints with an enlightened perspective—perspective informed by the supplementary and unique Latter-day Saint resources of additional scriptural records and living oracles—recognizing the approaches and conclusions of others as "scaffolding useful for research purposes,"[43] but centering one's full loyalty and trust in the modern prophetic word.

NOTES

1. G. E. Ladd, *The New Testament and Criticism* (Grand Rapids, Mich.: Eerdmans Publishing Co., 1966), p. 217.

2. *Our Bible and the Ancient Manuscripts* (New York: Harper & Brothers, 1958), p. 61.

3. *In Search of Truth: Comments on the Gospel and Modern Thought* (Salt Lake City: Deseret Book Co., 1963), pp. 81–82.

4. Kenyon, *Our Bible and the Ancient Manuscripts*, pp. 61–62.

5. For example, in the patristic period, Dionysius of Alexandria discussed the authorship of the book of Revelation; Abraham Ibn Ezra, a medieval Jewish commentator, doubted the Mosaic authorship of the Pentateuch; Martin Luther questioned the value of the epistle of James.

6. "The Historical and Literary Criticism of the New Testament," in *Biblical Criticism: Historical, Literary and Textual*, ed. R. K. Harrison, B. K. Waltke, D. Guthrie, and G. D. Fee (Grand Rapids, Mich.: Zondervan Publishing House, 1978), p. 87. An excellent study of all phases of New Testament biblical criticism is Raymond F. Collins, *Introduction to the New Testament* (New York: Doubleday & Co., 1983).

7. See, for example, C. H. Dodd, *The Interpretation of the Fourth Gospel* (Cambridge: Cambridge University Press, 1953); W. L. Knox, *Some Hellenistic Elements in Primitive Christianity* (Oxford: Oxford University Press, 1944); W. Schmithals, *Gnosticism in Corinth* (Nashville: Abingdon, 1971).

8. See Thomas Kuhn, *The Structure of Scientific Revolutions* (Chicago: University of Chicago Press, 1973); see also David Hackett Fischer, *Historians' Fallacies: Toward a Logic of Historical Thought* (New York: Harper & Row, 1970), ch. 6.

9. An illustration of this can be found in David R. Cartlidge and David L. Dungan, *Documents for the Study of the Gospels* (Philadelphia: Fortress Press, 1980).

10. See Robert L. Millet, "A Small Book that Spans Eternity," in *Studies in Scripture, Vol. 2: The Pearl of Great Price*, ed. Robert L. Millet and Kent P. Jackson (Sandy, UT.: Randall Book Co., 1985), pp. 6–8; Milton R. Hunter, *The Gospel Through the Ages* (Salt Lake City: Bookcraft, 1945).

11. This represents one of many possible answers to the question of cultural and religious similarities throughout world history. See Spencer J. Palmer, "Mormon Views of Religious Resemblances," *Brigham Young University Studies*, Vol. 16, No. 4 (Summer 1976), pp. 660–81; see also Milton R. Hunter, *The Gospel Through the Ages*, p. 40; Hugh Nibley, *The World and the Prophets* (Salt Lake City: Deseret Book Co., 1974), pp. 213–15. Many non-Latter-day Saint scholars are aware of underlying similarities in religious beliefs and practice from all over the world, and are sometimes at a loss to explain them.

12. Joseph Smith taught a similar doctrine in the School of the Prophets. See *Lectures on Faith* 3:4; 4:1.

13. John Warwick Montgomery, *History and Christianity* (San Bernardino, CA.: Here's Life Publishers, 1983), pp. 107–8, italics added. See also F. F. Bruce, *The New Testament Documents: Are They Reliable?* (Grand Rapids, Mich.: Eerdmans, 1974), pp. 7–9.

14. For an excellent summary of the causes of error in the transmission of texts, see Bruce M. Metzger, *The Text of the New Testament* (New York: Oxford University Press, 1969), pp. 186–206.

15. Gordon D. Fee, "The Textual Criticism of the New Testament," in Harrison et. al., *Biblical Criticism*, p. 127.

16. Metzger, *The Text of the New Testament*, p. 156.

17. See a brief article by E. J. Epp in *The Interpreter's Dictionary of the Bible*, 4 vols. plus supplementary volume (Nashville: Abingdon, 1976), Supplementary Volume, pp. 891–95.

18. Kenyon, *Our Bible and the Ancient Manuscripts*, p. 53.

19. "The Book of Mormon as a Co-Witness with the Bible and as a Guide to Biblical Criticism," *Sixth Annual Church Educational System Religious Educators' Symposium—the Book of Mormon* (Salt Lake City: The Church of Jesus Christ of Latter-day Saints, 1982), pp. 56–57. Bruce Metzger has written: "The manuscripts of the New Testament preserve traces of two kinds of dogmatic alterations: those which involve the elimination or alteration of what was regarded as doctrinally unacceptable or inconvenient, and those which introduce into the Scriptures 'proof' for a favourite theological tenet or practice." (*The Text of the New Testament*, p. 201.)

20. These figures are found in F. F. Bruce, *The New Testament Documents: Are They Reliable?*, p. 31.

21. For excellent treatments of the dating, formation, and areas of stress of the Gospels of Mark and Luke, see S. Kent Brown, "The Testimony of Mark," in *Studies in Scripture, Vol. 5: The Gospels*, ed. Kent P. Jackson and Robert L. Millet (Salt Lake City: Deseret Book Co., 1986), pp. 61–87; Richard Lloyd Anderson, "The Testimony of Luke," in *ibid.*, pp. 88–108.

22. See *The Nag Hammadi Library*, ed. James M. Robinson (New York: Harper & Row, 1977), pp. 117–30; F. F. Bruce, *Jesus and Christian Origins Outside the New Testament* (Grand Rapids, Mich.: Eerdmans, 1974), pp. 110–56.

23. For further possibilities concerning the Gospel of Thomas, see S. Kent Brown, "The Nag Hammadi Library: A Mormon Perspective," in *Apocryphal Writings and the Latter-day Saints*, ed. C. Wilfred Griggs (Provo, UT.: Religious Studies Center, Brigham Young University, 1986), pp. 260, 275 (n. 37).

24. See C. S. Mann, "Synoptic Relationships and the Supposed Priority of Mark," in *Mark*, vol. 27 in the Anchor Bible series (New York: Doubleday, 1986), pp. 47–66.

25. William R. Farmer, *Jesus and the Gospel* (Philadelphia: Fortress Press, 1982), pp. 3–7.

26. Two scholars have also been critical of the notion of a single sayings source. "It is not in the least necessary, we think, to suppose that there was a *single* block of material on which both Matthew and Luke drew. The vitality of oral tradition, the varying emphases cherished by various groups in the early Church, the care that was taken (to which the Johannine letters bear witness) to ascertain from reliable sources precisely what did happen in the public and private ministry of Jesus, the urgent need felt to preserve Christ's teachings in writing in the face of the difficult times—all these will have led to more than one tentative collection of oral material." Further, they contend that "it is far simpler to suppose that both Matthew and Luke used their own sources than to assume that one evangelist saw the other's work and proceeded to some radical editorial revision." (From W. F. Albright and C. S. Mann, *Matthew*, volume 26 in the Anchor Bible series [New York: Doubleday, 1971], "Introduction," pp. xivii, li.

27. See the comments of Frank M. Cross, Jr. in *The Ancient Library of Qumran and Modern Biblical Studies* (Grand Rapids, Mich.: Baker Book House, 1980), pp. 215–16, regarding the relationship of pre-Christian (Essene) motifs of light and darkness and the same elements in John's Gospel. One of

the more interesting (yet controversial) books published in some time is John A. T. Robinson, *Redating the New Testament* (Philadelphia: Westminster Press, 1976). Robinson challenges the traditional scholarship which places much of the New Testament in the late first century-early second century A.D. He proposes that the evidence (internal and external) suggests that all New Testament records could very well have been written by A.D. 70.

28. See Edgar V. McKnight, *What Is Form Criticism?* (Philadelphia: Fortress Press, 1969) for a brief treatment of the subject.

29. Norman Perrin, *What Is Redaction Criticism?* (Philadelphia: Fortress Press, 1969), pp. 15–16. A typical example of a form critical study is Arland J. Hultgren, *Jesus and His Adversaries* (Minneapolis: Augsburg Publishing House, 1979).

30. See Bruce R. McConkie, *Doctrinal New Testament Commentary*, 3 vols. (Salt Lake City: Bookcraft Publishers, 1965–73), 1:55–56.

31. See, for example, Dibelius, *From Tradition to Gospel* (New York: Scribners, 1933) and Bultmann, *History of the Synoptic Tradition* (New York: Harper & Row, 1963).

32. See Birger Gerhardsson, *The Origins of the Gospel Traditions* (Philadelphia: Fortress Press, 1979); Werner H. Kelber, *The Oral and the Written Gospel* (Philadelphia: Fortress Press, 1983).

33. From "Fragments of Papias," in *The Ante-Nicene Fathers*, 10 vols., eds. Alexander Roberts and James Donaldson (Grand Rapids, Mich.: Eerdmans Publishing Co., 1981), 1:153; italics added.

34. "Types of Christian Revelation," in *Literature of Belief: Sacred Scripture and Religious Experience*, ed. Neal E. Lambert (Provo, UT.: Religious Studies Center, Brigham Young University, 1981), pp. 63–64.

35. *Acts and the History of Earliest Christianity* (Philadelphia: Fortress Press, 1980), pp. 25–26. Another branch of New Testament biblical criticism which has just begun to surface in recent years is known as Canonical Criticism. Its major proponent, Brevard S. Childs of the Yale University Divinity School, contends that form criticism has failed to give adequate attention to the manner in which the earliest Christian documents were transmitted as a package, as canonical materials. See his *The New Testament as Canon: An Introduction* (Philadelphia: Fortress Press, 1985).

36. *The New Testament Documents: Are They Reliable?*, p. 33.

37. *The Resurrection According to Matthew, Mark, and Luke* (Philadelphia: Fortress Press, 1977), pp. 3–5. This book is a redaction critical study of the resurrection narratives. For another example, see Reginald H. Fuller, *The Formation of the Resurrection Narratives* (Philadelphia: Fortress Press, 1980).

38. See *A New Witness for the Articles of Faith* (Salt Lake City: Deseret Book Co., 1985), p. 402; cf. also the words of Spencer W. Kimball in *President Kimball Speaks Out* (Salt Lake City: Deseret Book Co., 1981), pp. 55–56.

39. See Robert L. Millet, "As Delivered from the Beginning: The Formation of the Canonical Gospels," in *Apocryphal Writings and the Latter-day Saints*, pp. 199–213; "The JST and the Synoptic Gospels: Literary Style," in *The Joseph Smith Translation: The Restoration of Plain and Precious Things*, eds. Monte S. Nyman and Robert L. Millet (Provo, UT.: Religious Studies Center, Brigham Young University, 1985), pp. 147–62.

40. Guthrie, "The Historical and Literary Criticism of the New Testament," pp. 107–8.

41. *Acts and the History of Earliest Christianity*, pp. 56–57.

42. Conference Report, April 1915, p. 100.

43. Joseph F. Smith, *Gospel Doctrine* (Salt Lake City: Deseret Book Co., 1986), p. 38.

The True Mormon Intellectuals 12

S. Michael Wilcox

First of all, let me say that I do not want to offend. I do not want to write with a spirit of contention or confrontation. I wish to edify and to clarify. I will try to do this as honestly and pointedly as I can.

I have heard the phrase "Mormon intellectual" used frequently in the last decade. It is often used by those who set themselves a bit apart from the rest of the membership of the Church by reason of their educational skills or learning. It is a term they have applied to themselves. There is often a spirit of criticism that pervades their writing. They often point out what they consider to be flaws in the doctrines, history, or practices of the Church; and the General Authorities frequently become the targets of their criticism. At times they display an attitude of desiring to correct or update or improve the philosophy, doctrine, or practices of the Church. They have their own voices, outlets, and sounding boards. They are often the center of controversy. They believe they are misunderstood and question whether it is possible to remain loyal to the Church and to scholarship at the same time. As Elder Boyd K. Packer intimated on one occasion, their position often seems to be, "The gospel is true;

S. Michael Wilcox is Assistant Professor of Ancient Scripture at Brigham Young University.

however . . ." instead of, "The gospel is true; *therefore*." When stating their position for freedom of thought over trust in prophets, some often play children's games, overdramatizing their perceived conflict by references to "crimes of obedience" like those of Dachau or My Lai, or to the surrender of conscience in the face of authoritarianism.

These skeptics are eloquent, scholarly, and diligent in the pursuit of learning. However, though they may not always mean to, they frequently sow seeds of doubt and skepticism among the uninformed. I have more than once seen them damage and sometimes destroy the tiny testimonies of newborn Saints. They are not a product of the modern world, but have existed at all periods of the earth's history.

I am writing this to those who are troubled by, attracted to, confronted with, or uneasy about the writings and lectures of self-named "intellectuals." I would like the reader to understand one truth—God's definition of intelligence, inasmuch as we can comprehend his definition. Once in possession of this principle, we will know where to find the "true Mormon intellectual." (I am afraid, however, that the true intellectuals I refer to would never choose this title to apply to themselves.)

A More Refined Definition of Intelligence

It is important that we understand God's definition of intelligence. I perceive that our modern "debunking" intellectuals want to give the impression that they have intelligence and that an attack against them is an affront to intelligence and scholarship. However, I believe that our modern "intellectuals" are not distinguished by any unusual ability in finding and exhibiting truth. On the contrary, in many ways they are further away from true intelligence than the vast majority of ordinary, faithful members of the kingdom.

I realize that my definition of intelligence will not match the definitions of men, of universities, or of scholarly journals. As Latter-day Saints, however, we are not as interested in men's philosophies as in God's eternal truths. Everything that is not eternal will one day be a mere memory of the past. It is the eternal that is always vital and pertinent.

Let us now go to the scriptures and seek understanding so that we will not be misled. When we try to define true intelligence from that source, we are immediately confronted with a number of words and concepts. Let's start with a most familiar scripture: "The glory of God is intelligence, or, in other words, light and truth. Light and truth forsake that evil one." (D&C 93:36–37.)

Intelligence is here equated with "light," "truth," and the "glory of God." We also learn that intelligence forsakes evil. Already we can see that intelligence is more than the accumulation of facts, degrees, or the reading of the "right books." This is important to understand, for Paul prophesied that in the last days men would be "ever learning, and never able to come to the knowledge of the truth" (2 Timothy 3:7). Learning and intelligence may not always mean the same thing, and obviously in the last days they will become confused with each other. It is truth in its highest definition that we are seeking.

A deeper study of the Doctrine and Covenants reveals more of the Lord's synonyms for intelligence: "For the word of the Lord is truth, and whatsoever is truth is light, and whatsoever is light is Spirit, even the Spirit of Jesus Christ" (D&C 84:45). Intelligence is thus associated with the Spirit, "even the Spirit of Jesus Christ." In section 88, verse 66, similar equations are made: "My voice is Spirit; my Spirit is truth; truth abideth and hath no end; and if it be in you it shall abound."

I realize these quotations do not critically define intelligence, but for me these additional descriptions help to formulate an idea of what the Lord means by the word. It is more than learning. It is truth, light, and spirit. It is deeply associated with the Lord Jesus Christ.

Keys to Receiving Intelligence

The key factors in receiving and maintaining true intelligence are given in those same sections of the Doctrine and Covenants that deal with light and truth: section 84, verse 46, teaches that "the Spirit enlighteneth every man . . . that hearkeneth to the voice of the Spirit." In other words, a person receives more light and truth as he obeys the light he has been given. Section 88, verse 67, teaches a similar truth: "And if your eye be single to my glory, your whole bodies shall be filled with light, and there shall be no darkness in you; and that body which is filled with light comprehendeth all things." Here we see that directing one's whole being toward God's "glory" will result in additional light and truth. An individual can be filled with "intelligence." Verse 68 continues with this line of reasoning and contains instruction on how to achieve a singleness of mind to the glory of God: "Therefore, sanctify yourselves that your minds become single to God."

Thus we see that the sanctification of the individual results in the blessing of light and truth. That sanctifying process, we know from the testimony of the scriptures, is contingent upon a person's acceptance of the atonement of Christ through repentance and baptism and the reception of the Holy Ghost. The Holy Ghost then continues to purify and teach an individual until he becomes Christlike.

Continuing in the Doctrine and Covenants, we read: "He that keepeth his commandments receiveth truth and light, until he is glorified in truth and knoweth all things" (D&C 93:28). Apparently obedience to the commandments is directly linked to the reception of true intelligence. That obedience becomes a sanctifying power that enables one to receive more and more intelligence. By contrast, Doctrine and Covenants 93:39 teaches that intelligence can be lost "through disobedience." This teaching is repeated in section 1: "He that repents not, from him shall be taken even the light which he has received" (D&C 1:33). This is taught as well by the Prophet Joseph Smith: "As far as we degenerate from God, we descend to the devil and lose knowledge."[1]

One more section of the Doctrine and Covenants should solidify our point and allow us to make some summarizing conclusions before proceeding.

> And that which doth not edify is not of God, and is darkness.
>
> That which is of God is light; and he that receiveth light, and *continueth in God, receiveth more light*; and that light groweth brighter and brighter until the perfect day.
>
> . . . And I say it that you may know the truth, that you may chase darkness from among you. (D&C 50:23–25; italics added.)

The key to receiving more light is an individual's "continuing in God." Once again, obedience is the key factor. There is a consistency throughout all the scriptures. The twelfth chapter of Alma in the Book of Mormon teaches these same truths. We have also received the knowledge in sections 50 and 93 of the Doctrine and Covenants that intelligence edifies and "chases" darkness away. If learning does not edify, it is "not of God."

Section 50 contains an additional insight about intelligence and truth: we can learn something about the atmosphere in which truth is taught when it comes from God. Truth taught in this proper atmosphere, attitude, or spirit, can be trusted and adhered to: "Verily I say unto you, he that is ordained of me and sent forth to preach the word of truth by the Comforter, in the Spirit of truth, doth he preach it by the Spirit of truth or some other way? And if it be by some other way *it is not of God*." (D&C 50:17–18; italics added.)

So it is not enough just to speak or teach the truth in itself. One must teach "by the Comforter" in a proper spirit. If anyone attempts to teach truth in any other way, the scriptures plainly indicate that "it is not of God." The Lord explains this to his Church in order for its members to know how to "chase darkness from among you" (D&C 50:25).

One may ask: How do I know if a teacher is teaching truth by the Comforter? The answer given in scripture is plain and should put to rest—for all who seek rest—the frequently debated topic of which utterances of General Authorities to accept as "scripture" (as it is defined in D&C 68:3–4), as opposed to those which represent private views. As a receiver of intelligence I have as much responsibility to listen "by the Comforter" as the teacher does to preach "by the Comforter": "And again, he that receiveth the word of truth, doth he receive it by the Spirit of truth or some other way? If it be some other way it is not of God." (D&C 50:19–20.)

As if to emphasize the simplicity of God's method of transmitting true intelligence, the next verse states: "Why is it that ye cannot understand and know, that he that receiveth the word by the Spirit of truth receiveth it as it is preached by the Spirit of truth? Wherefore, he that preacheth and he that receiveth, understand one another, and both are edified and rejoice together."

Our problem may lie in our inability to truly listen by the Holy Ghost, not in the Apostles and prophets' inability to teach by the Holy Ghost. The responsibility for cultivating the Spirit is ours: when we accept that responsibility and learn to listen with the Holy Ghost, we will "rejoice together" with our teachers and prophets. In the meantime let us not be guilty of pointing accusatory fingers; rather let us ask ourselves, as the Apostles once did, "Lord, is it I?"

Let us summarize what the scriptures teach. First, true intelligence is inextricably intertwined with light, truth, glory, the Spirit, and the voice of Jesus Christ. Second, intelligence forsakes evil, chases darkness, and always edifies. Third, the key to receiving intelligence and maintaining it is obeying the commandments, hearkening to the voice of the Spirit, continuing in God, sanctifying oneself, and having an eye "single" to God's glory. Fourth, intelligence may be lost through disobedience. Fifth, intelligence and truth, when of God, are always taught by the power of the Holy Ghost. Sixth, all members of the Church have the right and responsibility to receive truth by the Holy Ghost. A true Mormon intellectual's life, teachings, writings, and attitudes will reflect all of the above truths. If we link the above principles with the frequent scriptural condemnation associated with the spirit of contention, confrontation, and criticism, particularly when directed at the Lord's servants, we will be well on our way to new understanding and awareness.

The Light of the World or the *Light* of the World?

Many self-proclaimed intellectuals may disagree with this scriptural emphasis. They may retreat into a more worldly application of the term *intellectual*, claiming the right to examine the principles of the gospel only under a worldly light. They may feel restricted by the scriptural definition and choose to apply it to religious matters only.

If we are lecturing on, or writing about, or postulating on the dialogues of Plato, for instance, or the historical veracity of Plutarch's Lives, or the literary merits of Boswell, or the moral implications of Machiavelli, our leanings to the worldly definition of intellectualism and scholarship might be appropriate. But when we discuss or criticize the principles of light and truth revealed through the medium of the Lord's appointed prophets, we have entered another domain, and the Lord's emphasis must be the standard as we look for guidance. If we do not observe that standard, we will find ourselves in the position of a finite, limited, and often nearsighted world—judging, commenting on, and counseling an infinite, unlimited, and foresighted Deity. The foolishness of such a position is evident. What should we think of a man who counsels God and then is angry when the Lord does not take his advice? Though I respect the learning of these intellectuals and the rigors of their educational encounter, I do not equally respect their judgment. After all, does the learning of our specialized, much-acclaimed intellectuals really have anything to do with understanding the restoration of the gospel of Jesus Christ, the most important event in the history of the world next to the life and atonement of the Savior? Do all their meritorious labors with scholarship really give them any insight into the mind of a prophet like Joseph Smith, who once said: "It is my meditation all the day, and more than my meat and drink, to know how I shall make the Saints of God comprehend the visions that roll like an overflowing surge before my mind."[2] Has their commitment to the temples of modern and ancient learning really given them insight into the commitment evident in the testimony of an Apostle like Elder Boyd K. Packer, who stated:

> I also have come to know the power of truth and of righteousness and of good, and I want to be good. I'm not ashamed to say that—I want to be good. And I've found in my life that it has been critically important that this was established between me and the Lord so that I knew that He knew which way I had committed my agency. I went before Him and in essence said, 'I'm not neutral, and You can do with me what You want. If You need my vote, it's there. I don't care what You do with me, and You don't have to take anything from me because I give it to You—everything, all I own, all I am.' *And that makes the difference.*[3]

Does their undoubted ability to read the lines of scholarly thinking, no matter how great it is, in truth give them the depth necessary to read *between* the lines of the sermons and publications of a General Authority like B. H. Roberts, who wrote near the end of his life:

> In the truth of principles we have received from God we are strong; not so much, either, because of the little truth that has been revealed to us; the little knowledge to which we have attained, but more because of the great ocean of knowledge that we have access to, through one of the great principles we announce as a doctrine to the world, *namely: revelation*. Through the acceptance of that doctrine we have access to God's hidden treasure of knowledge; *which, in comparison to that which men in this world have received, is as some mighty ocean to a lakelet.*[4]

The True Intellectuals

In case the above descriptions and testimonies have not clearly exemplified the true Mormon intellectuals, the Lord plainly describes them in the Pearl of Great Price. The following quotation is rather lengthy, but I believe pertinent and necessary for total understanding:

> And the Lord said unto me: These two facts do exist, that *there are two spirits, one being more intelligent than the other; there shall be another more intelligent than they*; I am the Lord thy God, *I am more intelligent than they all*. . . .
>
> I dwell in the midst of them all; I now, therefore, have come down unto thee to declare unto thee the works which my hands have made, *wherein my wisdom excelleth them all*, for *I rule* in the heavens above, and in the earth beneath, *in all wisdom and prudence, over all the intelligences* thine eyes have seen from the beginning; I came down in the beginning in the midst of all the intelligences thou hast seen.
>
> Now the Lord had shown unto me, Abraham, *the intelligences* that were organized before the world was; and among all these *there were many of the noble and great ones*;
>
> And God saw these souls that *they were good*, and he stood in the midst of them, and he said: These I *will make my rulers*; for he stood among those that were spirits, and he saw that they were good; and he said unto me: *Abraham, thou art one of them*; thou wast chosen before thou wast born.
>
> And *there stood one* among them that was *like unto God*, and he said unto those who were with him: We will go down, for there is space there, and we will take of these materials, and we will make an earth whereon these may dwell;
>
> And *we will prove them herewith, to see if they will do all things whatsoever the Lord their God shall command them*. (Abraham 3:19, 21–25; italics added.)

From these verses we learn a number of things. First: God is more intelligent than man. His wisdom "excelleth them all." Second: Christ is "like unto God." Third: There are different degrees of intelligence among the Father's children. Fourth: The noble and great intelligences were designated by God to be "rulers," or prophets and Apostles on the earth, to convey (if we study all of Abraham 3) light, truth, and order to the lesser intelligences. These noble and great ones were to receive light and intelligence from Christ because he was "like unto God." Fifth: The purpose of the earth's existence will be to see if the intelligences can "prove" themselves by obedience to God. In order to do this the lesser intelligences must recognize superior intelligence—certainly that of God and Christ, but also that of the noble and great prophets and Apostles foreordained to be "rulers" on earth.

I don't know how the Lord could make the issue of intelligence any clearer. By his definition, the noble and great ones—the prophets and Apostles—are the true "intellectuals" of the earth. To find them I need only look to the First Presidency or the Quorum of the Twelve Apostles. These men are not infallible; they have never claimed to be; but a wise man will recognize their advanced state of intelligence and think long and hard before choosing to ignore or rebel against their counsel.

The Foolishness of Men—Modern and Ancient

It seems clear that a person of intelligence is distinguished in part by his or her ability to recognize a being or person of superior intelligence. This is crucial. Without that ability we can never learn; we will be unteachable. One who cannot recognize superior intelligence is a person to be pitied, not feared, for either he is too proud to defer to higher intelligence or else he is too foolish to see what is obvious to a person of real vision. And though he may be clever or eloquent or sophisticated in his criticism, ought we not to recognize his wisdom for what it truly is? Did not Paul teach the Corinthians: "I will destroy the wisdom of the wise, and will bring to nothing the understanding of the prudent. Where is the wise? . . . where is the disputer of this world? hath not God made foolish the wisdom of this world?" (1 Corinthians 1:19–20.)

Paul was referring to the affirmation of the Lord in Isaiah: "I am the Lord that maketh all things . . . that turneth wise men backward, and maketh their knowledge *foolish*; that *confirmeth the word of his servant, and performeth the counsel of his messengers*" (Isaiah 44:24–26; italics added).

As we said at the beginning of this chapter, self-proclaimed intellectuals are not a new phenomenon. They have always existed. They criticized, sought to instruct, and confronted the ancient prophets and Apostles. They are as perennial as a winter storm. They destroyed or weakened the faith of earlier Saints.

A few examples may be instructive. Paul reminded the Corinthian Saints about the difference between the power of truth and intelligence as it was taught in the spirit of men's wisdom and the intelligence of God taught in the spirit of His wisdom.

> And my speech and my preaching was not with enticing words of man's wisdom, but in *demonstration of the Spirit* and of power:
>
> That your faith should not stand in the wisdom of men, but in the power of God. . . .
>
> But the natural man receiveth not the things of the Spirit of God: for they are *foolishness* unto him: neither can he know them, because they are spiritually discerned. . . .
>
> Let no man deceive himself. If any man among you seemeth to be wise in this world, let him become a fool, that he may be wise.
>
> For the wisdom of this world is *foolishness* with God. (1 Corinthians 2:4–5, 14; 3:18–19; italics added.)

In his second epistle to the Corinthians Paul once again alluded to the self-proclaimed "wise" men of the ancient Church: "For we dare not make ourselves of the number, or compare ourselves with some that commend themselves: but they measuring themselves by themselves, and comparing themselves among themselves, are not wise. . . . For not he that commendeth himself is approved, but whom the Lord commendeth." (2 Corinthians 10:12, 18.)

Paul warned Titus of those who concentrated on the negative, those who strained at the gnats of doctrine or history while ignoring the camels of truth and righteousness that stood right in front of them. They were seeking those things "that turn from the truth."

> Unto the pure all things are pure: but unto them that are defiled and unbelieving is nothing pure; but even their mind and conscience is defiled.
>
> They profess that they know God; but in works they deny him. . . .
>
> But avoid foolish questions . . . and contentions, and strivings about the law; for they are unprofitable and vain. (Titus 1:15–16; 3:9.)

Peter also spoke of the false intellectuals of his time and the damage they did to those who heard them and allowed themselves to be deceived by their "wisdom."

> Presumptuous are they, selfwilled, they are not afraid to speak evil of dignities. . . .
>
> . . . These . . . speak evil of the things that they understand not; and shall utterly perish in their own corruption. . . .
>
> . . . Spots they are and blemishes, sporting themselves with their own deceivings while they feast with you. . . . Beguiling unstable souls. . . . These are wells without water. . . . They speak great swelling words of vanity. (2 Peter 2:10–18.)

The Assurance of Pure Intelligence

I state this clearly, leaving no room for doubt: I stand on the side of the true intellectuals, the Apostles and prophets. Perhaps some would accuse me of blind obedience. We do not believe in blind obedience in this Church, but we believe in trust, a trust that is born when one recognizes the intelligence of the "noble and great ones." Trust has a clearer and truer focus and vision than ordinary perception. It looks beyond the present and tries to see as Deity does. I will always try to be loyal to the true intellectual because of trust, not blind obedience. Let me explain why. This will not be a very scholarly explanation, but it will be an "intelligent" one. I am an employee of the Church Educational System, and some people say to me: "Oh, you have to feel about the General Authorities and the Church the way you do. You work for them, whereas I can do some independent thinking. You're too much of a Mormon to look objectively and honestly." When I hear that suggestion I am reminded of the opening paragraph of the *Histories* of Tacitus. He faced a similar dilemma: "But while we instinctively shrink from a writer's adulation, we lend a ready ear to detraction and spite, because flattery involves the shameful imputation of servility, *whereas malignity wears the false appearance of honesty*."[5]

I have had three personal encounters with General Authorities. When I was a deacon my mother told me Elder William J. Critchlow was coming to stake conference to speak. I lived in southern California. I remember that stake conference. We were late. We sat on the stage far from the podium. I could not see the speakers. When Elder Critchlow stood to speak I wanted to see him. My mother told me to take a folding chair and carry it up the aisle, place it in front of the podium, and listen to "one of God's servants." I did so. As I think back on it, it must have looked rather strange to Brother Critchlow and the audience. There was a twelve-year-old boy in the middle of the aisle, staring straight up at the podium. I don't remember much of what he said, but a spirit settled over me as he talked, a spirit that whispered, "This man is a man of God. You may believe him." When he was finished he came up to me and laid his hand on my shoulder; I felt the assurance of pure intelligence.

As a nineteen-year-old missionary in Lyon, France, I was told that Elder Boyd K. Packer was coming to a zone conference. All the missionaries were waiting in the meetinghouse for him. I was conversing with my companion with my back to the door when Elder Packer entered. Without seeing him, I felt him enter the room. I felt the influence of pure testimony and pure intelligence as it came from him. I knew that he was a chosen servant of God, "a noble and great one.'' He shook my hand and I felt the same assurance I did as a boy staring up at the pulpit during stake conference. It wouldn't have mattered which Apostle came into the room: the feeling would have been the same.

As a prospective seminary teacher, I was once interviewed by Elder LeGrand Richards. After he had asked a number of questions, he leaned back in his chair, studied me for a few moments and asked, ''Brother Wilcox, do you believe that Jesus was the living Son of God; that he lived and died to bring the Atonement and the Resurrection? Do you love the Savior? Is your heart and your mind sure that he is the Christ?''

I said, ''Yes, sir, I do believe and I am sure.''

He waited a moment or two, then smiled warmly with genuine delight and said, ''Isn't that wonderful! I do too.'' Then his smile turned and he was serious again. ''Do you believe,'' he questioned, ''that Joseph Smith was a living prophet of God? Do you believe he talked to the Father and Son in the Sacred Grove, that the angel Moroni visited him and gave him the plates from which he translated the Book of Mormon? And do you believe that book is the living word of truth and righteousness?''

He waited and listened while I said, ''Yes sir, I know that all that you have spoken is true.''

He studied me seriously, broke into his warm and welcoming smile, and said, ''Isn't that wonderful! Wonderful! I do too!'' Once more he turned serious and questioned, ''Do you believe this Church is directed by living prophets and Apostles who are guided by Christ, whose church this is? Do you accept their words and do you sustain with all your heart the Brethren who lead the Church? Do you believe in modern revelation?''

''Yes sir, I do,'' I answered.

Once again came the pause and then the smile. ''Isn't that wonderful! Wonderful! I do too.'' As he spoke, the assurance returned—the feeling of pure intelligence. That assurance has returned again and again. It comes with searching the scriptures. It comes with every general conference. It comes when I hear the humble testimonies of countless ordinary Saints as they speak of what they know. It may not be scholarly and it isn't conventionally intellectual. It is light and truth and spirit—the spirit of pure intelligence.

I left Elder Richards's office knowing that he knew and that I knew. I also knew that the Brethren have the full confidence of the Lord and, knowing that, I give them my undivided confidence and obedience—not in blindness but in sight that sees beyond earthly doubts or worldly inconsistencies.

Stumbling Blocks or Building Stones?

I believe there does not have to be a controversy or a dispute between scholarship and loyalty to the Church, between trust and independent thinking. The scriptures are plain. They demand of each individual a service and love for God "with all your mind." The Lord expects from us the best of all our abilities, including our intellects. This is a thinking man's religion and it can stand the most strenuous tests without faltering, but nothing of quality, truth, and goodness will ever be seen as pure through the eyes of those who strain at gnats in the darkness, ignoring the light in a spirit of self-proclaimed intellectualism. Within the framework of true intelligence let us seek unity and not disharmony, for the kingdom of God will always need the best minds and the best hearts. I believe that the spirit we all ought to exhibit, whether we are scholars or not, is that which was manifested by Paul in his letters to the Corinthians and to the Romans. During his time one dispute in particular centered around the eating of meat offered to idols. This is Paul's counsel to those who wish to make issues or sow the seeds of doubt when trust, unity, charity, faith, and selflessness are needed. To all members of the Church in every dispensation, Paul counsels:

> But *take heed lest by any means this liberty of yours become a stumblingblock to them that are weak. . . .*
>
> And through thy knowledge shall the weak brother perish, for whom Christ died?
>
> But *when ye sin so against the brethren*, and wound their weak conscience, *ye sin against Christ.*
>
> Wherefore, if meat make my brother to offend, I will eat no flesh while the world standeth, lest I make my brother to offend. (1 Corinthians 8:9, 11–13; italics added.)

And to the Romans he wrote:

> Him that is weak in the faith receive ye, but not to doubtful disputations. . . .
>
> For none of us liveth to himself, and no man dieth to himself. . . .
>
> But why dost thou judge thy brother? or why dost thou set at nought thy brother? for we shall all stand before the judgment seat of Christ.
>
> So then every one of us shall give account of himself to God.
>
> *Let us not therefore judge one another any more: but judge this rather, that no man put a stumblingblock or an occasion to fall in his brother's way. . . .*
>
> But if thy brother be grieved with thy meat, thou walkest not charitably if thou eatest. Therefore destroy not him with thy meat, for whom Christ died.
>
> *For the kingdom of God is not meat and drink; but righteousness, and peace, and joy in the Holy Ghost. . . .*

> *Let us therefore follow after the things which make for peace and things wherewith one may edify another. . . .*
>
> It is good neither to eat flesh, nor to drink wine, nor anything whereby thy brother stumbleth, or is offended, or is made weak. . . .
>
> We then that are strong ought to bear the infirmities of the weak, *and not to please ourselves.*
>
> *Let every one of us please his neighbour for his good to edification.*
>
> *For even Christ pleased not himself.* (JST, Romans 14:1, 7, 10, 12–13, 15, 17, 19, 21; 15:1–3; italics added.)

I hope I have not broken the spirit of Paul's counsel in this article. I believe that this counsel of Paul is in accord with the spirit of the talks given over the last few years by General Authorities on this topic. Those who choose to take offense at those talks have failed to see in them this spirit of edification and charity for one's neighbor. There are too many beautiful things about the gospel and the Church that bring unity, peace, and edification to be spending so much energy worrying about Mormon "intellectualism" and its place in the kingdom. Let us focus on the true, the good, and the beautiful, for that is what the kingdom of God is all about.

NOTES

1. Joseph Fielding Smith, comp., *Teachings of the Prophet Joseph Smith* (Salt Lake City: Deseret Book Co., 1976), p. 217.
2. *Teachings of the Prophet Joseph Smith*, p. 296.
3. Boyd K. Packer, *That All May Be Edified* (Salt Lake City: Bookcraft, 1982), p. 272; italics added.
4. From Truman Madsen, *Defender of the Faith: The B. H. Roberts Story* (Salt Lake City: Bookcraft, 1980), p. 369; italics added.
5. Tacitus, *The Histories*, Robert M. Hutchens, ed., in *Great Books of the Western World*, 54 vols. (Chicago: Encyclopedia Britannica, Inc., 1952), 15:189; italics added.

Faith and History 13

Louis Midgley

In the midst of the recent flowering of scholarship on the Book of Mormon and on Mormon history generally, some of which is very good, a few Latter-day Saints are busy reinterpreting the generative texts and founding events of the Mormon past in secular or naturalistic terms. Such efforts have begun yielding revisionist accounts.

Revisionist History—Transformed Faith

Some of these interpretations may appear sophisticated because they make use of explanations borrowed from the social and behavioral sciences, or from secular and sectarian religious studies, though usually without an examination of the consequences of such an undertaking and sometimes with little awareness of the limitations of such speculation. It is, of course, possible to fashion explanations in such terms. When viewed from within the horizon of the dominant ideas of our age, essentially secular or naturalistic accounts may appear plausible; they may also jeopardize the

---

Louis Midgley is Professor of Political Science at Brigham Young University.

integrity of the faith, and they certainly attempt to alter both its form and content.

The way Mormon history is written must be of concern to the Saints; we must be especially concerned about revisionist interpretations of the Book of Mormon. The reason why is that the truth of the faith both involves and depends upon statements about the past. And the moral imagination of the Saints—our concept of who and what we are—depends upon an understanding of the Book of Mormon, as well as of the events surrounding its coming forth. Revisionist accounts, especially those grounded in naturalistic explanations of the generative texts and founding events, transform the faith by recasting it in ways that compete with its own internal content and norms. Of course, secular or naturalistic treatments of the Book of Mormon and the other revelations central to the Restoration may still preserve the language of the special revelations. This may be accomplished by the simple device of interpreting the revelations as expressions of sentiment, as metaphorical or mythical, as instances of nineteenth-century frontier fiction, and so forth. But these approaches also entail a radical shift in the understanding of what constitutes revelation, and that new understanding is borrowed from sources exterior to the Restoration itself. Why are these approaches mistaken?

Scripture as a Call to Remembrance

The Latter-day Saint scriptures—part of which purport to be extensive ancient histories—include a complex set of categories, norms, and descriptions that constitute a way of life. Those histories and doctrines work together to provide, among other things, powerful images of Zion and Babylon, of the pure in heart who constitute the covenant people of God, and of a dark world in rebellion against God. The most important elements in the Book of Mormon are clearly not the historical details, although the function of that text is to preserve and enlarge the memory of those who now receive it of the mighty deeds of God on behalf of the covenant people; its prophetic warnings often take the form of accounts of the consequences of the turning away from the covenant with God. Without the historical component, the teachings and core message lose their divine warrant as God's revelation and they also are thereby rendered doubtful.

The Book of Mormon is unusually self-conscious about records and their role in the preservation of the memory of concrete events in which God has acted for sinful man, of the works of darkness that betray the covenant God made with Lehi and others. To learn of these things—and thereby to come to know and remember the prophetic warnings and promises—facilitates making and renewing our own covenants with God; it also provides a means whereby we may remain true to our covenants. To understand what it means to be God's covenant people, we must have before us texts that set out the choice we have between two essentially different ways, as well as the consequences of such choices. We must not neglect those texts but must diligently seek the truths they contain. To the extent that the Saints disregard the terms of their covenant with God, especially as set forth in the Book of Mormon and the other revelations of the Restoration, they expose themselves to the darkness of the world, and also thereby place themselves under divine condemnation for such neglect and recalcitrance.

Even though the Saints find in the Book of Mormon an indication that God has moved to restore the gospel and also frequently express a fondness for the scriptures, the lack of a genuine exegetical tradition leaves us exposed and hence vulnerable to revisionist fads. When the Book of Mormon is seen as merely a sign of the Restoration, the Saints then tend to neglect the messages, the prophetic teachings and warnings of the book. And in addition to the neglect of the sacred texts, certain of the dominant ideas of our age are in competition with the categories and explanations set out in the scriptures. The Saints are not entirely immune to such explanations. Naturalistic treatments of the themes sacred to the memories and identity of the Saints, or revisionist explanations and interpretations of texts crucial to the restoration of the gospel, threaten to decoy the hearts and minds of the Saints from the saving substance of the gospel of Jesus Christ.

Jesus Christ: Reality or Myth?

We are disciples of Jesus Christ because we believe that Jesus is the Christ—a living, resurrected Son of God and not merely a moral emblem or symbol in what some have now even begun calling "the Mormon myth." That Jesus is the Christ entails a network of assertions about the past which form the precondition and ground for faith. These statements, which are clearly historical, provide the actual content of the beliefs out of which trust in God grows and upon which it rests. Hence the statement that Jesus is the Christ is, at least partly, a statement that involves history. And, for the statement to be true in any genuinely meaningful sense, it must report accurately the essentials of what truly happened. Faith is thus believing something definite as well as definitely believing something; it is not merely a sentiment, nor is it only a formula pointing to "concerns."

A trust in God that is ultimately fruitful and not futile depends upon there actually having been a Jesus of Nazareth who, among other things, offered the perfect sacrifice for sinful man, and who through the power of God was raised from the dead on the third day. The same Jesus eventually restored his gospel to Joseph Smith by making available to us, through him, the Book of Mormon, as well as the other special revelations. The hopes and expectations of the faithful would be in vain if certain crucial events were not part of the past. Such hopes, as well as the related historical claims upon which they are grounded, are necessarily problematic, since they involve logical relationships between faith and the historical grounds of faith, which include certain statements about the past. This fact explains why the prophetic claims have been doubted, questioned, and challenged in various ways, as well as believed and defended.

The Past and the Future: The Grounds for Hope

Challenges to the historical statements which form the ground and precondition for the belief that in Jesus of Nazareth our Heavenly Father provided for our release from both sin and death call faith into question and make it difficult for the gospel to flourish. A testimony that Jesus is the Christ rests on the work within us of the Spirit, which imparts a witness that certain things are true about God's mighty acts in the past and also provides a hope for the future. A testimony is thus a witness or evidence of something; it must have a referent and content involving, among other things, the past; it is therefore at least partly concerned with the past. In that sense, a testimony is historical, or has historical content, even though it is not merely an inference from currently available historical materials, nor does it depend upon fashionable historical interpretations.

Flowing as it does from the crucial founding experiences of the restoration of the gospel of Jesus Christ, the Book of Mormon claims to be an authentic ancient history. The Saints commonly speak of a testimony of the truthfulness of the Book of Mormon. The witness of the Spirit that the fulness of the gospel of Jesus Christ is to be found in the Book of Mormon involves the truth of its message with the account it contains of a certain past. In addition, the account of its coming forth is in the realm of history. The story told by Joseph Smith of his having been the recipient of special revelations that provided him with access to authentic histories of God's dealings with his people also constitutes a historical framework that is itself part of the precondition and ground of faith for the genuine Latter-day Saint. The resulting network of historical statements provides not only a means for addressing the past but also a measure of confidence in a future embracing the works and plans of Deity. Whatever hope the Saints have for a future free from sin and beyond the grave requires that some things about the past are simply true; otherwise our faith is in vain, whatever else might be said about it.

The Question of Historical Vulnerability

Since the Book of Mormon—as well as certain other textual vehicles through which the heavens have once again been opened—claims to be authentic ancient history, it follows that the faith is necessarily exposed, at certain points, to disconfirmation by the work of historians. The Book of Mormon claims no immunity from historical criticism. But that kind of vulnerability seems to have led a few of the Saints, as it once did both Christian and Jewish theologians, to fashion ways to insulate faith from the ravages of skeptics bent on using historical scholarship to pull it from its foundations. Those who take this approach sometimes deny that faith has substantive content, and that move is accomplished by separating faith from history in order to dissolve the substance of faith. But, examined more closely, the vulnerability of historical faith to disconfirmation is also a clear advantage to it, for a faith that might possibly be false—and hence futile and barren—is also one that might be true in a way that makes a profound difference. The statement that Jesus is the Christ is thus a statement that makes a real difference—it involves a claim that simply cannot be ignored.

Opposition to the Book of Mormon on the cultural fringes of the community of Saints, as well as from outside the kingdom, seems to indicate that more than just the believers see the possibilities that are offered by an authentic Book of Mormon. Those confronted with the message of the Restoration must ask whether Jesus of Nazareth was the Son of God who even now holds in his hands the key to redemption from death and from our sins. Although such a claim, as well as the host of different statements it involves, may not be settled for us merely by the methods of the historian or be strictly demonstrable by historical evidences, those methods and evidences are not thereby irrelevant to its truth. Hence the attack on the faith, as well as its defense, always begins by asking whether the historical component is authentic, or whether the story told is accurate.

Joseph Smith began his work by telling a story about some rather strange things. Whatever the imponderables of his story, he provided us with an extraordinary text—the Book of Mormon. Is that book an authentic ancient history? Does it contain a true message? The question of the historical authenticity of the Book of

Mormon is necessarily the initial question, even if it is not in the final analysis the decisive one. A negative assumption or decision about the initial question closes the door to a faithful response to the decisive questions that each must answer concerning the core message of the book, its central teaching, and hence its truth for us.

Both the Saints and those who do not believe and who also wish to contend against the kingdom have sensed that the Restoration message is true if—and only if—the Book of Mormon is an authentic ancient history. And clearly these questions can be tested, if not settled, by the methods of the historian. We begin to become faithful Saints by receiving that book and embracing its message. Joseph Smith's story and the texts he offered thus provide both the grounds and some of the crucial content of faith. Of course, confidence in the Book of Mormon ultimately rests upon assurances that go beyond the arena of historians, but we cannot thereby turn away from the question of its historical authenticity and at the same time pretend to understand it or its place in the Restoration, or to comprehend its message. Though faith is ultimately trust in God, even that dimension of faith rests upon grounds and preconditions. To find reasons for or against the claims of the Book of Mormon, when we are confronted with those claims, touches upon the preconditions and grounds for a genuine trust in God.

Challenges to Faith

The foundations of the faith of the Saints, understood as the historical preconditions and grounds for our trust in God, are again being questioned by those who challenge or deny the authenticity of the Book of Mormon or the essential truthfulness of the story told by Joseph Smith. We should anticipate and perhaps even welcome such challenges. The Book of Mormon was, from the first, the vehicle and the prime witness for the Restoration, as well as the foremost target of skeptics. But in the past, those who rejected the claims of the Restoration and who struggled to debunk the Book of Mormon stood outside the kingdom. Those who denied that the Book of Mormon was an authentic ancient history—and, in that sense, the word of God—saw themselves and were seen by the faithful as standing outside the community of faith. Recently there has been a subtle shift; some of those who doubt or deny that God really restored anything, for one reason or another, want to remain within the Church—and some even present themselves as learned spokesmen for it.

There are now a few Latter-day Saints who insist that the Book of Mormon is fiction—that is, who deny that it is an authentic history—but who also deny that they have thereby challenged the foundations of the faith. They claim that they have come to understand the truth of the faith as no previous spokesmen have understood it. They borrow from non-LDS theologians or try to fashion their own theories of what constitutes divine revelation. From their perspective these theories permit the transformation of the Book of Mormon into a myth that is not authentic history and yet remains a vehicle for what amounts to their own inspiration and instruction. These savants insist that their learning can make available to those they consider primitive believers a new and deeper grasp of truths previously hidden in what they understand to be essentially fiction and hence buried beneath primitive literalisms. They argue that what Joseph Smith gave us—either intentionally or more probably unintentionally—is best understood as a "Mormon myth" in the sense of inspiring or "inspired fiction." They hold that the fabrication by Joseph Smith of fictional accounts of the past is what the Saints must now come to understand as divine "revelation" if they are to follow the lead of certain Protestant or Catholic theologians—a thing which they insist that the Saints should begin to do in order to gain credibility with the otherwise incredulous and bemused non-LDS world.

A fundamental modification of the content of the historical foundations of the faith can be seen in certain recent attempts to reinterpret Joseph Smith and the Book of Mormon. With the Book of Mormon understood as fiction or as a "Mormon myth," it is also necessary to transmogrify the Saints' understanding of Joseph Smith. Thus he must be seen as psychologically dissociative, or transformed into a mystic, or a rustic magician, rather than being seen as a genuine prophet. Revisionists insist that we must begin to see Joseph Smith as having imagined the story of the angel out of his presumed deep involvement in the occult, magic, and superstition common to his time. The "Joseph the Mystic," or the newer "Joseph the Magician," is pictured as both "religious" and "sincere"; but he was still a magical myth-maker, a mystic, and, at best, merely an inspired fiction writer or perhaps an inventive imitator or embellisher of ancient texts—certainly not a genuine seer, translator, and prophet. In some of these fashionable revisionist accounts Joseph Smith's prophetic special revelations are not denied outright, as they were in the past, but are subsumed under the more general category of ordinary religious experience in which prophets are understood as clever redactors, doctrinal embellishers, mystics, or superstitiously religious people.

Some Crucial Choices

In support of revisionist accounts of the Book of Mormon and the crucial generative events of the Restoration, we are now being offered a picture of perfectly harmless, wholly honest, tough-minded, competent scholars just telling it like it is. Such is the glossy portrait revisionists strive to paint of their own situation. Revisionists then set their kind over against sentimental and incompetent people whose work is merely traditional, apologetic, and "faith-promoting," and therefore neither honest nor competent. That picture is a rationalization for revisionism and also a trap for young players. The illusion is thus created that sound scholarship must necessarily lead to a fundamentally different understanding of the restored gospel. Efforts to scrutinize revisionist explanations and accounts are characterized as the work of anti-intellectual fundamentalists or of traditionalists bent on causing some personal harm to the purveyors of revisionist ideology. That characterization of the situation tends to lure the unwary into accepting the revisionist ideology because they desire at least the appearance of intellectual sophistication, they yearn to be on the cutting edge of the new views of Mormon history. They even, at times, give up on the gospel before they have had a chance to become sufficiently critical of the endless flux of fashions in scholarship—and before they have honestly called upon God to help them address the question of what is true. Revisionist ideology entices them into doubting what they already in some degree know to be true about the Book of Mormon and the restoration of the gospel of Jesus Christ.

We have always had "Cultural Mormons," marginal members who for different reasons can neither spit nor swallow when it comes to the gospel; they are clearly not sound guides. Neither their intellectual pretenses nor their passionate sincerity warrants our following their lead. Whether they know it or not, intellectuals are all caught between different and, at times, competing worlds, just as are merchants, business moguls, and everyone else who has been brushed by the gospel. Sometimes they fail to resolve in a satisfactory way the deep tensions generated by being confronted with competing worlds.

We need not, of course, fear or despise historical scholarship, but we may need to give close attention to and even be somewhat wary of some of the uses to which it can be put. The "iniquities" and "secret acts" of the rebellious—some of which have recently been, so to speak, "spoken from the housetops"—should make historians more cautious about certain fads. The Saints must be prudent when confronted with revisionist accounts of their past. And they must also be leery of fashionable new explanations of the Book of Mormon, especially when it seems that those accounts tend to turn it into fiction, especially when it is then claimed that such is what we must now believe constitutes divine revelation. The restoration of the gospel of Jesus Christ was made necessary, in the first place, precisely because of the effect of similar transformations in earlier ages.

The Spirit of Truth 14

Joseph Fielding McConkie

"Were you to ask me how it was I embraced Mormonism," said Brigham Young, "I should answer, for the simple reason that it embraces all truth in heaven and on earth, in the earth, under the earth, and in hell, if there be any truth there. There is no truth outside of it; there is no good outside of it; there is nothing holy and honorable outside of it; for wherever these principles are found among all the creations of God, the Gospel of Jesus Christ, and his order and Priesthood embraces them."[1] Joseph Smith stated the principle thus: "We believe in being honest, true, chaste, benevolent, virtuous, and in doing good to all men; indeed, we may say that we follow the admonition of Paul—We believe all things, we hope all things, we have endured many things, and hope to be able to endure all things. If there is anything virtuous, lovely, or of good report or praiseworthy, we seek after these things." (Articles of Faith 1:13.)

What Is Truth?

"What is truth?" Such was the question Pilate asked of Christ some two thousand years ago. The question does not identify Pilate

Joseph Fielding McConkie is Associate Professor of Ancient Scripture at Brigham Young University.

as an honest truth seeker. His was merely the profession of a skeptic, one whose interest in truth reached no further than a knowledge of what was politically expedient. John records no answer to the Roman procurator's question, nor was there reason for him to do so. Jesus had just said that "everyone that is of the truth" would hear his voice. Pilate was not interested in knowing about "the truth," which was to be found in Christ, but rather about facts as they related to a political decision that he was required to make.

To suppose that John left the question "What is truth?" unanswered is to miss the very purpose for which he wrote. The very first verse of his gospel announces that "the Word was God," and then follows with the announcement that the "Word was made flesh" (v. 14). John also introduced Jesus as "the true Light," saying that all received light from him (v. 9). Further, it was John who taught that those who lived by the word of Christ were his disciples and that they would know the truth and the truth would make them free (see John 8:31–32). "I am," John records Jesus as saying, "the way, the truth, and the life" (John 14:6). Indeed, the testimony of John was that as Jesus was the Word made flesh and the Light made flesh, He was thus the Truth made flesh. All truth, in the high spiritual sense that John used the word, centered in Jesus.

Truth in its highest scriptural sense was not intended to describe that which stood opposite error. Truth was an active rather than a passive word. It constituted an expression of what one did or what one was. Thus we find John reporting the Savior's words that he who does evil "hateth the light, neither cometh to the light," so that his deeds might be hidden, while "he that *doeth* truth cometh to the light, that his deeds may be made manifest, that they are wrought in God" (John 3:20–21; italics added). Again John writes, "God is light, and in him is no darkness at all. If we say that we have fellowship with him, and walk in darkness, we lie, and *do not* the truth." (1 John 1:5–6; italics added.) In both passages—and this is not a mistake in translation—John describes truth as something one *does* rather than something one believes.

The idea that *religion* consists of intellectual or verbal assent to a given set of beliefs is a perversion of the word. In its highest scriptural usage it carries no such meaning. Thus we find James saying: "Pure religion and undefiled before God and the Father is this, To visit the fatherless and widows in their affliction, and to keep himself unspotted from the world" (James 1:27). The pure religion of the New Testament peoples was found in what they did, not in what they professed. The watchword of Christians was: "By their fruits ye shall know them." To this the Savior added the warning: "Not every one that saith unto me, Lord, Lord, shall enter into the kingdom of heaven; but *he that doeth* the will of my Father which is in heaven. Many will say to me in that day, Lord, Lord, have we not prophesied in thy name? and in thy name cast out devils? and in thy name done many wonderful works? And then will I profess unto them, I never knew you: *depart from me, ye that work iniquity.*" The promise of salvation was given only to those who "heareth these sayings of mine, and *doeth* them." (Matthew 7:20–24; italics added).

This ancient sense of truth which laid stress upon that which a man *did* has not been lost in the revelations of the restored gospel. In the thirteenth Article of Faith Joseph Smith wrote that we believe in being "honest, true," etc. The thought is not redundant. To be honest is one thing, to be true quite another. In the standard dictionary of Joseph Smith's day under the listing for truth, we find that the primary sense of the root was to make "close and fast," or to "make straight."[2] Our word *true* is derived from the Old English "treowe," which meant "faithful," "trustworthy," "loyalty," or "fidelity."[3] This gives greater meaning to the testimony of Nephi when he speaks of the words of Christ as being "true and faithful" (2 Nephi 31:15), or to the testimony of the Lord himself when he declared that the prophecies and promises in the Doctrine and Covenants "are true and faithful" (D&C 1:37), or that the Book of Mormon contains the "truth and the word of God" (D&C 19:26). That is, Christ and his scriptural records are trustworthy, and obedient acceptance of them constitutes a covenant with God which he cannot break (see D&C 82:10).

Restoring the full strength of meaning to the word *truth* grants a richness to a host of passages that otherwise is lost. For instance, we are told that Alma "declare[d] the word with truth and soberness" (Alma 42:31). If we suppose that the "word"—meaning the gospel—and "truth" are the same thing then the expression is redundant. If we understand that "truth" carries the meaning of trustworthiness or loyalty, then we catch the full meaning of the expression. Alma taught the word, or the gospel, in a trustworthy or loyal manner; that is, he neither added to nor took from the word of god. This is a sermon within a sermon. Many a gospel teacher has yielded to the temptation to sensationalize a story to captivate the attention of his audience or to soften a doctrine out of fear of giving offense. Alma, we can infer, refused to do this. He taught the gospel in a faithful manner, doing so in simplicity and soberness.

Obtaining a Knowledge of Spiritual Things

As with truth, the word *knowledge*, even as used in the scriptures, has many shades of meaning. As with truth, much of the richness of its meaning needs to be restored. If we dare be so candid as to place blame for robbing the word *knowledge* of its purity, the original influence was Greek, while its modern oppressors are self-styled scholars. In the context of the Bible, knowledge—in its highest spiritual sense—had little to do with the intellect but was rather a matter of the heart. The Old Testament references to knowing God and to a man knowing his wife—meaning conceiving a child with her—both use the same Hebrew word (*yada*). As a man was to leave his father and mother and cleave unto his wife and thus become one flesh with her, so he was to leave the things of the world, cleave unto his God, and become one with him. As faithfulness in marriage was essential to the nurturing of love, so faithfulness in keeping gospel covenants was understood to be necessary in obtaining a knowledge of God. As love of spouse was strengthened in sacrifice and devotion, so the knowledge of God was obtained in living those covenants with exactness and honor. Thus a frequent characteristic of Hebrew prophecy was to describe apostasy through the metaphor of adultery and Israel's covenant with God as a marriage.

In the context of both the Old and the New Testaments, one's knowledge was measured by what he or she did. Jeremiah declared that to be just and righteous and to bless the poor and the needy was to know God (Jeremiah 22:15–16). Peter, having listed the attributes of godliness, said, "If these things be in you, and abound, they make you that ye shall neither be barren nor unfruitful in the knowledge of our Lord Jesus Christ" (2 Peter 1:8). "Hereby we do know that we know him," wrote John, "if we keep his commandments. He that saith, I know him, and keepeth not his commandments, is a liar, and the truth is not in him." (1 John 2:3–4.) It was understood by all that there could be no knowledge of God among those guilty of swearing, lying, killing, stealing, committing adultery, or breaking other sacred bonds (Hosea 4:1–4).

The idea of sacred knowledge being obtainable only in the living of sacred covenants finds eloquent expression in the revelations of the Restoration. Of these revelations the Lord himself declared that "there is no unrighteousness in them." Assurance was then given that all who will strip themselves of jealousies and fears, clothing themselves in humility and righteousness, shall rend the veil and know God, "not with the carnal neither natural mind, but with the spiritual." The natural man cannot "abide the presence of God," for such things are not "after the carnal mind." (D&C 67:10, 12.) It is with the restoration of the Melchizedek Priesthood that the "key of the knowledge of God" (D&C 84:19) is given anew to man. Again we see how closely such knowledge is linked to the making of sacred covenants and are reminded that such knowledge is obtainable only through obedience (see D&C 130:19).

Covenant Knowledge

Purity, not intellect, is the prime requisite for the knowledge of God. Knowledge that can be obtained independent of purity and righteousness is without the power of salvation. Only that knowledge that comes from God through the medium of the Holy Spirit has the power to sanctify the soul and prepare one to stand in the divine presence. Such is the "Spirit of truth," a spirit which the "world cannot receive" (John 14:17). "The Spirit of truth is of God," the Savior said. "I am the Spirit of truth, and John bore record of me, saying: He received a fulness of truth, yea, even of all truth; and no man receiveth a fulness unless he keepeth his commandments. He that keepeth his commandments receiveth truth and light, until he is glorified in truth and knoweth all things." (D&C 93:26–28.)

Thus Mormonism does, as Brigham Young declared, embrace all truth and all that is good. We reverence all truth as we reverence all acts of goodness, yet we do not suppose that all truths have the power of salvation in them any more than we suppose that good deeds supplant the need for the ordinances of salvation. As there is no equality among truths, some being of appreciably greater importance than others, so there is no equality among the good acts of men. Of Christ himself it was said that he must needs be baptized to "fulfil all righteousness" (2 Nephi 31:5; Matthew 3:15). Christ's greatest deeds consisted in obedient submission to the will of his Father, not *per se* in feeding the hungry or healing the sick and afflicted.

All the ethical discourses in the world are without the power to remit a single sin, even as the combined goodness of all who have ever lived is without the power to resurrect a single soul. Christ taught "the gospel of the kingdom" (Matthew 4:23), the "new covenant" of which Jeremiah spoke (Jeremiah 31:31), or the "everlasting covenant" of which Ezekiel wrote (Ezekiel 37:26). It is only in this covenant relationship that sins are remitted and the promises of heaven obtained. Heaven's truths, the truths of salvation, can only be obtained in a covenant relationship. To seek these truths some other way is adultery in the metaphor of the Old Testament or idolatry in the language of the Restoration. These are they of whom the Lord said: "They seek not the Lord to establish his righteousness, but every man walketh in his own way, and after the image of his own god, whose image is in the likeness of the world, and whose substance is that of an idol, which waxeth old and shall perish in Babylon, even Babylon the great, which shall fall" (D&C 1:16).

In the broad and general sense the gospel embraces all truth, as it embraces all that is "of good report or praiseworthy." In the high spiritual sense the gospel is limited to those principles by conformity to which we place ourselves on the path to exaltation. This is the reason the Lord said that the Book of Mormon contains the "fulness of the gospel" (D&C 20:9). No one would for a moment suppose that it or any other book could contain every truth. What it contains is a faithful account of those truths by obedience to which salvation comes.

Conclusion

Describing the manner of his conversion President Brigham Young said:

> If all the talent, tact, wisdom, and refinement of the world had been sent to me with the Book of Mormon, and had declared, in the most exalted of earthly eloquence, the truth of it, undertaking to prove it by learning and worldly wisdom, they would have been to me like the smoke which arises only to vanish away. But when I saw a man without eloquence, or talents for public speaking, who could only say, "I know, by the power of the Holy Ghost, that the Book of Mormon is true, and Joseph Smith is a Prophet of the Lord," the Holy Ghost proceeding from that individual illuminated my understanding, and light, glory, and immortality were before me. I was encircled by them, filled with them, and I knew for myself that the testimony of the man was true. But the wisdom of the world, I say again, is like smoke, like the fog of the night, that disappears before the rays of the luminary of day, or like the hoar-frost in the warmth of the sun's rays. My own judgment, natural endowments, and education bowed to this simple, but mighty testimony.[4]

This is the spirit of truth, the spirit by which a knowledge of God comes. The fulness of this spirit and knowledge can be found only in a covenant relationship—one in which we take upon ourselves the name of Christ, one in which we learn to think as he thought, believe as he believed, act as he acted, and do as he did. Such is the process of salvation; such is the manner in which we become one with him; such is the spirit of truth.

NOTES

1. *Journal of Discourses*, 11:213.
2. *Noah Webster's First Edition of an American Dictionary of the English Language* (Reprinted by the Foundation for American Christian Education, Anaheim, California, 1967).
3. Eric Partridge, *Origins: A Short Etymological Dictionary of Modern English* (New York: Greenwich House: Distributed by Crown Publishers, Inc., 1983), p. 740.
4. *Journal of Discourses*, 1:90.

Index

— F —

— G —

— H —